WELFARE BENEFITS

WELFARE BENEFITS

Kevin Browne, LLB, Solicitor

Published by

College of Law Publishing,
Braboeuf Manor, Portsmouth Road, St Catherines, Guildford GU3 1HA

© The College of Law 2009

British Library Cataloguing-in-Publication Data

A catalogue record for this book is available from the British Library.

ISBN 978 1 905391 72 1

Typeset by Style Photosetting Ltd, Mayfield, East Sussex

Printed in Great Britain by Ashford Colour Press Ltd, Gosport, Hampshire

Preface

As a practising solicitor, advising on welfare benefits was one of the most challenging but rewarding areas of my work. Now as a lecturer on the subject, I tell people that studying and understanding welfare benefits is a bit like completing a three-dimensional jigsaw puzzle. The picture on the box is very detailed and it takes time to find all the right pieces and put them together correctly. I hope that students and advisers will find this book a helpful start to that process.

A welfare benefits adviser must be able to identify if a client is entitled to one or more benefits. This is a skill that, in this book, I call 'claimant profiling'. To carry it out properly, a person needs to have studied and understood the conditions of entitlement for each welfare benefit. These conditions are normally set out in legislation. They are like a checklist of legal tests and all of them have to be ticked off before the benefit is payable.

The aim of this book is to provide a simple introduction to the social security system in England and Wales. It does not cover all benefits, neither does it cover all the provisions of those benefits within its ambit. In particular, it deals mainly with new claims, and contains little on transitional provisions which may preserve or protect rights to benefits for those claimants who started to receive a benefit before a change in the law which would now disentitle them or require them to be treated differently. In **Chapter 1** the welfare benefits system is outlined. **Chapter 2** then deals with various topics that are common to the non means-tested benefits. In the next seven chapters the benefits are collected together by client group, such as the unemployed, disabled, retired, bereaved etc. **Chapter 10** then considers the inter-relationship of immigration law and welfare benefits, and in particular the immigration requirements for claiming and exporting a welfare benefit. Readers may wish to consult *Immigration Law* for more details. The Appendices contain practical and, I hope, useful source materials.

Welfare benefits law is always changing. In this edition, I have tackled the two major developments that have occurred since the last edition, namely employment and support allowance (which has replaced incapacity benefit and income support for those unable to work) and local housing allowance for claimants of housing benefit who have a private landlord. These now take up much of **Chapters 4** and **9** respectively.

Readers may wish to consult previous editions of this book (when it had the title of *Welfare Benefits and Immigration Law*) for the law on incapacity benefit. I have only covered its replacement, contributory employment and support allowance, in this edition.

This edition is dedicated to my mother.

KEVIN BROWNE
The College of Law
Store Street

August 2008

Contents

APPENDICES   189

Table of Cases

Table of Statutes

Table of Secondary Legislation

Table of Abbreviations

AA	attendance allowance
AA Regs 1991	Social Security (Attendance Allowance) Regulations 1991
BACIFHE	British Accreditation Council for Independent Further and Higher Education
BB	bereavement benefits
CA	carer's allowance
CAA	constant attendance allowance
CB	child benefit
CBJSA	contribution-based jobseeker's allowance
CESA	contributory employment and support allowance
CLS	Community Legal Service
CPAG	Child Poverty Action Group
CP Regs 1987	Social Security (Claims and Payments) Regulations 1987
CPR 1998	Civil Procedure Rules 1998
CSA	Child Support Agency
CTB	council tax benefit
CTB Regs 1992	Council Tax Benefit (General) Regulations 1992
CTB Regs 2006	Council Tax Benefit Regulations 2006
CTC	child tax credit
DA Regs 1999	Social Security and Child Support (Decisions and Appeals) Regulations 1999
DfES	Department for Education and Skills
DfWP	Department for Work and Pensions
DLA	disability living allowance
DLA Regs 1991	Social Security (Disability Living Allowance) Regulations 1991
EC	European Community
ECHR	European Convention on Human Rights
ECtHR	European Court of Human Rights
ECJ	European Court of Justice
EEA	European Economic Area
EO	employment officer
EU	European Union
GP	general medical practitioner
HA 1985	Housing Act 1985
HB	housing benefit
HB Regs 2006	Housing Benefit Regulations 2006
HMRC	HM Revenue and Customs
HND	Higher National Diploma
HRA 1998	Human Rights Act 1998
HRP	home responsibilities protection
IA 1971	Immigration Act 1971
IBJSA	income-based jobseeker's allowance
ICA Regs	Social Security (Invalid Care Allowance) Regulations 1976
ICB	incapacity benefit
IDB	industrial disablement benefit
I(EEA) Regs 2006	Immigration (European Economic Area) Regulations 2006
IRESA	Income-related employment and support allowance
IS	income support
IS Regs 1987	Income Support (General) Regulations 1987
IW Regs 1995	Social Security (Incapacity for Work) (General) Regulations 1995
JA 1995	Jobseekers Act 1995

JA Regs 1996	Jobseeker's Allowance Regulations 1996
JSA	jobseeker's allowance
LAG	Legal Action Group
LEL	lower earnings limit
LSC	Legal Services Commission
MA	maternity allowance
MB	maternity benefits
NHS	National Health Service
NICs	National Insurance contributions
NINo	National Insurance number
NIRP	National Insurance retirement pension
NVQ	National Vocational Qualification
OB Regs 1979	Social Security (Overlapping Benefits) Regulations 1979
PAYE	pay as you earn
PCT	primary contributions threshold
PD Regs 1985	Social Security (Industrial Injuries) (Prescribed Diseases) Regulations 1985
SERPS	state earnings-related pension scheme
SFD	Social Fund Directions
SMP	statutory maternity pay
SMP Regs 1986	Statutory Maternity Pay Regulations 1986
SP	State Pension
SSA 1998	Social Security Act 1998
SSAA 1992	Social Security Administration Act 1992
SSCBA 1992	Social Security Contributions and Benefits Act 1992
SS(GB) Regs 1982	Social Security (General Benefit) Regulations 1982
SS(I&A)CA Regs 2000	Social Security (Immigration and Asylum) Consequential Amendments Regulations 2000
SSP	statutory sick pay
UEL	upper earnings limit
UKBA	United Kingdom Border Agency
WTC	working tax credit

Chapter 1

Introduction to Welfare Benefits

1.1 The nature of welfare law

Welfare benefits law is a complex and rapidly changing area of law, which is often little understood by solicitors. It has evolved piecemeal over a very long period of time. Because of this, the legislation needed to put the schemes in place has also been created piecemeal. This explains the extraordinary diversity of the different benefits, and the arbitrary nature of their rules. The legislation itself is very full; not so much the primary, statute law, but the enormous volume of statutory instruments created under that primary law, where the detail is to be found.

1.2 Overview of the benefits system

1.2.1 The types of benefits

Welfare benefits are traditionally classified as either means-tested or non means-tested. The latter are grouped into three types: contributory, statutory, and other non means-tested. Here, the benefits are grouped in these categories, but generally in the book they are grouped by client group, with appropriate benefits of different types considered together. This should help the reader to grasp the relationship between the different benefits.

At **1.7** there are checklists, which can be used to find quickly the benefits appropriate to a particular client's needs. They cross-refer to the detailed discussion of each benefit.

At **1.9** the skill of 'claimant profiling' is outlined. When reading the rest of this book the reader should consider how he will best be able to develop and use that skill.

1.2.2 Contributory benefits

The contributory benefits are dealt with in detail in **Chapters 2 to 5** of the book. In order to qualify for any contributory benefit, the claimant must have paid (or be treated as having paid) National Insurance contributions:

(a) of an appropriate class;

(b) at an appropriate time;

(c) of the appropriate level.

These contribution conditions, which are explained in **Chapter 2**, vary according to the benefit in question.

1.2.2.1 Contribution-based jobseeker's allowance

The contributory form of jobseeker's allowance (see **Chapter 3**) is payable to those who have been employees and become unemployed. It can be paid for a maximum of 26 weeks. It should therefore be thought of as a short-term unemployment benefit.

1.2.2.2 Contributory employment and support allowance

Contributory employment and support allowance (see **4.3**) is payable to people who for a recognised medical reason are unable to work (known as 'limited capability for work'). A claimant must undergo a medical test by a Government-appointed doctor and score sufficient points (see **4.4**). A claimant must also have a suitable record of National Insurance contributions (see **2.3.3.2** and the summary at **4.3.2**).

Note that there is also a limited form of non-contributory employment and support allowance for adults who become disabled during youth (under 20, or 25 in some circumstances) and thereby have limited capability for work (see **4.3.3**).

1.2.2.3 State Pension

State Pension (see **5.2.1**) is the familiar 'old age pension' to which most people will be entitled once they reach retirement age. It will be paid for the rest of their lives.

1.2.2.4 Bereavement benefits

The bereavement benefits (see **5.4**) are a range of benefits for those whose spouse or civil partner has died. Uniquely among contributory benefits, entitlement depends not on the claimant's own contributions, but those of the spouse or civil partner who has died.

1.2.3 Statutory benefits

An employee has no rights at general law to be paid on any day on which he does not work. Until the statutory benefits were introduced, any rights to sick pay and maternity pay were entirely contractual. Now, most employees have the right to statutory sick pay for up to 28 weeks (see **4.2**), and statutory maternity pay (see **6.3**).

1.2.4 Other non means-tested benefits

The rest of the benefits in this group are dealt with in **Chapters 4 and 6** of the book. Most of them are for people with disabilities. Their names are a starting point to understanding the purpose of the benefit and are worth committing to memory.

1.2.4.1 Disability living allowance

Disability living allowance (see **4.6** to **4.8**) is the most important benefit for people with disabilities who become disabled while under the age of 65. It is, in fact, two benefits consisting of: the 'care component', for people who need physical help and/or supervision; and the 'mobility component', for people who are either effectively unable to walk, or need guidance or supervision in order to walk out of doors.

1.2.4.2 Attendance allowance

Attendance allowance (see **4.9**) is like the care component of disability living allowance, for those who first become disabled at age 65 or older.

1.2.4.3 Non-contributory employment and support allowance

This version of employment and support allowance is to help young adults aged 16 or over who become incapable of work before reaching 20, or sometimes 25 years of age. See **4.3.3**.

1.2.4.4 Industrial disablement benefit

This benefit (see **4.10**) is paid to employees who become disabled as a result of an accident at work or from contracting a prescribed industrial disease.

1.2.4.5 Maternity allowance

Maternity allowance (see **6.4**) is a benefit for women who stop working to have a baby, and do not qualify for statutory maternity pay.

1.2.4.6 Carer's allowance

Carer's allowance (see **6.7**) is paid to a volunteer who is effectively working full time to look after a person in receipt of either disability living allowance care component or attendance allowance.

1.2.4.7 Child benefit

Child benefit (see **6.6**) is paid to people with children who are under 16 or up to 20 in certain prescribed circumstances.

1.2.5 Earnings replacement benefits

Some of the above-mentioned non means-tested benefits have been specifically designed to assist people who no longer have earnings because they have become unemployed, incapable of work, pregnant, a full-time carer or have reached retirement age. The exceptions to that principle are widowed parent's allowance and bereavement allowance, which replace the earnings of the deceased spouse.

These so-called 'earnings replacement benefits' are:

(a) contribution-based jobseeker's allowance;
(b) contributory employment and support allowance;
(c) maternity allowance;
(d) carer's allowance;
(e) retirement pension;
(f) widowed parent's allowance and bereavement allowance.

It is important to be able to identify these benefits since, as a general rule, an individual is not entitled to more than one at any time (but see further **2.6**). Moreover, if both members of a couple are each entitled in their own right to such a benefit, the amount of any increase in that benefit may be affected (see **2.4**).

1.2.6 Means-tested benefits

The means-tested benefits require the claimant to undergo a means test as part of the route to qualification. These benefits are described in **Chapters 7 to 9** of the book.

1.2.6.1   Income support

Income support (see **Chapter 8**) is the benefit of last resort for anyone who is capable of work but is not required, under the rules for claiming benefit, to be available for work. That includes carers and single parents of young children. It is usually paid to top up other benefits such as carers allowance, or child tax credit, or on top of part-time earnings (fewer than 16 hours per week). One important feature of the benefit is that it can provide help to owner-occupiers in meeting their housing costs (notably mortgage interest repayments).

1.2.6.2   Income-related employment and support allowance

This is a top-up benefit for people on a low income who are not required to be available for work for a recognised medical reason. They might be in receipt of statutory sick pay (see **4.2**) or contributory employment and support allowance (see **4.3**). A claimant must undergo a medical test by a Government-appointed doctor and score sufficient points (see **4.4**). Like income support, one important feature is that owner-occupiers may receive help with certain housing costs, particularly mortgage interest payments.

1.2.6.3   Income-based jobseeker's allowance

This form of jobseeker's allowance is an identical twin of income support, for those who have to be available for work (see **Chapter 8**).

1.2.6.4   Housing benefit

Housing benefit (see **9.3**) is payable to those who are under a legal liability to pay rent for the dwelling occupied as their home.

1.2.6.5   Council tax benefit

Although called a benefit, council tax benefit (see **9.4**) is actually a rebate against the liability to pay council tax on the occupation of residential property.

1.2.6.6   Pension credit

Although called a credit, this is a benefit designed to ensure that pensioners have a guaranteed level of income (the 'guarantee credit' element) and are not prejudiced, but indeed are rewarded, if they have made some retirement provision in addition to the basic State Pension (the 'savings credit' element). Like income support, income-related employment and support allowance, and income-based jobseeker's allowance, it can provide help to owner-occupiers in meeting their housing costs (see **5.3**).

1.2.6.7   Child tax credit

Although called a tax credit, this is a benefit paid to low-income families with one or more children or qualifying young persons. See **9.8**.

1.2.6.8   Working tax credit

Again, strictly, this is a benefit available to low-paid workers, including those who are disabled. See **9.10**.

1.2.7   Other income-related benefits

In addition to these benefits and credits, there are other payments and benefits in kind which are means-tested. The most important of these are the so-called 'passport benefits', such as free prescriptions and school meals, and the social fund which makes grants and loans towards some one-off expenses. These are both described in **Chapter 9**.

1.3 Sources of welfare benefits law

The law of welfare benefits is unusual in that the same law applies to the whole of Great Britain: not just England and Wales, but Scotland as well. The rest of the UK has separate welfare law systems. We shall see something of the relationship between these systems and the British system in **Chapter 10**. For the rest of this part of the book, we shall be dealing exclusively with British law.

1.3.1 Statute

All welfare law is statutory in origin. The statutes dealing with welfare benefits are principally enabling statutes. Most of the detailed law is contained in statutory instruments (see **1.3.2**).

The principal statutes are set out below.

1.3.1.1 Social Security Contributions and Benefits Act 1992

The Social Security Contributions and Benefits Act 1992 (SSCBA 1992) is the statute that creates the main benefits and deals with the rules for entitlement to them. It has been heavily amended by subsequent legislation.

1.3.1.2 Jobseekers Act 1995

The Jobseekers Act 1995 (JA 1995) created the jobseeker's allowance (see **Chapters 3, 7 and 8**), which replaced the earlier unemployment benefit in 1996. This is a free-standing Act: it supplements, rather than amends, the SSCBA 1992.

1.3.1.3 Social Security Administration Act 1992

The Social Security Administration Act 1992 (SSAA 1992) is concerned not with benefits but the way the benefits system works. It deals with claims, decision-making, appeals, payment methods and other administrative measures.

1.3.1.4 Welfare Reform and Pensions Act 1999

The 1999 Act introduced the stakeholder pension schemes (see **5.2.4.2**) and made changes to the regulatory framework for occupational and personal pensions. It also set out the scheme of bereavement benefits (see **5.4**) and made reforms to other benefits.

1.3.1.5 Tax Credits Act 2002 and State Pension Credits Act 2002

These Acts, supplemented in the usual way by numerous statutory instruments, set out the provisions concerning entitlement to these three tax credits.

1.3.1.6 Welfare Reform Act 2007

This Act introduced the employment and support allowance (see **Chapters 4, 7 and 8**), as well as the local housing allowance for housing benefit purposes (see **Chapter 9**).

1.3.2 Statutory instruments

Most welfare benefit law is created by statutory instruments, made under the enabling provisions of one of the Acts listed in the last section. Each of the major benefits (see list at **1.2**) has its own main set of regulations, usually including the word 'general' in the title. Each set of regulations is usually longer than the whole parent statute. There are also regulations to cover transitional provisions, whenever there is one of the frequent changes of law. There are also a large number of regulations to govern the details of administration and payment.

1.3.3 Case law

Where there is complex legislation, there is room for the courts to be asked to interpret it. The review and appeals systems for welfare law are described below (see **1.4.3** and **1.4.4**). Welfare law cases may reach the civil courts at Court of Appeal level, and regularly reach the House of Lords or European Court of Justice. Decisions of the higher courts are binding on the decision-making authorities (see **1.4.4**) in accordance with the usual rules on precedent. In addition, decisions of the second appeal tier, the Social Security Commissioners, are binding on tribunals of first instance and decision-makers as well.

What follows is a typical example of the way the three tiers of authority work together.

Example

Your client, aged 49, wants to claim income support. You are holding £19,000 in your client account, which is due to him following a successful personal injury claim. How does this affect his right to income support?

Section 134(1) of SSCBA 1992 provides that a claimant shall not be entitled to income support if his capital exceeds a 'prescribed amount'. That word 'prescribed' tells us to look in regulations to find what amount has been prescribed.

Regulation 45 of Income Support (General) Regulations 1987 (IS Regs 1987) provides that the prescribed amount is £16,000. But how is that calculated? Calculation of capital is covered by reg 46, which provides for some items which would otherwise be treated as capital to be disregarded. The twelfth item in Sch 9, where these items are listed, reads:

> Where the funds of a trust are derived from a payment made in consequence of any personal injury to the claimant, the value of the trust fund and the value of the right to receive any payment from the trust.

What is the nature of money held by a solicitor on behalf of his client? Does the solicitor hold it on trust for the client, in which case the £19,000 is disregarded? Or is it a simple chose in action like a bank account, in which case it disqualifies him from benefit? In *Commissioner's Decision CIS 600/1995,* the Commissioner held that it was the latter.

Now the picture is complete, and you can give your client the bad news.

1.4 Welfare benefits administration

1.4.1 Making a claim

1.4.1.1 Department for Work and Pensions

The Department for Work and Pensions (DfWP) has the primary responsibility for most of the administration of the benefits system, and most benefits are funded out of its departmental budget. The social security budget is the largest single item of central government expenditure.

1.4.1.2 Jobcentre Plus

The DfWP is responsible for the administration of both forms of jobseeker's allowance. It also works through an executive agency, known as 'Jobcentre Plus', which runs and manages Jobcentres and regional offices. See also **1.4.1.5**.

1.4.1.3 HM Revenue and Customs

HM Revenue and Customs (HMRC) has various roles within the welfare benefits system. It deals with the collection and recording of National Insurance contributions (see **2.2**), and provides information to the DfWP when it needs to check entitlement to contributory benefits. It is responsible for the administration of child benefit (see **6.6**) and the child tax and working tax credits (see **9.6**).

1.4.1.4 Local authorities

As a general rule, local government is responsible for the administration of housing benefit and council tax benefit. The local authorities concerned are those which act as housing authorities: district and borough councils where these still exist, otherwise London boroughs, unitary authorities and metropolitan districts. The councils fund the payments partly out of their own council tax receipts and partly out of support grants from central government.

1.4.2 Backdating

If a claimant wishes to claim a benefit, he must do so on the appropriate form. The claim is made only when the form is received at an office of the appropriate department, accompanied by all the information requested on the form.

If a person lacks the ability to make a claim, the DfWP can authorise a third party, usually a relative or friend, to do so. This person is known as an appointee and he takes on all the rights and obligations of a claimant, for example to appeal a decision and to notify the DfWP of changes in circumstances.

There are strict time limits for claiming benefits. The basic rule is that a benefit must be claimed as soon as the claimant becomes entitled to it. There are only limited powers to backdate a claim before the date on which the appropriate office receives the claim form. Different rules apply to different benefits, as set out below.

1.4.2.1 Child benefit, industrial disablement benefit, State Pensions, bereavement benefits, maternity allowance, employment and support allowance, child tax credit, working tax credit

These benefits can be backdated for up to three months before the date of application. No reason for the late claim is required. The claimant must show that he fulfilled all the conditions of entitlement for the benefit at the date to which he wishes the benefit to be backdated.

1.4.2.2 Income support, jobseeker's allowance

These benefits may be backdated for a maximum of one month before the date of the claim if that is 'consistent with the proper administration of benefit' according to any of the grounds detailed in the Social Security (Claims and Payments) Regulations 1987 (CP Regs 1987), reg 19(7). These include:

(a)   the appropriate office where the claimant would be expected to make a claim was closed (eg due to a strike) and alternative arrangements were not available;

(b)   the claimant was unable to attend the appropriate office due to difficulties with his normal mode of transport and there was no reasonable alternative available;

(c)   there were adverse postal conditions;

(d)   during the month before the claim was made the claimant's partner, parent, son, daughter, brother or sister died.

Alternatively, these benefits may be backdated for a maximum of three months before the date of the claim but only if the conditions of CP Regs 1987, reg 19(4)(a),(b) and (5) are met. Regulation 19(4) provides that the prescribed time for claiming the benefit shall be extended, subject to a maximum extension of three months, to the date on which the claim is made, where:

(a)   any of the circumstances specified in reg 19(5) applies or has applied to the claimant; and

(b)   as a result of that circumstance or those circumstances the claimant could not reasonably have been expected to make the claim earlier.

Hence a two-step test must be carried out. First, as required by reg 19(4)(a), the claimant must establish one or more of the circumstances justifying backdating that are set out in reg 19(5). Secondly, reg 19(4)(b) provides that it must be shown that as a result of any such circumstance the claimant could not reasonably have been expected to make the claim earlier. Note that in *Commissioner's Decision CIS 4354/1999,* Commissioner Mesher held that if a claimant could reasonably have been expected to make a claim even one day earlier than the actual date of the claim, then the second test under reg 19(4)(b) is not met.

Regulation 19(5) provides an exhaustive list of the circumstances referred to in reg 19(4) which are:

(a)   the claimant has difficulty communicating because:
    (i)   he has learning, language or literacy difficulties; or
    (ii)   he is deaf or blind,
and it was not reasonably practicable for the claimant to obtain assistance from another person to make his claim;

(b)   except in the case of a claim for jobseeker's allowance, the claimant was ill or disabled, and it was not reasonably practicable for the claimant to obtain assistance from another person to make his claim;

(c)   the claimant was caring for a person who is ill or disabled, and it was not reasonably practicable for the claimant to obtain assistance from another person to make his claim;

(d)   the claimant was given information by an officer of the DfWP which led the claimant to believe that a claim for benefit could not succeed;

(e)   the claimant was given written advice by a solicitor or other professional adviser, a medical practitioner, a local authority, or a person working in a Citizens' Advice Bureau or a similar advice agency, which led the claimant to believe that a claim for benefit could not succeed;

(f)   the claimant or his partner was given written information about his income or capital by his employer or former employer, or by a bank or building society, which led the claimant to believe that a claim for benefit could not succeed;

(g)   the claimant was required to deal with a domestic emergency affecting him and it was not reasonably practicable for him to obtain assistance from another person to make his claim; or

(h)   the claimant was prevented by adverse weather conditions from attending the appropriate office.

If the reason is not one which is listed, then backdating is impossible, however good and understandable the reason for the delay.

1.4.2.3   Disability living allowance and attendance allowance

By ss 65(4) and 76(1) of the SSCBA 1992 neither of these benefits can be backdated.

1.4.2.4   Carer's allowance, housing benefit, council tax benefit and pension credit

As a general rule, these benefits can be backdated for up to three months before the date of application. No reason for the late claim is required. The claimant must show that he fulfilled all the conditions of entitlement for the benefit at the date to which he wishes the benefit to be backdated. Note that housing benefit and council tax benefit claimed by someone under 60 may be backdated for up to six months.

1.4.2.5   Statutory maternity pay

If the employer accepts the claim, he must pay it from the start of the maternity pay period (see **6.3.4**).

1.4.2.6   Statutory sick pay

If the employee gives notice of sickness in time (see **4.3.5**), he must be paid from his first qualifying day. If he is late but gives notice within one month of the time limit, the claim can be backdated to the first qualifying day if there was 'good cause' for the delay (eg the employee had a serious accident or heart attack).

1.4.3   Decision-making, revision and supersession

Every claim for a centrally administered benefit is considered by an officer of the appropriate department, on behalf of the Secretary of State, who will decide whether the claimant is entitled to benefit, and if so, how much. Once the decision has been made, it is sent to the claimant, usually with an explanation. What are his rights if he thinks it is wrong?

1.4.3.1   Written reasons

His first right is to ask for written reasons for the decision, if they are not sent to him at the same time. The request must be made within one month of receipt.

1.4.3.2   Revision

The Secretary of State may revise a decision within one month of notification, on his own initiative or in response to an application by the claimant. No particular grounds are needed for revision.

1.4.3.3   Supersession

A decision may also be superseded at any time, on application or on the Secretary of State's initiative, on certain specified grounds. These are:

(a)   that the decision was wrong in law;
(b)   that the decision was made in ignorance of, or under a mistake of, a material fact;
(c)   that it is a decision against which no appeal lies (see **1.4.4**);
(d)   that there has been a change of circumstances since it was made; or
(e)   that the decision concerns a sanction for jobseeker's allowance (see **3.3.5**).

If supersession results in more benefit being payable, the extra benefit may be backdated, normally for a month (longer in official error cases). A decision of the Secretary of State may supersede a decision of a tribunal or commissioner, where there are grounds for supersession.

There are similar provisions for revision of decisions for housing benefit and council tax benefit, by the appropriate officer of a local authority.

1.4.4 Appeals and judicial review

The claimant's next step may be to appeal against the decision. His rights of appeal vary according to the benefit in question, and the nature of the disputed decision.

1.4.4.1 Discretionary social fund

Decisions about the discretionary social fund are in the discretion of the Secretary of State. The claimant may ask for revision or supersession, but judicial review is the only route to a challenge through the courts.

1.4.4.2 Benefits and tax credits

The Commissioners for HM Revenue and Customs deal with appeals arising from disputes between employer and employee over statutory sick pay and statutory maternity pay.

For benefits, there is a right of appeal to a tribunal, provided that the disputed decision is one which is appealable. Whether or not a decision is appealable is defined in Schedules to the Social Security Act 1998 (SSA 1998).

The commonest decisions against which there is no right of appeal are:

(a)   whether the contribution conditions for a contributory benefit have been met (see **2.3**);

(b)   whether and how an overpayment of benefit which is legally recoverable will actually be recovered (see **7.11**);

(c)   whether a claim should be backdated for up to one month if it is received within that period after a preliminary enquiry (see **1.4.2**).

The only control over these non-appealable decisions is to ask first for a review, and then, if that is unsuccessful, to seek judicial review. If a claimant wrongly appeals against one of these decisions, the appeal will be struck out, as a tribunal has no jurisdiction.

1.4.5 How to appeal to a tribunal

An appeal must be made in writing, on a prescribed form, and must contain details of the decision appealed against and the grounds for appeal. The appeal must be made within one month of the decision being notified (ie sent, not received). Late appeals can only be admitted in exceptional circumstances.

The Tribunals Service, which administers the tribunal system, is an executive agency of the Ministry of Justice. The tribunal always includes one lawyer, who may sit alone in cases which do not require any other professional input. The lawyer sits with a doctor if the case involves the question of capacity for work; with two hospital consultants if the case involves the degree of disability following an industrial accident; and with one doctor and a lay member in cases involving disability living allowance and attendance allowance. The lay member in disability cases will either have a disability himself, or will have experience of working with people with disabilities – for example, a social worker, occupational therapist, or advice worker.

Procedure at the tribunals is informal. Guidance can be found on the Tribunals Service's website (see **1.6.3**). Appellants are asked beforehand whether they want an oral hearing or the matter to be dealt with on the papers. If they do not opt for an oral hearing, they are not given one, though the tribunal may order an oral hearing if it considers the matter cannot be fairly resolved without oral evidence. The tribunal gives its decision on the day of the hearing, in a short handwritten notice. Either the Secretary of State or the appellant may, within 21 days, ask for a full written statement of the findings of fact and reasons for the decision.

Cases with no realistic prospects of success are weeded out at an early stage, so that they do not waste tribunal time. The commonest ill-founded appeals are against a refusal to backdate an application for benefit where there is no reason within reg 19(5) of CP Regs 1987 (see **1.4.2.2**), or against the amount of a means-tested benefit which has been correctly calculated.

1.4.6   The higher tiers of appeal

1.4.6.1   Social Security Commissioners

Appeals from a tribunal lie to the Social Security Commissioners. A claimant may appeal from the decision of a tribunal only if it was wrong in law. This includes procedural irregularities, such as the failure to make explicit findings of fact, or apparent bias on the part of the tribunal. To appeal, the claimant must obtain a full written statement (see **1.4.5**), and needs leave.

The Commissioner may hold a complete rehearing of the case, make his own findings of fact and substitute his decision for that of the tribunal, or he may quash the decision and remit the case for rehearing by a different tribunal.

1.4.6.2   Court of Appeal and above

Appeals from the Commissioners on points of law lie to the Court of Appeal and then to the House of Lords in the usual fashion. Welfare law cases may also reach the European Court of Justice, since there are many European aspects of social security law (see also Chapter 10).

1.4.6.3   Human Rights Act 1998 and the European Convention on Human Rights

There have been more appeals from the decisions of tribunals as a result of the coming into force of the Human Rights Act 1998 (HRA 1998). This imports into English law the European Convention for the Protection of Human Rights and Fundamental Freedoms 1950, and specifically Article 6, which states:

> In the determination of his civil rights and obligations ... everyone is entitled to a fair and public hearing within a reasonable time by an independent and impartial tribunal established by law.

Procedural irregularities and bias will be even more likely to give rise to appeals as a result of this provision.

See further **1.11**.

1.4.7   Getting paid

1.4.7.1   DfWP benefits

Most DfWP benefits used to be paid by an order book, cashed at the Post Office. Forgery of order books is increasingly common and, for security reasons, the DfWP prefers to pay direct into claimants' bank accounts, usually four-weekly. The manner of payment is a non-appealable decision.

1.4.7.2 Mortgage interest

Mortgage interest payments as part of income support, or income-related employment and support allowance or income-based jobseeker's allowance (see **8.3.3**) are paid direct to the lender.

1.4.7.3 Housing benefit and council tax benefit

Council tax benefit, and housing benefit for local authority tenants, take effect as a rebate rather than an actual payment. Rent for private accommodation is usually paid direct to the tenant.

1.4.7.4 Income-based jobseeker's allowance and social fund payments

The element of jobseeker's allowance which represents anything other than mortgage interest is paid by a fortnightly Girocheque, posted to the claimant, or collected by him if there are problems with post (eg because he is of no fixed abode or he lives in a hostel where Giros are likely to be stolen). The same payment methods are used for social fund payments. However, by 2010 this system will be replaced by payments to the claimant's bank account, or otherwise by way of a pre-paid plastic 'credit' card which can be cashed at a post office.

1.5 Benefits for people entering and leaving the UK

Chapter 10 covers the rights to benefits of those entering the UK, whether for the first time or returning after a period of absence. In addition, 'exporting' particular benefits is considered. This is the area of law which brings together both immigration and welfare law. As to the former, see *Immigration Law*.

1.6 Welfare law bibliography

The following suggestions are offered for a bibliography for welfare law.

1.6.1 Legislation, cases and commentary

Annotated selections of statutes, statutory instruments and case extracts are useful for the study of detailed law. They are essential for the successful preparation of an appeal or other challenge to a decision, whether on the substantive law or procedural grounds. The main selections are Bonner, Hooker and White, *Non Means-Tested Benefits: the Legislation* (Sweet & Maxwell); Mesher and Wood, *Income Related Benefits: the Legislation* (Sweet & Maxwell); Rowland, *Medical and Disability Appeal Tribunals* (Sweet & Maxwell).

The first two are updated annually, the third only when there is a major change in the law. These deal only with the centrally administered benefits.

For locally administered housing benefit and council tax benefit, the Child Poverty Action Group (CPAG) publishes *CPAG's Housing Benefit and Council Tax Benefit: the Legislation* by Findley and Ward.

The DfWP publishes its own handbook for decision-makers (see further at **1.6.3**).

1.6.2 Textbooks and advisers' manuals

The market leader in this subject is the CPAG's *Welfare Benefits and Tax Credits Handbook*. This well-established book has many virtues: it is updated annually to take account of annual changes in the law; it is written in a friendly, direct manner which is addressed to claimants rather than advisers, though with full footnotes and references to original sources; and, not least, it is astonishingly cheap for so authoritative a book. It represents the absolute minimum library for anyone purporting to give advice on welfare law.

The CPAG also publishes an *Immigration and Social Security Handbook* which covers the area of overlap between welfare and immigration law.

The Disability Rights Alliance publishes a large-format *Disability Rights Handbook*. This covers all benefits but naturally concentrates on benefits for the disabled. It is fuller than the CPAG *Handbook* on some subjects of concern to people with disabilities, such as the funding of residential care and war pensions, both of which are outside the scope of this book.

1.6.3 Keeping up to date

Welfare law changes rapidly. Much of the legislation is contained in statutory instruments, which can be changed at very short notice. A means of keeping up to date is thus essential.

Two good journals are CPAG's *Welfare Rights Bulletin,* which updates the *Handbook,* and *Legal Action,* the journal of the Legal Action Group (LAG). Both these journals provide information about new legislation and review recent case law.

There are numerous websites covering various welfare law issues. You might start with those listed in the table below.

Organisation	Website
Department for Work and Pensions including *Decision Maker's Guide, Housing Benefit Guidance Manual, Social Fund Guide* and *Overpayments Guide*	www.dwp.gov.uk
Government services (includes disability living allowance, attendance allowance and carer's allowance)	www.direct.gov.uk
Her Majesty's Revenue and Customs including *Tax Credits Manual, Tax Credits Guidance Manual* and *Child Benefit Technical Manual*	www.hmrc.gov.uk
Jobcentre Plus	www.jobcentreplus.gov.uk/JCP/index.html
Pension Service	www.thepensionservice.gov.uk
Sure Start	www.surestart.gov.uk
Tribunal Service including *Appeals Guide*	www.appeals-service.gov/uk

Organisation	Website
Citizen's Advice online	www.adviceguide.org.uk
Rightsnet (welfare advice/updating/ courses)	www.rightsnet.org.uk
Child Poverty Action Group (welfare advice/updating/ courses)	www.cpag.org.uk
Dial UK (disability advice)	www.dialuk.info
One parent family advice	www.oneparentfamilies.org.uk
Age Concern	www.ageconcern.org.uk
Disability Alliance	www.disabilityalliance.org
Legal Action Group	www.lag.org.uk
Commissioners' decisions	www.osscsc.gov.uk
Court of Appeal judgments	www.hmcourts-service.gov.uk/cms/civilappeals.htm
House of Lords judgments	www.publications.parliament.uk/pa/ld/ldjudgment.htm
ECJ judgments	www.europa.eu.int/cj/en/transitpage.htm

1.7   Which benefit? A quick guide

Too ill to work, working age:	go to Checklist 1
Physical or mental disability, any age:	go to Checklist 2
Unemployed or working part time:	go to Checklist 3
Low income:	go to Checklist 4

Checklist 1: too ill to work

(a)   *Statutory sick pay* for employees for first 28 weeks (**4.2**).

(b)   *Contributory employment and support allowance* for others for first 28 weeks and anyone after that. All claimants need to meet the National Insurance contribution conditions (**4.3**).

(c)   *Non-contributory employment and support allownace* generally only for those young adults aged 16 and over whose disability began before reaching the age of 20 or, exceptionally, 25 (**4.3.2**).

(d)   *Income-related employment and support allowance* subject to means test (**Chapter 8**).

(e)   *Consider also benefits in Checklist 2.*

Checklist 2: physical or mental disability

(a)   *Disability living allowance care component* for care or supervision if under 65 at first claim (**4.7**).

(b)   *Attendance allowance* for care or supervision if 65 or over at first claim (**4.9**).

(c)   *Disability living allowance mobility component* for problems with walking out of doors if at least 3 and under 65 at first claim (**4.8**).

(d)   *Industrial disablement benefit* for employees injured or contracting a prescribed disease at work (**4.10**).

(e)   *Working tax credit* for employee with a disability (**9.6**).

(f)   *Consider also carer's allowance for full-time voluntary carers (6.7) and benefits in Checklists 1 and 3.*

Checklist 3: unemployed or working part time

(a)   *Contribution-based jobseeker's allowance* for first 26 weeks subject to contribution conditions and labour market conditions (**Chapter 3**).

(b)   *Income-based jobseeker's allowance* subject to means test, labour market conditions and partner's hours of work (**Chapter 8**).

(c)   *Income support* if not required to satisfy labour market conditions (eg carer or single parent) subject to means test and partner's hours of work (**Chapter 8**).

(d)   *Child tax credit* if responsible for a child or qualifying young person (**9.6**).

(e)   *Consider also the benefits in Checklist 4.*

Checklist 4: low income

All these benefits are subject to a means test. Consider first whether any of the benefits in the other three checklists may apply.

(a)   *Income support or income-related employment and support allowance* if not required to satisfy labour market conditions. Can include mortgage interest payments (**Chapter 8**).

(b)   *Income-based jobseeker's allowance* as Checklist 3. Can include mortgage interest payments (**Chapter 8**).

(c)   *Housing benefit* if there is a legal liability to pay rent (**9.3**).

(d)   *Council tax benefit* for residential occupiers (**9.4**).

(e)   *Pension credit* for a pensioner (**5.3**).

(f)   *Working tax credit* for low-paid employee (**9.6**).

(g)   *Child tax credit* if responsible for a child or qualifying young person (**9.6**).

(h)   *'Passport' benefits* (9.17).

(i)   *Social fund* (9.18).

1.8   Fact analysis

The welfare law adviser must be able to *ask the right questions.* Very often, the client will have a long and complicated story to tell. The adviser must listen carefully, ask probing questions, spot the legal issues that arise in the case and suggest possible courses of action. Look again at the example under **1.3.3**. The right question to ask is: does the £19,000 constitute capital for income support purposes? As we have seen, to be able both to ask and answer that question, the adviser must be aware of the relevant provisions to be found in statute, regulations and case law.

1.9   Claimant profiling

As was stated at **1.8**, a welfare benefits adviser must be able to ask the right questions. This includes being able to identify that a client may be entitled to a whole range of different welfare benefits. I call this skill 'claimant profiling'. It centres on understanding the key conditions of entitlement for each welfare benefit and then asking the right questions in order to determine whether or not the claimant has any entitlement. At the end of each chapter there is set out a short suggested profile of the typical recipient of the benefits discussed.

1.10 The claimant's 'partner'

Historically, a claimant's partner for welfare benefit purposes has meant his or her spouse or person of the opposite sex with whom he or she is living in a relationship akin to marriage.

The Civil Partnership Act 2004 provides for couples of the same sex to enter into a civil partnership. So now, for welfare benefit purposes, couples in a civil partnership are treated in the same way as married couples. Equally, same-sex couples who are not in a civil partnership but who are living together as if they were civil partners, are treated in the same way as opposite-sex unmarried couples who are living together as husband and wife.

As to the often vexed question of cohabitation, see further **7.10**.

1.11 Human rights

How does the entitlement to a social security benefit engage rights under the European Convention on Human Rights (ECHR)? The preferred choice of the European Court of Human Rights (ECtHR) in locating a Convention right in cases of economic discrimination by the State has been via Article 1 of the First Protocol. It has long been accepted that State benefits under a contributory scheme are within the article. In the case of *Stec v UK*, Application No 65731/01, the Grand Chamber of the ECtHR (confirmed by the judgment of the Court on 12 April 2006) took the opportunity in its admissibility decision to resolve previous doubts, by holding that non-contributory benefits are to be treated in the same way. The position was explained as follows.

> 54. . . . [Article 1 of the First Protocol] does not create a right to acquire property. It places no restriction on the Contracting State's freedom to decide whether or not to have in place any form of social security scheme, or to choose the type or amount of benefits to provide under any such scheme . . . If, however, a Contracting State has in force legislation providing for the payment as of right of a welfare benefit — whether conditional or not on the prior payment of contributions — that legislation must be regarded as generating a proprietary interest falling within the ambit of [Article 1 of the First Protocol] for persons satisfying its requirements . . .

So it may be possible to argue discrimination in respect of a welfare benefit under Article 14 of the ECHR. As the Grand Chamber stated in *Stec*:

> 55. In cases . . . concerning a complaint under Article 14 in conjunction with [Article 1 of the First Protocol] that the applicant has been denied all or part of a particular benefit on a discriminatory ground covered by Article 14, the relevant test is whether, but for the condition of entitlement about which the applicant complains, he or she would have had a right, enforceable under domestic law, to receive the benefit in question . . . Although Protocol No 1 does not include the right to receive a social security payment of any kind, if a State does decide to create a benefits scheme, it must do so in a manner which is compatible with Article 14.

However, the chances of succeeding under Article 14 appear to be slim. In the joined appeals of *R v Secretary of State for Work and Pensions, ex p Carson and Reynolds* [2005] UKHL 37, [2005] 2 WLR 1369, Ms Carson had moved to South Africa and received her UK State Pension there, but because there was no reciprocal agreement (see **10.2.2**) with South Africa under which cost of living increases were payable, her UK pension was not increased in line with increases paid to pensioners in the UK. Ms Reynolds was under the age of 25 and for that reason she received a lower rate of jobseeker's allowance than if she had been over the age of 25. Both appellants complained of discrimination.

The House of Lords rejected both claims. Of Ms Carson's claim, Lord Hoffmann said (at paras 18 and 33):

> The denial of a social security benefit to Ms Carson on the ground that she lives abroad cannot possibly be equated with discrimination on grounds of race or sex. It is not a denial of respect for her as an individual. She was under no obligation to move to South Africa. She did so voluntarily and no doubt for good reasons. But in doing so, she put herself outside the primary scope and purpose of the UK social security system . . . What matters in my opinion is that (1) there is no question in this case of discrimination on a ground such as race or gender which denies Ms Carson the right to equal respect (2) in applying a scheme of social security, it is rational and internationally acceptable to distinguish between inhabitants of the UK and persons resident abroad (3) the extent to which the claims, if any, of persons resident abroad should be recognised is a matter for parliamentary decision.

As to Ms Reynolds' claim, Lord Rodger of Earlsferry said (at para 45):

> Ms Reynolds complains of discrimination in terms of Article 14 because, for some of the time when she was under 25 years of age, she received less by way of jobseeker's allowance than people of 25 and over. In other words, she was discriminated against on the ground of her age. There is no doubt that the relevant Regulations, endorsed by Parliament, deliberately gave less to those under 25. But this was not because the policymakers were treating people under 25 years of age as less valuable members of society. Rather, having regard to a number of factors, they judged that the situation of those under 25, as a class, was different from that of people of 25 and over, as a class. For example, in broad terms, those under 25 could be expected to earn less and to have lower living costs. Moreover, paying them a smaller amount of benefit would encourage them to live with others, rather than independently – something that was regarded as desirable in terms of general social policy. The scheme also had certain administrative advantages. In my view, having regard to these and other factors, it was open to ministers and Parliament, in the exercise of a broad political judgment, to differentiate between the two groups and to set different levels of benefit for them. Drawing the bright demarcation line at 25 was simply one part of that exercise. It follows that the difference in treatment of which Ms Reynolds complains easily withstands scrutiny and there is no unlawful discrimination in terms of Article 14.

What about Article 8 of the ECHR? The point was taken in *Carson and Reynolds* but dropped after the High Court stage ([2002] EWHC 426 (Admin) 37). As had been indicated by Maurice Kay J in *Tucker v Secretary of State for Social Security* [2001] EWCA Civ 1646:

> Any attempt to rely upon Article 8 alone to sustain a Convention right to a welfare benefit faces difficulty. The Strasbourg jurisprudence tends not to interpret the obligation on the state to respect family life in such a way as to require financial support.

Thus in 1987, in *Vaughan v UK*, Application No 12639/87, the applicant complained to the Commission that his supplementary benefit had not included a component to cover the travelling cost of contact visits to his home on the part of his children. It was held:

> Insofar as the applicant complains that there has been a violation of his right to respect for family life under Article 8 of the Convention, the Commission considers that the right to respect for family life does not impose an obligation on States to provide financial assistance for the purpose of ensuring that individuals can enjoy family life to the fullest.

Chapter 2

Introduction to Non Means-Tested Benefits

2.1 The scope of this chapter

2.1.1 Contents of this chapter

This chapter will consider the following topics:

(a) a reminder of the main non means-tested benefits;

(b) National Insurance contributions;

(c) contribution conditions for contributory benefits;

(d) increases for dependent adults;

(e) the incompatible and overlapping benefit rules.

These topics are common to several benefits within this group, and it makes sense to deal with them separately from the basic rules for the benefits themselves.

2.1.2 The non means-tested benefits

The benefits which are commonly called 'non means-tested' are of three types: contributory, non-contributory and statutory. The lists that follow cross-refer to the main treatment of each benefit. You may find it helpful to refer to the brief summary of the benefits in **Chapter 1**.

2.1.2.1 Contributory benefits

(a) Contribution-based jobseeker's allowance (**Chapter 3**).

(b) Contributory employment and support allowance (**4.3**).

(c) State Pension (**5.2**).

(d) Bereavement benefits (**5.4**).

2.1.2.2 Non-contributory benefits

(a) Non-contributory employment and support allowance (**4.5**).

(b) Disability living allowance (**4.6** to **4.8**).

(c) Attendance allowance (**4.9**).

(d) Industrial disablement benefit (**4.10**).

(e) Maternity allowance (**6.4**).

(f) Carer's allowance (**6.7**).

(g) Child benefit (**6.6**).

2.1.2.3 Statutory benefits

(a)   Statutory sick pay (**4.2**).

(b)   Statutory maternity pay (**6.3**).

2.2 National Insurance contributions

2.2.1 What are National Insurance contributions?

Every person in Great Britain is allocated a unique National Insurance number of two letters, six digits and a final letter. The number is used for income tax reference purposes as well as for benefits and contributions. HMRC collects contributions paid by employers and employees, alongside the tax deducted under the Pay As You Earn (PAYE) system for Schedule E income tax. It assesses self-employed people for liability to pay earnings-related contributions on the basis of the information contained in their tax returns. Contributions are paid by reference to the tax year (ie 6 April to 5 April).

2.2.2 The jargon

Before we examine the topic of contributions, we need to define some specialist jargon terms.

2.2.2.1 'Lower earnings limit' (LEL)

The lower earnings limit is a very low level of weekly earnings below which an employee is not involved in the National Insurance system at all. For 2008/09 it was £90.

The LEL is a very important concept. As we will see, it is used as the basic measure for potential entitlement to the contribution-based benefits. However, it is usually National Insurance contributions (NICs) paid in the past which are relevant and so it may be necessary to know the LEL for previous tax years. For example:

Tax year	LEL: £
2007/2008	87
2006/2007	84
2005/2006	82
2004/2005	79

2.2.2.2 'Primary contributions threshold' (PCT)

Primary Class 1 contributions are paid by employees, by deduction at source from their gross pay by their employers. For 2008/09 the PCT was £105. If an employee earns between the LEL and PCT, he does not pay any Class 1 contributions but he is treated as if he has paid such. That will be important if he later comes to claim a contributory benefit. An employee will pay Class 1 contributions at a prescribed percentage on the amount of his earnings that exceed the PCT up to the upper earnings limit (UEL) (see **2.2.2.4**) and at 1% of earnings above the UEL.

2.2.2.3 'Secondary contribution threshold'

Secondary Class 1 contributions are a tax on employers, payable in respect of their employees. The threshold at which payments start is usually the same as the primary threshold. We shall not be concerned further with secondary contributions, since they do not affect a claimant's right to benefit.

2.2.2.4 'Upper earnings limit'

The UEL is the figure which defines the maximum amount of contributions payable by employees at a prescribed rate depending on whether or not they are part of the additional State Pension scheme (see **5.2.3**). Above the UEL, contributions are paid at the flat rate of 1% of earnings. In 2008/09 it was £770.

2.2.2.5 'Earnings factor'

The earnings factor is the total amount of gross earnings on which an employee pays his National Insurance contributions in any tax year. An employee pays a fixed percentage of his gross earnings by way of primary Class 1 contributions. The more he earns, the more he pays. In benefits jargon terms, the higher his earnings, the higher his earnings factor. This can be important in helping him to qualify for contributory benefits if his contribution record has gaps in it. High earnings over a short period of employment can produce as high an earnings factor in a couple of months as low earnings in a complete year.

Example

(a)   Bob is employed for just June, July and August 2008 for the tax year 6 April 2008 to 5 April 2009. He is paid £2,000 each month. He therefore has an earnings factor of £6,000 for that tax year.

(b)   Janet is employed for the whole of the tax year 6 April 2008 to 5 April 2009. She is paid £500 each month. She also has an earnings factor of £6,000 for that tax year.

Self-employed people also have an earnings factor. Each weekly Class 2 NIC payment (see **2.2.3.2**) gives rise to an earnings factor equal to that year's weekly LEL. So, a person who is self-employed for the whole of a tax year (ie 52 weeks) will have an earnings factor of 52 times the LEL for that tax year.

2.2.3 Who is liable to pay compulsory contributions?

Although NICs are a form of tax on earned income, not everyone, even if working for pay, is liable to pay contributions. Every person in the population falls into one of three categories.

(a)   Those who are liable to pay compulsory NICs.

(b)   Those who are not liable to pay NICs but will not suffer as a result of non-payment.

(c)   Those who are not liable to pay NICs but may suffer as a result of non-payment.

Anyone who is aged between 16 and retirement age, and who is working and earning, is prima facie liable to pay contributions in respect of their earnings. How much they pay, and which of the various classes of compulsory NICs, depends on whether they are employed or self-employed, how much they are earning, and some other factors specific to each type of contribution. In reading the following account you may need to refer to the jargon section at **2.2.2**.

2.2.3.1 Employees

Employees pay primary Class 1 contributions on a fixed percentage of all their earnings over the primary contribution threshold. The employer deducts the contributions from the gross pay, together with Schedule E income tax, before payment. The rate of deduction varies according to whether the employee is or is not a member of a private pension scheme (see **5.2**).

If an employee earns between the LEL and PCT, he is deemed to have paid Class 1 NICs on those earnings (see further **2.2.6**).

Class 1 contributions are the only type which can be used as the basis of a claim for all the contributory benefits.

Historically, married women had the right to pay Class 1 contributions at a nominal rate, which did not entitle them to any benefits. However, since 5 April 1977 the only people who still have this right are women who were exercising it in 1977, who are still married to the same man as they were in 1977, and who have been paying contributions at that rate continuously ever since.

2.2.3.2   Self-employed workers

All self-employed people are liable to pay Class 2 contributions on their earnings from self-employment. The contributions are at a very low weekly flat rate which is regarded as producing an earnings factor equivalent to the lower earnings limit. For example, Doris is self-employed for 30 weeks in a tax year. Each week she made a Class 2 NIC payment. Her earnings factor for that tax year was 30 times the LEL.

It is possible for a self-employed person with very low earnings to apply for a certificate of exemption from paying contributions on the grounds of low earnings. This is rarely done, because it jeopardises entitlement to future benefit claims that are described at **2.2.5**.

Class 2 contributions can be used as a basis for a claim for all the contributory benefits except contribution-based jobseeker's allowance.

2.2.3.3   Higher-earning self-employed people

Self-employed people whose profits exceed a level roughly equal to the primary contribution threshold must also pay profit-related Class 4 contributions. This is a fixed percentage of all profits between the Class 4 threshold and a figure equal to the upper earnings limit.

Class 4 contributions are truly income tax under another name. They make no difference whatsoever to entitlement to any benefit.

2.2.4   People who have no need to pay contributions

There are two important groups who are not liable to pay contributions and suffer no detriment whatsoever as a result. This is so, even if they are working and earning in excess of the levels at which contributions are normally compulsory. The first group is children under the age of 16, the second anyone who has reached retirement age (60 for a woman, 65 for a man).

2.2.5   People who may suffer from not paying contributions

Everyone else who is not liable to pay compulsory contributions is theoretically at risk, because they will not have the contribution record needed to claim future benefits. People find themselves in this position for one of two reasons. They may not be working at all, for whatever reason – choice, illness or disability, unemployment, looking after children or invalids – or they may be working, but on earnings so low they are not liable to pay contributions. Some of these people will be given a form of automatic protection: others will have to make their own arrangements.

2.2.5.1 Low-paid employees

An employee may pay no contributions because his earnings are below the primary contribution threshold. Provided he earns at least the lower earnings limit, he is deemed to be paying full Class 1 NICs on an earnings factor equivalent to his actual gross pay. For benefit purposes, these deemed contributions are treated as actual contributions.

2.2.5.2 Contribution Class 1 credits

Contribution Class 1 credits may be awarded to people who do not pay actual contributions and are not deemed to do so. Credits can assist in qualifying for all the contributory benefits. On their own, however, they are not sufficient to enable a person to claim incapacity benefit or contribution-based jobseeker's allowance, which need a minimum number of actual or deemed contributions.

Three classes of people may be awarded contribution Class 1 credits.

(a) Those who are unemployed, registered with the Jobcentre, signing on and complying with the rules for jobseeker's allowance (see **Chapter 3**). This applies whether or not they are actually receiving any benefit.

Example

Mike was a self-employed taxi driver who can no longer drive because he has lost his licence. His wife Jenny works full-time as a teacher. How can Mike protect his contribution record?

Mike cannot claim contribution-based jobseeker's allowance because, being self-employed, he does not have the right contribution record (see **2.3.3**). He cannot claim income-based jobseeker's allowance because his wife is in full-time work (see **Chapter 8**). But, if he fulfils all the other rules for jobseeker's allowance, he will get a Class 1 NIC credit for each week that he signs on.

(b) Those who are unable to work because of illness, who are not on paid sick leave from an employer, and who are providing evidence of illness in the form of medical certificates to the DfWP. Again, this applies whether or not they are entitled to receive any benefit.

Example

Sunita, aged 45, cannot work because she has broken her wrist. She has not worked since her child was born 15 years ago. Her husband Ajay is a full-time engineer with a salary exceeding £40,000 pa. How can she protect her contribution record?

Sunita will not be entitled to contributory employment and support allowance because she will not have paid the right contributions at the right time (see **2.3**). She will not be entitled to income-related employment and support allowance because of her husband's job (see **Chapter 8**). But if she is providing evidence of illness to the DfWP, she will receive a Class 1 NIC credit for each week that she is unable to work.

(c) A person who is in receipt of carer's allowance (see **6.7**) will also be awarded Class 1 credits for each week the benefit is paid.

Example

Anne starts caring for her elderly mother in the autumn of 2007. She is awarded carer's allowance and receives it for 20 weeks during the tax year 2007/08 and for the entire tax year 2008/09. Anne will have 20 Class 1 NIC credits for 2007/08 and 52 Class 1 NIC credits for 2008/09.

2.2.5.3   Young person's Class 3 credits

A young person, aged at least 16 and under 19, is potentially liable to pay contributions, and would be doing so if he was working. If he stays on at school or college during that period, there may be a period of up to three years of his life when he is not paying contributions, which could affect his future rights to retirement pension (see **2.3.6.1**). As long as his parents are receiving child benefit for him, he will receive Class 3 credits for up to three years. Young person's credits can only assist in qualifying for retirement and bereavement benefits.

2.2.5.4   Home responsibilities protection

A parent of young children who is staying at home to look after those children, or a carer receiving income support, will be awarded 'home responsibilities protection', which was introduced in April 1978. It is awarded automatically to anyone whose records show that they are, throughout a tax year, receiving child benefit for a child under 16, or income support as a carer, and are not paying contributions or getting deemed contributions or credits under any of the rules already described. It helps them to qualify for retirement and bereavement benefits only, by reducing the number of years' contributions needed to qualify for full benefits. Note that in certain limited circumstances, the partner of the child benefit claimant may be able to claim the home responsibilities protection instead: see the Social Security Pensions (Home Responsibilities) Amendment Regulations 2008 (SI 2008/498). How this works is explained in detail at **2.3.6.3**.

2.2.5.5   Class 3 (voluntary) contributions

Anyone else who wishes to protect future rights to retirement pension and bereavement benefits must pay voluntary Class 3 contributions. These contributions are paid weekly at a flat rate. Self-employed people with earnings below the small earnings threshold (see **2.2.3.2**) would get a better deal from Class 2 contributions, as these carry the right to CESA with them, and are much lower.

2.2.6   Contributions and benefits: a summary

If an employee earns less than the LEL, he is not liable to pay Class 1 NICs.

If an employee earns between the LEL and the PCT, he is treated as if he had paid Class 1 NICs on those earnings. These Class 1 contributions are deemed to be paid contributions and so can count towards meeting the first condition to qualify for contribution-based jobseeker's allowance (CBJSA) and contributory employment and support allowance (CESA) (see **2.3.3**).

If an employee earns more than the PCT he pays Class 1 NICs on his earnings.

A self-employed person earning more than the small earnings exemption will pay Class 2 NICs. If he makes a high level of profit he also pays Class 4 NICs, but these are irrelevant when considering any benefit entitlement.

Class 1 credits may assist a person in claiming any contributory benefit (but for CBJSA and CESA can only help meet the second condition: see **2.3.3**).

Class 2 credits may assist a person claiming any contributory benefit apart from CBJSA (and for CESA such can only help meet the second condition: see **2.3.3**).

Class 3 credits can only help a person in claiming bereavement benefits and a retirement pension.

Home responsibilities protection (HRP) must be established for an entire contribution year. Each year of HRP is deducted from the number of years otherwise required to obtain full bereavement benefits or State Pension.

2.3 Contribution conditions

2.3.1 What are contribution conditions?

The right to receive CBJSA, CESA and State Pension depends upon the claimant's contribution record. For each benefit, it is important that the claimant has paid, is deemed to have paid, or is credited with:

(a)   the right *number or value* of contributions;

(b)   of the right *class*;

(c)   at the right *time.*

These rules collectively are called the contribution conditions and they vary with different benefits. The decision whether the contribution conditions are satisfied in any given case is the classic example of a decision against which there is no right of appeal (see **1.4.4**).

Bereavement benefits and certain retirement pensions take account of the record of the deceased spouse.

2.3.2 Terminology

Before we look at the contribution conditions, we need to define some further specialist jargon terms.

2.3.2.1 'Contribution year'

A contribution year is the period of 12 months and is identical to the tax year: 6 April in one year to 5 April in the next.

2.3.2.2 'Benefit year'

The benefit year is the period of 12 months within which the claimant makes a claim for any particular benefit for the first time. It begins on the first Sunday in January (eg the benefit year 2009 begins on 4 January). For CBJSA, the relevant benefit year is that in which the jobseeking period begins. For CESA, it is the year in which the period of limited capability for work begins.

2.3.2.3 'Working life'

The working life of any individual is from the sixteenth birthday (school leaving age) to retirement age (60 for a woman, 65 for a man). The basic length of the working life is thus 44 years for a woman and 49 for a man, but see **5.2.1.1**.

2.3.3 Contribution-based jobseeker's allowance and contributory employment and support allowance

The contribution conditions for CBJSA and CESA are the most complicated.

2.3.3.1 Contribution-based jobseeker's allowance

The contribution conditions for CBJSA are:

(a)   the claimant must have actually paid Class 1 NICs in respect of one of the last two contribution years ending before the beginning of the relevant benefit year and producing an earnings factor of at least 25 times that year's LEL ('the first condition'); *and*

(b)   the claimant must have either paid or been credited with Class 1 NICs in each of the last two contribution years ending before the beginning of the relevant benefit year and producing an earnings factor of at least 50 times the LEL each year ('the second condition').

Summary of key points

(a)   Only employees may claim CBJSA as only Class 1 NICs count.

(b)   The relevant contribution years are the last two years ending before the relevant benefit year starts.

(c)   Deemed payments count as actual payments.

(d)   Class 1 credits can help meet only the second condition.

Example

Robert is made redundant in June 2009. He signs on and receives CBJSA. His jobseeking period therefore begins in the benefit year 2009. The relevant contribution years to be considered are 6 April 2007–5 April 2008 (that is the contribution year which ends immediately before the relevant benefit year begins) and 6 April 2006–5 April 2007. Let us assume that Robert was employed for both of those years and earned gross £12,000 each year. Does he meet the first condition? Yes, as in fact he paid Class 1 NICs in each year on an earnings factor of £12,000 which exceeds the 2007/08 minimum required of £2,175 (25 × £87) or, in the alternative, the 2006/07 minimum required of £2,100 (25 × £84). Does he also meet the second condition? Yes, given he paid Class 1 NICs in each year on an earnings factor of £12,000 which exceeds the 2007/08 minimum required of £4,350 (50 × £87) and the 2006/07 minimum required of £4,200 (50 × £84).

2.3.3.2   Contributory employment and support allowance

The contribution conditions for CESA are:

(a)   the claimant must have actually paid Class 1 or 2 NICs in respect of one of the last three contribution years ending before the beginning of the relevant benefit year and producing an earnings factor of at least 25 times that year's LEL ('the first condition'); *and*

(b)   the claimant must have either paid or been credited with Class 1 or 2 NICs in each of the last two contribution years ending before the beginning of the relevant benefit year and producing an earnings factor of at least 50 times the LEL each year ('the second condition').

Summary of key points

(a)   Both employees and the self-employed may claim CESA as Class 1 and 2 NICs count. Class 1 deemed payments count as actual payments.

(b)   The relevant contribution years for the first condition are the last three ending before the relevant benefit year starts; whilst the relevant contribution years for the second condition are the last two ending before the relevant benefit year starts.

(c)   Class 1 and 2 credits can help meet only the second condition.

Example

Alice becomes unable to work in June 2009. She claims CESA as she is self-employed and so not entitled to SSP. Her period of limited capability for work therefore begins in the benefit year 2009. The relevant contribution years to be considered for the first condition are 6 April 2007–5 April 2008 (that is the contribution year which ends immediately before the relevant benefit year begins); 6 April 2006–5 April 2007 and 6 April 2005–5 April 2006. Let us assume that Alice was self-employed for the whole of 2005/2006 and paid a Class 2 contribution each week, but that in 2006/2007 and 2007/2008 she cared for her aged mother full time and received carer's allowance each week (so each year she was credited with 52 Class 1 NICs). Does she meet the first condition? Yes, as in fact she paid Class 2 NICs in one of the relevant contribution years (ie 2005/2006) on an earnings factor of 52 times the LEL which exceeds the minimum required of 25 times the LEL. Does she also meet the second condition? Yes, given she received Class 1 NIC credits in both relevant contribution years of 2006/07 and 2007/08 on an earnings factor of 52 times the LEL and the minimum required was 50 times the LEL.

2.3.4   Statutory sick pay and qualifying for CESA

We shall see in **Chapter 4** that most employees cannot claim CESA for the first 28 weeks of their illness, because they are entitled to statutory sick pay (SSP) instead. If the illness lasts more than 28 weeks, employees may then claim CESA. Note that the contribution record used for this claim for CESA is the one that applied at the time they first became ill and not when their SSP ended.

2.3.5   Carers

2.3.5.1   Carers and CBJSA

A carer who is looking after a person who is sick or disabled for 35 hours or more a week is likely to be receiving carer's allowance (see **6.7**). He may well be out of the labour market for many years. When his caring responsibilities end with the death, recovery or hospitalisation of the person he has been caring for, he may well wish to return to paid employment. Until he does so, he will sign on to protect his contribution record. But how can he claim CBJSA?

He will have contribution credits with his carer's allowance, and normally credits alone cannot qualify for CBJSA (see **2.3.3.1**). But, by a special concession, a carer may link his claim back to the beginning of the claim for carer's allowance, which is then treated as being the relevant benefit year to consider his contribution record. If at that date, however long ago, he satisfied the conditions for CBJSA, he may claim the benefit now.

2.3.5.2   Carers and CESA

If a person is entitled to carer's allowance before becoming unable to work, the first contribution condition (see **2.3.3.2**) is modified such that he must have paid the correct amount of Class 1 or 2 NICs for any one contribution year whatsoever during his working life. He can, of course, use any Class 1 credits (see **2.2.5.2**) received to meet the second condition.

2.3.6   Retirement and bereavement benefits

To claim either State Pension or bereavement benefits, the claimant needs to show a contribution record for most of the relevant working life. For a claim for State Pension, that is usually the claimant's own working life; for bereavement benefits, the working life in question is that of the spouse who has died. All classes of contributions (except Class 4) and credits count equally for these benefits.

Working life usually means from school-leaving age until retirement age (ie 16 to 60 for women (44 years) and 16 to 65 (49 years) for men), but see **5.2.1.1**. Bereavement benefits may be paid when a husband or wife has died well under retirement age, particularly bereavement allowance (see **5.4.4**). The working life is then from 16 to the date of death.

So what happens if there is a contribution record, but it does not cover the whole of the working life?

2.3.6.1   Total years' contributions necessary for full benefit

It is never necessary to have a record for every year of the working life. In the following table, the first column shows the number of years in the relevant working life, and the second the maximum number of years which can be missed for the claimant still to get the benefit at the full rate.

Working life	Permissible gap
years	*years*
1–10	1
11–20	2
21–30	3
31–40	4
41 and over	5

2.3.6.2   State Pension: contribution conditions

For the different types of pensions, see **Chapter 5**.

First, we need to consider who must have paid or been credited with NI contributions. This person is called the 'contributor'. For a category A pension, the contributor is the claimant. However, for a category B pension, the contributor can be the claimant or a spouse, or a deceased spouse's record can be used. Secondly, note that the contribution conditions are:

(a)   the contributor must have actually paid in any one contribution year whatsoever before death or pensionable age, Class 1, 2 or 3 NICs producing an earnings factor of at least 52 times that year's LEL ('the first condition'); and

(b)   the contributor must have either paid or been credited with Class 1, 2 or 3 NICs for each of the requisite number of years producing an earnings factor of at least 52 times the LEL for each year ('the second condition').

Example

Errol has just retired at the age of 65. He came to England from Trinidad as a spouse 22 years ago and has worked and paid contributions in England ever since. How much pension can he claim?

Errol's working life is 49 years (ie 65 minus 16). His permissible gap is 5 years (see table at **2.3.6.1**) so he would need contributions for 44 years to claim a full pension. He has only 22 years' contributions, so he can only claim a pension at 22/44 or one half of the full normal rate.

Currently, as seen, women need to have 39 qualifying years and men 44 years to get the full State Pension. However, under the Pensions Act 2007, this will be reduced to 30 years for anyone reaching pensionable age after 2010.

2.3.6.3   Home responsibilities protection

Home responsibilities protection (see **2.2.5.4**) works by reducing the total number of years' contributions needed for a full pension.

Example

Judith is 50 years of age and due to retire in 10 years' time. She worked and paid contributions from leaving university at the age of 21 for 8 years before having children. She then did not work for 15 years, and returned to work at the age of 44. She has worked ever since. How much pension can she claim, assuming she continues to work and pay contributions until she retires, aged 60?

Judith's working life will be 44 years (ie 60 minus 16). Normally she would need a contribution record for 39 of them to get a full pension as her permissible gap is 5 years – see table at **2.3.6.1**. The number of years she will have worked will be only 24 (ie 8 years before having children and 16 years before retiring). So at first sight it might seem that she will not get much more than just over half a standard rate pension. However, the 15 years she spent bringing up her children is deducted from the usual target of 39 years to reduce it to 24. As she will have worked and paid contributions for 24 years she will receive her full pension.

2.3.6.4   Bereavement benefits: contribution conditions

The only NIC requirement for a bereavement payment (see **5.4.5**) is that the late spouse or civil partner must have actually paid in any contribution year whatsoever Class 1, 2 or 3 NICs on an earnings factor of at least 25 times the LEL.

The NIC requirements for a widowed parent's allowance (see **5.4.3**) or a bereavement allowance (see **5.4.4**) are that for each benefit the late spouse or civil partner must have either:

(a)   paid in any contribution year whatsoever Class 1, 2 or 3 NICs on an earnings factor of 52 times the LEL; and

(b)   paid Class 1, 2 or 3 NICs or been credited with NICs on an earnings factor of 52 times the LEL for each of the 'requisite number of years' (see the above chart);

or in the alternative he or she died of an industrial injury or disease (see **4.10**).

If the requisite number of years is not met, then the amount of widowed parent's allowance or bereavement allowance is reduced proportionately. For example, a spouse dies aged 28. That spouse's working life is 12 years (ie 28 (age at death) minus 16 (school leaving age)). The requisite number of years is 12 minus 2 (see table at **2.3.6.1**), ie 10 years. Assume the spouse only paid and/or was credited with the correct number of NICs for eight contribution years. Only eight-tenths or 80% of the benefit is payable. Do not forget that should the spouse have died of an industrial injury or disease then the full benefit is payable.

2.4   Increases for adult dependants

2.4.1   What are increases?

A non means-tested benefit is usually paid at a single flat rate for the claimant alone, irrespective of his family circumstances. However, if he has a partner living in the household, he may be able to claim an additional sum on top of his own benefit. This additional sum is called an increase. The detailed provisions concerning unmarried partners and those living as civil partners are beyond the scope of this book. Note that the term 'dependant' here is somewhat misleading. What it means is that before an increase is payable you must first consider any earnings replacement benefit paid to, or earnings received by, the claimant's partner.

2.4.2 Which non means-tested benefits carry an adult dependant increase?

The following benefits are relevant:

(a)   maternity allowance (see **6.4**);

(b)   carer's allowance (see **6.7**); and

(c)   State Pensions (see **5.2**).

There are two key questions always to ask.

2.4.2.1 Does the overlapping earnings replacement benefit rule apply?

If the adult dependant for whom the increase is claimable receives an earnings replacement benefit (see **1.2.5**) in his or her own right then:

(a)   if the amount of the increase is the same or less than the amount of the adult dependant's earning replacement benefit, the increase is not payable; but

(b)   if the amount of the increase exceeds the amount of the adult dependant earning replacement benefit, the difference is payable.

Example (using 2008/09 figures)

Mrs Morgan receives maternity allowance. Her husband receives contribution-based jobseeker's allowance of £20.00 (he has part-time earnings and receives an occupational pension reducing it to this figure – see **3.4**). Mrs Morgan can claim an increase with her maternity allowance for Mr Morgan. However, Mr Morgan's contribution-based jobseeker's allowance is £20.00 and so only the *difference* between the increase of £39.40 and that contribution-based jobseeker's allowance of £20.00 is paid (ie £19.40). If Mr Morgan's contribution-based jobseeker's allowance had been £39.40 per week or more then no adult dependant increase in his wife's maternity allowance would be payable.

2.4.2.2 Does the adult dependant have earnings?

For State Pensions, if the amount of the adult dependant's net earnings exceeds a prescribed threshold figure (for 2008/09 it was £60.50 per week), the increase is not payable at all.

For maternity allowance and carer's allowance the increase is not payable if the amount of the adult dependant's net earnings equals or exceeds the amount of the increase. If the net earnings are less than the increase, the increase is payable in full.

Example (using 2008/09 figures)

Mrs Richards receives carer's allowance. Her husband's net earnings are £50 per week. No carer's allowance adult dependant increase is payable to Mrs Richards as her husband's earnings exceed the amount of the increase (£30.20).

2.4.3 Summary

When considering if an adult dependant increase is payable ask:

(1)   Does the adult dependant for whom the increase is claimable receive an earnings replacement benefit in his or her own right?

(2)   Does the adult dependant for whom the increase is claimable have earnings?

2.5 Incompatible non means-tested benefits

As a general rule, a claimant may be entitled to any non means-tested benefit for which he meets the conditions of entitlement. However, the right to one particular non means-tested benefit may prevent the entitlement to another such benefit. These benefits are known as incompatible non means-tested benefits and are set out in the following table.

Benefit claimed	Incompatible with
Contributory employment and support allowance or maternity allowance or State Pension or statutory sick pay or statutory maternity pay	Contribution-based jobseeker's allowance
Contributory employment and support allowance or maternity allowance or statutory sick pay or contribution-based jobseeker's allowance	Statutory maternity pay
Contributory employment and support allowance or statutory sick pay or contribution-based jobseeker's allowance	State Pension
Contributory employment and support allowance or maternity allowance or State Pension or statutory maternity pay or contribution-based jobseeker's allowance	Statutory sick pay
Widowed parent's allowance	Bereavement allowance

2.6 Overlapping non means-tested benefits

As we have seen in **2.5**, whilst as a general rule a claimant may be entitled to any non means-tested benefit for which he meets the conditions of entitlement, some benefits are incompatible. Where non means-tested benefits are compatible (ie can be claimed together), certain provisions, 'the overlapping benefit rules', may affect their rate of pay.

The non means-tested benefits that may be affected by these rules are the so-called earnings replacement benefits (see **1.2.5**). Where a claimant is entitled to claim two or more such benefits, the DfWP makes an adjustment to the rate of pay. If a contributory benefit is payable to the claimant, then that is paid in preference to a non-contributory benefit. However, if the amount of the contributory benefit payable is less than that of the non-contributory benefit, the difference between the two is paid in addition to the contributory benefit. In all other cases the amount of the highest benefit is paid.

There are two non means-tested benefits that have their own unique 'overlapping' rule. The benefits concerned are disability living allowance care component and constant attendance allowance. This is discussed at **4.11**.

The overlapping rules affect only the amount of benefit payable and not the entitlement to it. So, if a claimant meets the conditions of entitlement for both CESA and carer's allowance, he will be paid CESA (the contributory benefit which is more than the non-contributory benefit of carer's allowance) but is treated as still entitled to carer's allowance. As a result, he would still receive a carer's premium if entitled to income-related employment and support allowance (see **7.7.4**).

2.7 Claiming more than one non means-tested benefit: a summary

Subject to the fact that certain non means-tested benefits are incompatible (see **2.5**) or overlap (see **2.6**), a claimant may receive any number of the non means-tested benefits for which he meets the conditions of entitlement. If still on a low income, the claimant may be entitled to one or more means-tested benefits as well.

Examples

(a)   Andrew is 30 years of age and he is made redundant. The earnings replacement benefit (see **1.2.5**) he will wish to claim is contribution-based jobseeker's allowance. He may well not qualify for any other non means-tested benefits. He may therefore need to top up what he receives by also claiming the means-tested version of jobseeker's allowance, namely income-based jobseeker's allowance (see **Chapter 8**).

(b)   Brenda is 35 years of age and she has a serious accident at work. As a result, she is unable to work. Her employer pays her SSP (see **4.2**) for the first 28 weeks she is off work. Due to her disability she cannot return to work. The earnings replacement benefit she will wish to claim is CESA (see **4.3**). She may well be entitled to other non means-tested benefits due to her disability. If she has care and/or mobility needs she can claim disability living allowance (see **4.6**). As her accident arose out of her employment she may be entitled as well to industrial disablement benefit (see **4.10**). If the amount of her non means-tested benefits is inadequate, she may be able to top it up with the means-tested benefit of income-related employment and support allowance (see **Chapter 8**).

Chapter 3

Jobseeker's Allowance

3.1 Introduction

3.1.1 What is jobseeker's allowance?

Jobseeker's allowance (JSA) is the latest name for the benefit which until 1996 was called 'unemployment benefit'. However, the change from the passive-sounding 'unemployment benefit' to the active 'jobseeker's allowance' is not just playing with words: it represents a real change in the ethos of the benefit. It is a benefit for people who are actively trying to find work. There are many safeguards to ensure that the benefit is paid only to those who can demonstrate a genuine commitment to find work.

3.1.2 One benefit, two elements

Jobseeker's allowance has two elements. Each should be seen as a separate benefit. The first is contribution-based jobseeker's allowance (CBJSA), which is a contributory, non means-tested earnings replacement benefit (see generally **Chapters 1** and **2**). The second element is income-based jobseeker's allowance (IBJSA), a non-contributory means-tested benefit which is calculated in the same way as income support. This is discussed in **Chapter 8**, where its differences from CBJSA are set out in full.

Here we shall note five points about the similarities and differences, but the rest of the chapter concentrates on CBJSA.

(a) The rules on conditions of entitlement (see **3.2**) and disqualification from benefit (see **3.3**) apply in exactly the same way to both elements.

(b) Entitlement to CBJSA is unaffected by capital or by a partner's income; entitlement to IBJSA may be affected by either.

(c) The CBJSA can be paid only for a maximum of 26 weeks; IBJSA may be paid for many years, until the claimant reaches retirement age.

(d) The CBJSA is available only to those with the appropriate National Insurance contribution record (see **2.3.3.1**); IBJSA depends on a means test.

(e) The IBJSA may be paid if CBJSA is not payable (eg if the contribution conditions are not satisfied), or IBJSA can be paid to top up CBJSA, or IBJSA may be paid after CBJSA runs out at the end of 26 weeks.

3.2   Conditions of entitlement

3.2.1   What are the conditions of entitlement for CBJSA?

To qualify for CBJSA, the claimant must satisfy the contribution conditions (see **2.3.3.1**). He must then satisfy the conditions set out in s 1 of the JA 1995:

(a)   he must have signed a jobseeker's agreement (see **3.2.3**);

(b)   he must not be in 'remunerative work' (see **3.2.4**);

(c)   he must be available for work and actively seeking employment (the 'labour market conditions': see **3.2.5 to 3.2.8**);

(d)   he must not be disqualified from benefit for any reason (see **3.3**);

(e)   he must be capable of work and under retirement age (65 for men, 60 for women); and

(f)   as a general rule, he must not be under 19 years of age at school, college or on a non-advanced course. There are exceptions which are outside the scope of this book;

(g)   he must satisfy the residence requirements (see **Chapter 10**).

3.2.2   Making a claim for jobseeker's allowance

When a person becomes unemployed, his first step should be to visit the nearest Jobcentre Plus to enquire about claiming JSA. The claimant will be given a form to complete, and an appointment with an employment officer (EO) who carries out casework with unemployed claimants.

Among other information needed for processing the claim, the form requires him to suggest the type of work he wants to look for and how he proposes to go about finding it. This information will be used at the interview with the EO, as the starting point for arriving at a jobseeker's agreement (see **3.2.3**).

On receipt of the claim form, the EO may contact the last employer to find more about the circumstances in which the claimant lost his employment, and what payments he received on leaving, since the answers to these enquiries may affect his rights to benefit (see **3.3.3**).

3.2.3   The jobseeker's agreement

The jobseeker's agreement is intended to be a genuine agreement negotiated between the claimant and the Secretary of State, via the EO. It imposes obligations on the claimant in return for the payment of benefit, and provides him with clear guidance on what he must do in order to try to find work.

3.2.3.1   Form and content

The form and content of the agreement are specified in s 9 of the JA 1995, with details in regs 31–44 of the Jobseeker's Allowance Regulations 1996 (SI 1996/207) (JA Regs 1996). A copy of the standard form is reproduced in **Appendix 1**. The agreement must be in writing – in practice, a standard printed form is used, filled in with the appropriate details. It must be signed by the claimant and by the EO on behalf of the Secretary of State. The claimant receives a copy to keep. The agreement is likely to be varied as circumstances change, especially where the claimant remains unemployed for a long time. All variations must also be agreed, reduced into writing, and signed, with a copy given to the claimant.

The agreement contains, among other information:

(a)   a list of the types of employment for which the claimant is going to look;

(b)   any restrictions on types of employment, hours of work, distance travelled, or expected pay levels, which have been agreed with the EO (see **3.2.7**);

(c)   the steps that the claimant will take each week to attempt to find work (see **3.2.8**).

The agreement will also give the claimant the name of the EO who will be his regular contact. Lastly, it must explain his rights to challenge any part of the agreement.

3.2.3.2   Challenging the agreement

The claimant can receive no benefit until he has signed the agreement. If the claimant and the EO cannot agree on any term of the agreement, the claimant has the right to have the disputed term referred to a decision-maker, to decide whether his objections are well founded.

There is an ultimate right of appeal to a tribunal if the claimant is still unhappy after the review, but such appeals are extremely rare. The jobseeker's agreement may be backdated to the date of the first contact if the claimant's objections are accepted. Meanwhile, he has nothing to live on, and may have to apply for hardship payments (see **8.11**).

3.2.4   'Remunerative work' (JA 1995, ss 51–53)

It is easy to understand that a person cannot be entitled to a benefit intended for the unemployed if he is, in fact, working. But what if he is doing only a little part-time work? What if he is doing voluntary work to fill the time while he is unemployed? He is still allowed to claim the benefit (subject to meeting the other conditions) if he is not in 'remunerative work'. The number of hours worked is the starting point for the definition of this term. Work is not 'remunerative work' if it is for an average of less than 16 hours per week, including meal breaks taken at work.

Even if the claimant is working for 16 hours or more per week, it is still not 'remunerative' unless it is done for payment or in the expectation of payment. Voluntary work and hobbies are largely excluded. 'Payment' includes payment in kind if it is given in exchange for work, such as free meals or lodgings. 'Expectation of payment' means more than a mere hope that payment will be made and such expectation must be realistic. For example, a writer who writes a first novel in the hope it will be published will not be considered to be in remunerative work but, if it were a second novel, payment would be a realistic expectation and he will be treated as being in remunerative work.

The regulations are sufficiently wide to allow remunerative work to encompass work done that does not result in payment, as in *Kazantzis v Chief Adjudication Officer* (1999) *The Times*, 30 June. In that case, it was held that the time spent by a taxi driver waiting in the taxi office for customers counted as remunerative work, despite the fact that the taxi driver would not be paid for that time and did not expect payment for that time. The Court of Appeal decided that the waiting time was an essential part of the employment, just as the time spent by a shopkeeper tidying shelves would be, and therefore the hours spent in such activities should be included in calculating whether a claimant worked 16 hours or more per week.

Certain claimants are deemed not to be in remunerative work despite the number of hours worked. These include charity workers and volunteers; those on training schemes and part-time fire-fighters or auxiliary coastguards, or lifeboatmen or members of the territorial army, or local authority councillors.

A claimant who is not in remunerative work may still not get benefit. The CBJSA is subject to an earnings rule (see **3.4**): if the claimant is earning as much as he would receive in benefit, he can have no benefit. In addition, he must also satisfy the 'labour market conditions' (see **3.2.5**).

3.2.5 The labour market conditions

The claimant has signed his jobseeker's agreement, and is not in remunerative work. He must now show that he is available for work (JA 1995, s 6) and actively seeking employment (JA 1995, s 7). These two conditions are collectively known as 'the labour market conditions'.

The JA Regs 1996, at regs 5–22, define both conditions in detail, and include extensive deeming provisions, to enable claimants to be treated as available or seeking work when they are not, and vice versa. We shall look at some of these provisions in context.

3.2.6 'Available for work'

'Work', in this context, means work as an employee which it is reasonable for the claimant to do. The claimant will normally be expected to be available to work at least 40 hours per week.

Being available for work usually means 'immediately' available. There should be nothing to prevent the claimant from receiving job offers and acting on them straight away (ie within an hour or two). There are exceptions to this rule, including:

(a)   if the claimant provides a paid or unpaid service but is not a volunteer or carer (see below), he is allowed to start work after 24 hours' notice ('services' in this context may include giving someone a regular lift to the shops);

(b)   if the claimant is a carer (see **3.2.7.5**) or doing voluntary work, he is allowed to start work after one week's notice ('voluntary work' means work done for a charity or other non-profit making organisation, or for anyone who is not part of the claimant's family, for which no payment is received other than reimbursement of reasonable expenses);

(c)   if the claimant is working part time and is required to give notice, he will be allowed to work out that notice.

The JA 1995 and the JA Regs 1996 specify the following circumstances in which a person is conclusively deemed to be not available for work.

(a)   *If he is incapable of work due to illness or disability.* However, he may be deemed to be capable of work for a period of illness lasting not more than two weeks. This avoids the need to switch benefits for a short-term illness.

(b)   *If he is a student on a full-time course.* For students in further education (up to A level), 'full time' is at least 21 hours per week supervised study. There is no definition for higher education (degree level and similar). It is a question of fact, on which the opinion of the teaching institution is persuasive but not conclusive.

(c)   *If he is outside Great Britain,* unless the purpose of his absence is to attend a job interview within the EEA (see **10.4.4** and **10.4.9**).

3.2.7 Restricting availability

As a general rule, a claimant may restrict his availability for employment. He may do so by placing restrictions on the nature of the employment for which he is available and the terms or conditions of employment for which he is available (including the rate of remuneration). However, he must show that he has reasonable prospects of securing employment notwithstanding those restrictions (JA Regs 1996, reg 8). We shall now consider particular types of restrictions.

3.2.7.1 Restricting availability during any 'permitted period'

A claimant may be allowed to restrict his availability to his usual employment for a limited period. The permitted period starts on the date of the claim and may last from one week to a maximum of 13 weeks. Whether the claimant is entitled to any permitted period – and, if so, its length – is determined by the EO, who will consider the claimant's usual occupation, his relevant skills or qualifications, the length of any training undertaken for that occupation, his record of employment, whether the employment was continuous, and the availability and location of that type of employment. Generally speaking, the longer the claimant has been working in his usual occupation and the higher the degree of skill, training and qualification, the longer the permitted period will be. If there is little or no skill involved in the job at all, then a permitted period may not be allowed. The claimant's prospects of returning to work will depend on such things as his age, experience, the number and location of vacancies, and the number of people who can fill those vacancies. A qualified teacher who has taught for 15 years should be allowed to look for teaching work for the maximum 13 weeks; a labourer who has been a hod carrier on a building site for six months would be lucky to be allowed one week.

3.2.7.2 Restricted level of pay

The claimant may refuse to accept a job during any agreed permitted period which pays below the level of his gross pay which he used to receive, but only if he had been receiving that amount for a long period. The most recent level of pay received will be ignored as the claimant will not be used to receiving it. For example, a claimant spends five years in the same job for which he is paid £20,000 per annum. In the last two months before he is laid off he receives a pay rise of £500 giving him a salary of £20,500. His usual level of pay for the permitted period purposes is £20,000.

Whether or not a permitted period is granted, note that the level of pay cannot be restricted after the initial six-month period of the claim unless such is reasonable because the claimant is disabled (see **3.2.7.6**).

3.2.7.3 Restricting availability by hours of work

As indicated above a claimant must be willing to work at least 40 hours per week. The claimant may choose a pattern of availability as long as it gives him a reasonable prospect of securing employment and it is recorded in his jobseeker's agreement. For example, if a bank clerk restricts his hours of work to between midnight and 8 am on six days a week, it might seriously reduce his prospects of employment unless he can show that work is available with 24-hour telephone or Internet banking. If a claimant is not prepared to work for at least 40 hours per week, he will be unavailable for work and will not receive benefit unless he has caring responsibilities (see **3.2.7.5**), and/or he has physical or mental disabilities (see **3.2.7.6**). Such a claimant must be willing to accept employment of less than 40 hours per benefit week.

3.2.7.4 Religious beliefs and conscientious objections

A claimant may place restrictions on the type of employment he is willing to do because of religious or conscientious objections, which are sincerely held. For example, a claimant may not wish to work on a holy day, or a Jewish butcher may wish to work only for a kosher butcher. Again, the restrictions will be acceptable as long as the claimant can show that he has a reasonable prospect of securing employment despite the restrictions.

3.2.7.5 People with caring responsibilities

A person with caring responsibilities may restrict the total number of hours for which he is available for employment to less than 40 hours in any week provided:

(a)   in that week he is available for employment for as many hours as his caring responsibilities allow and for the specific hours that those responsibilities allow; and

(b)   he has reasonable prospects of securing employment notwithstanding that restriction.

In this context, 'caring responsibilities' means responsibility for caring for a child or for an elderly person, or for a person whose physical or mental condition requires him to be cared for, who is either in the same household or a close relative. A close relative here is a spouse or other member of an unmarried couple, parent, step-parent, grandparent, parent-in-law, son, stepson, son-in-law, daughter, stepdaughter, daughter-in-law, brother, sister, grandchild or the spouse of any of the preceding persons or, if that person is one of an unmarried couple, the other member of that couple.

3.2.7.6 People with disabilities

A person who has a disability may not have limited capability for work (see **4.3**), but may be restricted in what he can actually achieve at work. He may restrict his availability for types of work, hours and travelling to any extent which is reasonable in the light of his physical or mental disabilities. It does not matter that this may make it almost impossible to find work.

Thus, an unskilled labourer with lower-back pain may refuse any job involving prolonged standing or repeated bending and lifting, or a young woman with chronic fatigue syndrome may need to rest for an hour, two or three times in a working day. This may make these people virtually unemployable, but if the restrictions are justified, they must be permitted. A finding that a person does not have limited capability for work for ESA purposes (see **4.4**) is binding for the purposes of jobseeker's allowance.

3.2.8 'Actively seeking employment'

The jobseeker's agreement also specifies the steps that claimants must take each week in order to find employment. By s 7 of the JA 1995, the claimant will normally be expected to take more than two steps every week. Typical 'steps' include:

(a)   visiting Jobcentre Plus at least once a week;

(b)   registering with an employment agency;

(c)   reading the 'situations vacant' columns of specified local or national newspapers, or trade and professional journals;

(d)   telephoning or visiting potential employers;

(e)   preparing a CV, learning interview techniques, practising writing application letters;

(f)   applying for a certain number of vacancies each week.

A claimant must show that he is actively seeking work within a reasonable daily travelling time of his home and which he is capable of doing. The claimant must take all reasonable steps to give him the best chance of finding work. Whether the steps taken are reasonable will be determined by the EO, who will consider such things as the claimant's skills and qualifications, disabilities, the time that has passed since the claimant last worked and the effectiveness of previous steps taken. The steps taken must give the claimant his best chance of securing employment, which means that a step will not count if the claimant has undermined his own chance of being offered the job, for example, by acting abusively towards a prospective employer, or by spoiling an application. Some steps will be more relevant to some claimants than to others. For example, it would be pointless if a highly skilled or qualified person went to the Jobcentre on a daily basis during his permitted period when prospective employers are unlikely to advertise positions there. Equally, it would be pointless for a builder's mate to read the situations vacant column in a computer magazine.

The claimant may be required to keep a diary of his 'steps' to help discussions with his EO.

A claimant can safely ignore a job vacancy which falls outside the terms he has agreed with the EO. But if he refuses or fails to apply for a job which does fall within the agreed parameters, he may be penalised by a loss of benefit (see **3.3.5**), especially if he does this more than once.

3.3 Disqualification from benefit

3.3.1 What are the grounds for disqualification?

A claimant may have any benefit refused or withdrawn if it becomes obvious he is not entitled to it. For jobseeker's allowance, leaving aside fraudulent claims, the common most reasons for disqualification are as follows.

(a)   He has not yet signed a jobseeker's agreement (see **3.2.3**).

(b)   Doubt has arisen over whether he satisfies the labour market conditions (see **3.2.5–3.2.8**).

(c)   He has missed an appointment for signing on or to see an EO.

(d)   He has monies from his former employer which are treated as income, so that he is deemed to be in remunerative work.

(e)   He is involved in an industrial dispute.

(f)   A sanction has been imposed on him because of some aspect of his conduct during or before the start of his claim.

We need now to consider items (c) to (f) of this list.

3.3.2 Missed appointments

Regulation 23 of the JA Regs 1996 provides that a claimant must attend at any appointment notified to him by the Secretary of State. If he fails to do this then, under reg 25, his benefit will be stopped immediately, unless he attends the Jobcentre within five working days and shows 'good cause' why he failed to attend. Forgetfulness and confusion over the date is not good cause, but other factors such as illness, emergencies and transport problems may be. If the claimant cannot show good cause, he will have to make a new claim to benefit, and will probably lose at least one week's money.

This problem usually arises with claimants who miss their usual signing-on day. Every new claimant for JSA receives a card, which gives him details of the day and time he must attend, every two weeks, at the Jobcentre to sign on. Signing on involves signing a form to confirm that he has attended and that he has notified the Employment Service of any change in his circumstances. The card counts as notification of an appointment within the meaning of reg 23.

Claimants see an EO every 13 weeks. The first interview will coincide with the end of the period of the right to restrict availability to the usual occupation; the second with the expiry of the contribution-based benefit. The interviews are likely to result in changes to the jobseeker's agreement to include new tactics for job hunting, a wider range of types of employment, and possibly to consider retraining. These appointments too are covered by reg 23.

3.3.3 Payments on termination of employment

When an employee leaves employment, he may receive all or any of the following:

(a)   Pay for the last period worked before leaving.

(b)   A payment to compensate him for loss of earnings, where he is dismissed without notice. This payment may be made voluntarily by his employer, or in a negotiated settlement, or by a court or tribunal in an unfair or wrongful dismissal claim.

(c)   A redundancy payment, in a lump sum or instalments.

(d)   A cash payment for his accrued rights to paid holiday which he has not taken before leaving.

Of these, items (b) and (d) are treated as pay for the period they cover. The claimant is deemed to be in remunerative work (see **3.2.4**) during that period. Redundancy pay is not income for this purpose, even if paid by instalments.

Example

Karin has been made redundant, without notice. She has a redundancy payment of £4,000, six weeks' pay in lieu of notice and two weeks' pay for her holiday entitlement, which she was due to take next month. The six weeks' pay was paid only after her solicitor threatened to sue the employer. How long will it be before she can receive JSA?

The six weeks' pay is a compensation payment. Karin is treated as being in remunerative work during this period and the two weeks of her holiday pay period. She cannot claim JSA for eight weeks in total. But she should still sign on to get credits for her contribution record.

3.3.4 Industrial disputes

An employee who is out of work because of an industrial dispute at his place of work will not be entitled to benefit, unless he has no interest in the dispute being settled.

Example

Sandie and her brother Alex both work at a car factory. The factory is closed because the assembly workers are on strike for more pay. Alex, who is an assembly worker, cannot receive JSA because he has an interest in the outcome of the dispute. Sandie, who works in the canteen, can receive it because her pay will not be affected by the resolution of the dispute.

3.3.5 Sanctions (JA 1995, s 19)

A sanction denies the claimant JSA temporarily because of some aspect of his conduct. When a claimant is sanctioned, it does not break the claim but suspends it for the period of the sanction. The period varies according to the type of conduct and its seriousness.

3.3.5.1 Fixed-period sanctions

Fixed-period sanctions are for minor breaches such as:

(a) failure to comply with a specific instruction from an EO (such instructions are called 'jobseeker's directions');

(b) failure to attend on a training course for which the claimant has been enrolled; or

(c) leaving the course before it finishes.

The claimant will escape sanction if he can show 'good cause' for the failure. If there is no good cause, he will be sanctioned for two weeks the first time, four weeks on subsequent occasions. Whether there was good cause is a question of fact, and may be the subject of an appeal to a tribunal.

3.3.5.2 Discretionary period sanctions

For a more serious breach, the period of sanction is in the discretion of the Secretary of State, up to a maximum of 26 weeks. Discretionary period sanctions apply in three main circumstances.

(a) Voluntary unemployment. Employees are expected not to give up a job and throw themselves onto the National Insurance Fund without 'just cause', which means more than 'good cause'. It will include health reasons (including mental health), bullying and harassment, with or without physical assaults, and leaving to go to another job which then falls through. Not liking the job, or feeling 'I could do better than this' is not 'just cause'.

(b) Loss of employment for misconduct. The misconduct must be relevant to the employment, though not necessarily arising from it. It can involve fraud, persistent lateness, malingering, failure to obey reasonable orders and violence, and any act which means the claimant cannot carry out his job.

Example

James, a shop assistant, is convicted and fined for driving while uninsured. His colleague Paula is convicted of stealing from the shop. Both are dismissed. James's crime has no obvious effect on his ability to do his job, and no sanction should be applied. Paula has committed a serious breach of the duty of trust between employer and employee, and will probably be sanctioned for the maximum 26 weeks.

(c) Failing without good cause to apply for or take up a suitable opportunity of employment notified through the Jobcentre. The job must be within the terms of the jobseeker's agreement. The usual reason for refusal is that the pay is very low, although under reg 72 of JA Regs 1996, this is very rarely good cause.

With discretionary sanctions, the claimant may appeal both against the sanction itself and the period. Tribunals have been known to increase the period on appeal.

3.3.5.3 Effect of a sanction

A claimant who is sanctioned cannot receive either form of JSA during the sanction period. The period eats into any award of CBJSA, so that a person who is dismissed for misconduct with a maximum sanction of 26 weeks will never receive any CBJSA at all.

3.3.6 Hardship payments

A person who is disqualified from JSA may literally have nothing to live on. Means-tested hardship payments may be available to the following groups only:

(a)   those whose claim has not been decided because they have not yet signed a jobseeker's agreement, or there is doubt about the labour market conditions;

(b)   those who have been found not to satisfy the labour market conditions; and

(c)   those who have been sanctioned.

Hardship payments are discussed in more detail, including the means test, at **8.11**.

3.4   Amount of contribution-based jobseeker's allowance

The CBJSA is a non means-tested benefit. The amount of capital held by the claimant and any partner is irrelevant. Likewise, the fact that a claimant's partner may be in remunerative work is irrelevant.

The CBJSA is paid at three different rates depending on whether the claimant is aged under 18, between 18 and 24, or 25 and over. It is paid just for the claimant. There is no additional allowance for any partner. If the claimant has a partner who is not in remunerative work, he may be entitled to IBJSA (see **8.2.3**) to top up his CBJSA.

We have seen that a claimant can work part-time. However, his part-time earnings will be taken into account when the benefit is calculated. Only the first £5 is disregarded. Also, if the claimant receives a pension payment under a personal pension or occupational pension scheme which exceeds a prescribed figure (it was £50 in 2008/09), then the excess is taken into account and reduces the amount of the CBJSA.

Example (using 2008/09 figures)

Fred has claimed CBJSA. He works part-time doing a few gardening jobs and is paid £25 weekly. He also receives an occupational pension of £70 a week. Fred's CBJSA will be the personal rate of pay according to Fred's age *minus* £20 (ie his part-time earnings of £25 after disregarding £5) and *minus* £20 (ie the excess of his occupational pension above £50).

3.5   The New Deal

The New Deal is a series of initiatives taken by the Government designed to reduce the number of benefit claimants by helping people to find work. Everyone on New Deal gets a personal adviser who is their point of contact throughout the programme. There are two types of schemes. The first is for people who would otherwise be claiming benefits as unemployed, which is compulsory for those to whom it applies. The second group of schemes is aimed at people who are not classified as unemployed but are receiving benefits and would like to get back into work. Full details may be found at www.jobcentreplus.gov.uk.

3.6   Contribution-based JSA and other benefits

The CBJSA is treated as income when calculating the child tax credit and working tax credit (see **9.6**).

The CBJSA is treated as income when calculating income-based JSA, income support, income-related employment and support allowance, housing benefit and council tax benefit (see **7.3**).

The CBJSA is incompatible with (ie it cannot be claimed by an individual with) CESA, maternity allowance, retirement pension, SSP and statutory maternity pay (see **2.5**).

The CBJSA is an earnings replacement benefit (see **1.2.5**) and so may affect the entitlement of a spouse to any adult dependant increase in an appropriate benefit (see **2.4**).

The CBJSA and IBJSA can be claimed together. As indicated above, CBJSA will count as income when calculating any entitlement to IBJSA.

3.7 Claimant profile: CBJSA

Contribution-based JSA is a short-term earnings replacement benefit for an employee who has recently lost his job. It is payable only to an employee who has the correct Class 1 National Insurance payment history. The claimant must visit Jobcentre Plus and sign a jobseeker's agreement.

Chapter 4

Limited Capability for Work and Disability

4.1 Introduction

This chapter looks at non means-tested benefits for people who are sick and/or disabled. Traditionally the benefits fall into two groups. First, those payable because a person cannot work. A person who is employed or self-employed may fall sick or become disabled, and as a result may be unable to work. His inability to work may be for a few days or weeks, but it may be much longer, even permanent. Secondly, there is a group of benefits that have nothing to do with a person's inability to work but focus on the level of the claimant's disability.

4.1.1 Benefits covered by this chapter

4.1.1.1 Limited capability for work

The following are the benefits which may be paid to a person who has limited capability for work because of a physical or mental disease or disablement.

(a) Statutory sick pay (SSP), for most employees during the first 28 weeks of illness or disability.

(b) Contributory employment and support allowance (CESA), for anyone who meets the contribution conditions, including the self-employed (see **2.3.3.2**), and employees whose entitlement to SSP has ended. Remember SSP is payable for only 28 weeks, so if an employee is still unable to work he will wish to move on to CESA if he qualifies for it.

(c) Non-contributory ESA for a young adult aged 16 or over who does not meet the contribution conditions for CESA but has a long-lasting disability which began before the age of 20, or sometimes 25. See **4.3.3**.

A person who does not qualify for any of these benefits, but who has limited capability for work and satisfies the means test, may be entitled to income-related employment and support allowance (see **Chapter 8**). A person entitled to one of these benefits but otherwise on a low income may also be entitled to income-related employment and support allowance.

4.1.1.2 Disability

A person who suffers from a disability may receive one or more of the following benefits. These benefits are payable whether or not the person receives SSP or CESA.

(a)   Disability living allowance care component (DLA care), for those under 65 at first claim who need care or supervision.

(b)   Disability living allowance mobility component (DLA mobility), for those aged at least 3 and under 65 at first claim, who effectively cannot walk or cannot find their way around out of doors.

(c)   Attendance allowance (AA): like DLA care component for those aged 65 or over at first claim.

(d)   Industrial disablement benefit, for employees who have suffered an accident or contracted an occupational disease in the course of their employment.

4.1.1.3 Examples

Alan has influenza and cannot go to work for six weeks. During this period of illness his employer pays him SSP.

Brenda has a bad car accident and is hospitalised for three months. Fortunately she makes a full recovery and is back at work after 35 weeks. During this period of limited capability for work she is paid SSP for the first 28 weeks and CESA for the remaining seven weeks.

Clive has a serious accident at work. He is paid SSP for the first 28 weeks that he is off work. Due to his permanent disability he cannot return to work. He is then paid CESA. Those benefits have addressed his inability to work. But his disability may result in his being entitled to other non means-tested benefits as well. If he has care and/or mobility needs, he may receive disability living allowance. If the accident arose out of and during the course of his employment, he might be paid industrial disablement benefit. Moreover, if his income is low, he might be able to top it up with the means-tested benefit of income-related ESA.

4.2 Statutory sick pay

4.2.1 General conditions of entitlement

At general law, an employee has no right to be paid if he is not actually working, unless there is an express provision to the contrary in his contract. The right to sick pay is no exception. However, by statute, almost all employees are entitled to receive SSP from their employers for the first 28 weeks of any period of incapacity for work. The contract cannot exclude this right.

4.2.2 Qualifying conditions (SSCBA 1992, ss 151–154)

To qualify for SSP, an employee must:

(a)   be earning gross not less than the current lower earnings limit (see **4.2.3**);

(b)   not be employed on a temporary contract lasting less than three months (see **4.2.4**);

(c)   satisfy the own occupation test (see **4.2.5**);

(d)   have been sick for at least four days;

(e)   give notice to his employer of his sickness in the time stipulated in his contract of employment or otherwise within seven days (see **4.2.5**); and

(f)   produce evidence of his illness (see **4.2.5**).

4.2.3   The earnings condition

For the eight weeks prior to the claim, the employee's normal weekly gross earnings must not be less than the lower earnings limit (see **2.2.2.1**). If a person has not been employed that long but has received at least one pay packet, his earnings are averaged over the period those wages cover.

4.2.4   Short-term contracts

If a person's contract of employment is for less than three months, he is not entitled to SSP. However, employers cannot use this as a vehicle to avoid liability for the benefit. If a person has actually been continuously employed for more than three months, he cannot be excluded on this basis even if his contract was originally for a short term. Equally, a person employed on a fixed-term contract exceeding three months or permanently can claim even if he has not actually worked for three months under that contract.

4.2.5   Own occupation test

Most employers allow their employees to confirm their illness and inability to work for the first three days. HMRC Form SC2, employee's statement of sickness, can be used. After that it is usual to require a medical certificate from the employee's doctor. The medical test used is known as the 'own occupation test', that is, whether the employee is incapable by reason of some specific disease or bodily or mental disablement of carrying out the work for which he is employed. The test applies irrespective of how long the claimant has been employed.

4.2.6   Administration and payment

Statutory sick pay is payable only if an employee has at least four consecutive days off work because he is sick or otherwise unable to work. Those days do not have to be working days. So if Fred, an employee, normally works from Monday to Friday, 9am to 5pm, and he falls sick on Wednesday evening, you count Thursday, Friday, Saturday and Sunday as the first four days of his illness. However, payment does not start immediately. This is because SSP is payable only for days an employee normally works, and it is not payable for the first three of those days (often known as waiting days). So, to continue with our example of Fred, his three waiting days are Thursday, Friday and the following Monday. If he is still ill on the Tuesday, his SSP will then start.

Statutory sick pay is paid at a flat rate. It is paid by the employer through the employee's pay packet, net of tax and NICs. It is very commonly, and equally lawfully, paid in one of three ways:

(a)   the employee may receive his full normal pay for three or six months, with SSP as part of that pay;

(b)   the employee may receive full normal pay for a similar period but with SSP on top, so he is actually better off than when working;

(c)   the employee may receive SSP alone.

Once the period of 28 weeks has expired, no further SSP is payable unless the employee works for at least eight weeks continuously. An employee who is still unable to work after 28 weeks may move on to CESA (see **4.3**) if he meets the conditions of entitlement.

4.2.7   Statutory sick pay and other benefits

Statutory sick pay counts as income when calculating any entitlement to income support or income-based JSA (see **7.3**).

It counts as income when calculating the working tax credit and child tax credit (see **9.6**) and pension credit (see **5.3**).

It is treated as earnings when calculating any entitlement to housing benefit or council tax benefit and so any appropriate earnings disregard can be made (see **7.3**).

It counts as earnings for carer's allowance (see **6.7**) and increases for adult dependants (see **2.4**).

4.3   Contributory employment and support allowance

4.3.1   Conditions of entitlement

To be entitled to CESA a claimant must:

(a)   be aged 16 or over but under pension age (65 for men and 60 for women);

(b)   have limited capability for work (see **4.4**);

(c)   not be entitled to jobseeker's allowance (see **Chapter 3**) or income support (see **Chapter 8**);

(d)   not be part of a couple required to make a joint claim for income-based jobseeker's allowance (see **8.2.4**);

(e)   not be entitled to SSP (see **4.3**);

(f)   meet the residence conditions (see **Chapter 10**); and

(g)   meet the National Insurance contribution conditions (see **2.3.3.2** and immediately below).

4.3.2   A reminder of the National Insurance contribution conditions

Table 4.1 below is a reminder of the National Insurance contributions required for a claimant to be entitled to CESA.

Table 4.1   National Insurance contribution conditions

National Insurance contributions	When paid	Prior to	Earnings factor of
(1) *Actual or deemed* Class 1 or 2	Any one of last 3 contribution years	start of relevant benefit year	25 × LEL for the relevant contribution year
AND			
(2) *Actual, deemed or credited* Class 1 or 2	in *each* of last 2 contribution years	start of relevant benefit year	50 × LEL for each contribution year

Table 4.2 below is a reminder of the National Insurance contributions required for a claimant to be entitled to CESA if the claim is made in the benefit year 2009.

Table 4.2   Required NICs for CESA claim in 2009

National Insurance contributions	Contribution years	Earnings factor
(1) *Actual or deemed* Class 1 or 2	*Either* of 2007/08 or 2006/07 or 2005/06	£2,175 (25 × LEL of £87) or £2,100 (25 × LEL of £84) or £2,050 (25 × LEL of £82)
AND		
(2) *Actual, deemed or credited* Class 1 or 2	in *each* of 2007/08 and 2006/07	£4,350 (25 × LEL of £87) and £4,200 (50 × LEL of £84)

4.3.3   Non-contributory ESA

4.3.3.1   Persons disabled in youth

A young person who becomes disabled in his youth such that he cannot work will, of course, not be able to build up a National Insurance history to meet the requirements summarised above. So reg 9 of the ESA Regulations 2008 introduces this version of the benefit as a concession.

4.3.3.2   Conditions of entitlement

A claimant must:

(a)   be aged 16 or over; but

(b)   be under the age of 20 or, in prescribed cases, 25 (see below) on a day which forms part of the period of limited capability for work; and

(c)   have had limited capability to work (see **4.4.2**) throughout a period of 196 consecutive days; and

(d)   not be receiving full-time education.

There are complex qualifying conditions for an applicant whose period of limited capability for work began when aged between 20 and 25. Broadly, these are intended to cover young people who become unable to work whilst studying and so do not have the appropriate NIC record for the contributory version of ESA. As a general rule, the claimant must have been registered on and attending a course of full-time advanced or secondary education, or vocational or work-based training, for at least three months before he attained the age of 20 years. The course must have ended either immediately before the official date the claim began, or within one of the last two contribution years before the benefit year which would have governed a claim for the contributory version of the benefit (see above and **2.3.2.2**)), whichever is the later.

4.3.4   ESA: contributory and/or income-related

There is only one payment of ESA made to a claimant but this may be made up of CESA and/or IRESA. In this chapter we focus on the contributory version that usually requires National Insurance contributions to have been paid in the past. Income-related ESA has two main conditions of entitlement that are the same, namely, the claimant must have limited capability for work and must not be in remunerative work. But additionally the claimant must pass a means test and so have a low income and a limited amount of capital. For a quick review of both types of ESA, see **8.2.3.2**.

4.4 Work capability assessment

4.4.1 Introduction

To be entitled to ESA (contributory and/or income-related) a claimant must have 'limited capability for work' (see **4.4.2**). This means that due to a physical or mental condition, it is not reasonable to require the claimant to work.

If it is not reasonable to require a claimant to work, the next question is whether or not it is reasonable to require the claimant to take any steps to help him find work. This is known as 'limited capability for work-related activity' (see **4.4.3**).

Both these matters are determined by way of a medical examination of the claimant by a Government-appointed doctor or nurse. The doctor or nurse carries out what is known as a work capability assessment (WCA).

4.4.2 Limited capability for work

Regulation 19(1) of the Employment and Support Allowance Regulations 2008 (SI 2008/794) states:

> The limited capability for work assessment is an assessment of the extent to which a claimant who has some specific disease or bodily or mental disablement is capable of performing the activities prescribed in Schedule 2 or is incapable by reason of such disease or bodily or mental disablement of performing those activities.

Schedule 2 is reproduced in **Appendix 2** to this book. There are 11 physical activities listed in Pt 1 and 10 mental activities (mental, cognitive and intellectual functions) in Pt 2. Each activity is divided into a list of 'descriptors' which measure the level of disability associated with the task and allocates points accordingly. Take, for example, activity 3, concerning bending or kneeling. If the claimant cannot bend to touch his knees and straighten up again, he scores 15 points. If he cannot bend, kneel or squat, as if to pick a light object, such as a piece of paper, situated 15cm from the floor on a low shelf, and to move it and straighten up again without the help of another person, he scores 9 points. If he cannot bend, kneel or squat, as if to pick a light object off the floor and straighten up again without the help of another person, he scores 6 points.

Note that in assessing the extent of a claimant's capability to perform any activity listed in Pt 1 of Sch 2, the claimant is assessed as if he was wearing any prosthesis with which the claimant is fitted or, as the case may be, wearing or using any aid or appliance which he normally wears or uses.

So how does the points system work? The claimant's application form will have included his own self-assessment of his score. The doctor or nurse, on examining the claimant, should decide which activities apply to him and then address each from descriptor (a) downwards, stopping at the first that applies to the claimant. This is because only the descriptor with the highest score in respect of each activity counts. Take, for example, activity 1, walking with a walking stick or other aid if such aid is normally used. What if a claimant cannot walk more than 150 metres on level ground without stopping or severe discomfort? This does not meet descriptors (a), (b), (c) or (d). Note that (d) is where the claimant cannot walk more than 100 metres on level ground without stopping or severe discomfort. Descriptor (e) is that the claimant cannot walk more than 200 metres on level ground without stopping or severe discomfort, and so this is met.

What if a claimant satisfies a descriptor for only part of a day? Take, for example, activity 6 on manual dexterity. What if a claimant, on getting up in the morning, can fill his bathroom sink by turning a 'star-headed' tap with his left or right hand, but by the evening the pain in his left hand is so bad that he cannot turn a 'star-headed' tap with that hand. Is descriptor (g) met? Arguably it is, as reg 27 provides that:

> A claimant who at the commencement of any day has, or thereafter develops, limited capability for work as determined in accordance with the limited capability for work assessment is to be treated as having limited capability for work throughout that day.

So how many points does a claimant have to score to have limited capability for work? The answer is 15 points. It does not matter whether the points are scored in Pt 1 and/or Pt 2. For example, a claimant might score 6 points in Pt 1 and 9 points in Pt 2, giving a total of 15 points.

Only a few people are deemed by reg 20 to have limited capability for work. These include a claimant who is terminally ill (defined by reg 2 as suffering from a progressive disease and where death in consequence of that disease can reasonably be expected within six months), or who is receiving treatment by way of intravenous, intraperitoneal or intrathecal chemotherapy.

4.4.3   Limited capability for work-related activity

Regulation 34(1) of the Employment and Support Allowance Regulations 2008 states that:

> . . . where, by reason of a claimant's physical or mental condition, at least one of the descriptors set out in Schedule 3 applies to the claimant, the claimant's capability for work-related activity will be limited and the limitation will be such that it is not reasonable to require that claimant to undertake such activity.

Schedule 3 is reproduced in **Appendix 3** to this book. There are 11 activities in the schedule. If any one descriptor applies to the claimant then the test is met.

What if the claimant's condition fluctuates, or there are periods of remission? Regulation 34(2) states that:

> A descriptor applies to a claimant if that descriptor applies to the claimant for the majority of the time or, as the case may be, on the majority of the occasions on which the claimant undertakes or attempts to undertake the activity described by that descriptor.

Take, for example, the descriptor for activity 3, that the claimant cannot pick up and move a 0.5 litre carton full of liquid with either hand. Arguably a claimant satisfies this descriptor if, say, every three out of four times he tries using either hand to take a 0.5 litre carton of milk out of the fridge, he drops it.

Note that in determining whether any relevant descriptor listed in Sch 3 applies, the claimant is assessed as if he was wearing any prosthesis with which the claimant is fitted or, as the case may be, wearing or using any aid or appliance which he normally wears or uses.

A very limited number of people are deemed by reg 35 to have limited capability for work-related activity. These include a claimant who is terminally ill, or who is receiving treatment by way of intravenous, intraperitoneal or intrathecal chemotherapy.

4.4.4 Support group or work-related activity group?

If a claimant satisfies both the limited capability for work test and the limited capability for work-related activity test, he is placed in what is known as 'the support group'. This affects how much CESA he is paid (see **4.5.1**) and means he is not required to take any steps to help find work.

If a claimant satisfies only the limited capability for work test (and not the limited capability for work-related activity test) he is placed in what is known as 'the work-related activity group'. This affects how much CESA he is paid (see **4.5.1**) and means he is required to take steps to help find work (see **4.5.2**).

4.5 Administration and payment of CESA

4.5.1 Rates of pay

4.5.1.1 The assessment phase

The first 13 weeks of the claim are known as the assessment phase. During this time the claim is processed and the medical for WCA (see **4.4.1**) purposes should take place. Contributory ESA is paid at a flat rate during the assessment phase, and the amount depends on whether the claimant is aged between 16 and 24, or 25 and over. For 2008/09 the figures were £47.95 and £60.50 respectively.

4.5.1.2 The main phase

After the assessment phase ends and the claimant has been assessed as having limited capability for work, the claimant moves into the so-called main phase of ESA. Here, payment of CESA is as follows:

(a) All claimants, regardless of their age, are paid at one flat rate. For 2008/09 this was £60.50.

(b) A claimant in the support group (see **4.4.4**) receives an additional amount known as the support component. For 2008/09 this was £29.

(c) A claimant in the work-related activity group (see **4.4.4**) receives an additional amount known as the work-related activity component. For 2008/09 this was £24.

Do not forget that a claimant in either group may during the assessment and main phases have such a low income that he is entitled to income-related ESA (see **Chapter 8**). This is especially likely if the claimant owns his own house or flat and has allowable housing costs, such as mortgage interest or service charges (see **8.3**).

4.5.2 Work-related activities

A person in the work-related activity group is required to attend one or more appointments with a health care professional to discuss moving into work and any health-related issues. This is known as a work-focused health-related assessment.

A person in the work-related activity group is also required to attend a series of appointments with a personal adviser. These are designed to assess that person's prospects of obtaining work, to assist and encourage him to obtain work, to identify activities he might undertake to obtain work, to identify training, educational or rehabilitation opportunities which may make it more likely that he will obtain work or be able to do so, and to identify current or future work opportunities, including self-employment opportunities, that are relevant to the claimant's needs and abilities. Each appointment is known as a work-related activity interview. At the end of the first interview the claimant is given a written action plan. This is a record of the interview and any work-related activity that the claimant is willing to take. The record is updated at all subsequent interviews.

If a claimant fails to attend a work-focused health-related assessment or a work-related activity interview without good cause, his ESA will be reduced until he does attend. As to what may constitute good cause, see regs 53 and 61 respectively. For the first four weeks the sanction is loss of 50% of the amount of the work-related activity component (see **4.5.1.2**) and thereafter 100%. The reduction is made first to any CESA received and, if that is reduced to nil, then to income-related ESA.

4.5.3 Deduction from CESA for a pension payment

What if a claimant receives a weekly amount by way of a personal or an occupational pension, including any periodical payment received under a permanent health insurance policy arranged by a former employer? By reg 74 ,if that weekly payment exceeds a prescribed figure (in 2008/09 it was £85) then the amount of CESA payable is reduced by 50% of the excess.

So, for example, if a claimant receives a weekly pension payment of £105, that exceeds £85 by £20 and 50% of that is £10. So the amount of CESA would be reduced by £10.

4.5.4 Effect of work on the entitlement to ESA

As a general rule, a claimant is not entitled to ESA of either type for any week in which he works. However, certain types of work are ignored. These include:

(a)   work as a councillor;

(b)   domestic tasks carried out in the claimant's own home, or the care of a relative;

(c)   any activity the claimant undertakes during an emergency to protect another person or to prevent serious damage to property or livestock;

(d)   work for which the earnings in any week do not exceed £20.00;

(e)   work for which the earnings in any week do not exceed £92.00 and which is part of the claimant's treatment programme and is done under medical supervision while the claimant is an in-patient, or is regularly attending as an out-patient, of a hospital or similar institution, or which is supervised by a person employed by a public or local authority or voluntary organisation engaged in the provision or procurement of work for persons who have disabilities;

(f)   work done where the claimant receives no payment of earnings and where the claimant is engaged by a charity or voluntary organisation, or is a volunteer, and the Secretary of State is satisfied that it is reasonable for the claimant to provide the service free of charge;

(g)   work done in the course of participating in a work placement approved in writing by the Secretary of State before the placement starts.

Note that when calculating income-related ESA, if the claimant falls within (d) or (e) above, the amount earned up to the limit is disregarded.

4.5.5 Waiting days, linking rules and disqualification

A claimant is not entitled to ESA for the three days at the beginning of a period of limited capability for work. However, there is no waiting period if the claimant's entitlement to ESA commences within 12 weeks of receiving income support, State pension credit, jobseeker's allowance or carer's allowance, or SSP coming to an end.

What about linking periods? Any period of limited capability for work which is separated from another such period by not more than 12 weeks is treated as a continuation of the earlier period.

In certain limited circumstances set out in reg 157, a claimant may be disqualified from receiving ESA for up to six weeks. This includes, for example, if the limited capability for work results from his own misconduct, unless it is due to pregnancy or a sexually transmitted disease; or a claimant fails without good cause to attend for, or submit to, recommended medical or other treatment (excluding vaccination, inoculation or major surgery) which would be likely to remove the limitation on the claimant's capability for work.

4.5.6 ESA: a summary of the key questions

- *Question 1*: does the claimant score at least 15 points on the capability for work test (see **Appendix 2**)? If not, then he is not entitled to ESA (of either type). Consider jobseeker's allowance (contribution-based JSA in **Chapter 3** and income-based JSA in **Chapter 7**). But if the claimant is on a low income and a carer receiving or entitled to carer's allowance, or a lone parent with a child aged under 12, consider income support (see **Chapter 7**). If the claimant does score at least 15 points, answer question 2.

- *Question 2*: does the claimant pass the limited capability for work-related activity test (see **Appendix 3**)? If not, the claimant is in the work-related activity group, receives the work-related activity component during the main phase and is required to attend a work-focused health-related assessment and a series of work-related activity interviews. If he does pass the test, the claimant is in support group, receives the support component during the main phase and is not required to attend a work-focused health-related assessment nor any work-related activity interviews.

- *Question 3*: CESA or income-related ESA or both? For CESA, does the claimant have a recent NIC record (see **2.3.3.2** and **4.3.2**)? For income-related ESA, does the claimant have a low income and capital of less than £16,000 (see **8.2.1.2**)?

4.5.7 Contributory ESA and other benefits

Contributory ESA is treated as income when calculating income support, income-based JSA, housing benefit and council tax benefit (see **7.3**), and the tax credits (see **9.6**).

Contributory ESA is taken into account when assessing entitlement to the pension credit, but it is not treated as qualifying income for the savings credit element (see **5.3**).

Contributory ESA is incompatible with contribution-based JSA, State Pension, SSP and statutory maternity pay (see **2.5**).

Contributory ESA is an earnings replacement benefit (see **1.2.5**) and so may affect the entitlement of a spouse to an adult dependant increase for an appropriate benefit (see **2.4**).

4.6 Disability living allowance

4.6.1 Background

Disability living allowance (DLA) has two components, a care component and a mobility component.

Either component of DLA may be claimed separately, or they may be claimed together. Many claimants are also in receipt of CESA, but there are also many people in receipt of DLA who are in full-time or part-time work.

The award can be for an indefinite or fixed period.

4.6.2 DLA and other benefits

Disability living allowance does not count as income when calculating child tax credit and working tax credit (see **9.6**), the pension credit (see **5.3**), income support, income-related ESA, income-based JSA, housing benefit and council tax benefit (see **7.3**).

Disability living allowance does not affect the payment of any other non means-tested benefit, except that the DLA care component overlaps with constant attendance allowance (see **2.6** and **4.11**).

Someone caring for a recipient of DLA care component at the middle or highest rate may be entitled to carer's allowance (see **6.7**).

4.7 DLA care component

4.7.1 Conditions of entitlement (SSCBA 1992, s 72)

A person is entitled to the care component if he:

(a)   is under 65 when first claiming; and

(b)   is severely disabled physically or mentally (see **4.7.3**); and

(c)   has been so disabled for a continuous period of three months immediately before the claim and is likely to continue to be so throughout the next six months or is terminally ill (see **4.7.4**); and

(d)   passes an additional test if under 16 years of age (see **4.7.5**); and

(e)   is not subject to immigration control and satisfies the residence conditions (see **Chapter 10**).

4.7.2 Bodily functions

A person may be entitled to DLA care component because he needs help in carrying out his bodily functions (although this is not the only qualifying test). The amount of help that might be needed determines the rate of pay (see **4.7.3**). The interpretation of this term has led to a large amount of case law and so we shall consider that first.

In *R v National Insurance Commissioner, ex p Secretary of State for Social Services (Packer's Case)* [1981] 1 WLR 1017, Lord Denning MR said (at 1022):

> Attention is different from 'activity' or 'attendance'. It connotes something personal to the disabled person. 'Bodily functions' include breathing, hearing, seeing, eating, drinking, walking, sitting, sleeping, getting in or out of bed, dressing, undressing, eliminating waste products – and the like – all of which an ordinary person – who is not suffering from any disability – does for himself. But they do not include cooking, shopping or any of the other things which a wife or daughter does as part of her

domestic duties: or generally which one of the household normally does for the rest of the family. It is the words 'in connection with' which give rise to the difficulty. They are very uncertain. Some kinds of attention are closely connected with 'his bodily functions': other kinds are too remote. It is a question of degree upon which different minds may reach different conclusions ... I would hold that ordinary domestic duties such as shopping, cooking meals, making tea or coffee, laying the table or the tray, carrying it into the room, making the bed or filling the hot water bottle, do not qualify as 'attention ... in connection with [the] bodily functions' of the disabled person. But that duties that are out of the ordinary – doing for the disabled person what a normal person would do for himself – such as cutting up food, lifting the cup to the mouth, helping to dress and undress or at the toilet – all do qualify as 'attention ... in connection with [the] bodily functions' of the disabled person.

In 1997, the House of Lords considered this issue when dealing with joint appeals in the cases of *Cockburn v Chief Adjudication Officer; Secretary of State for Social Security v Fairey (also known as Halliday)* [1997] 1 WLR 799. In Mrs Cockburn's case the tribunal had found that

Mrs Cockburn cannot walk unaided and cannot get out of bed except with difficulty and she cannot dress herself properly without assistance. Mrs Cockburn is incontinent and as a result of this, a lot of washing is generated which Mrs Cockburn is unable to do herself and relies on her daughter.

Lord Clyde commented that attention to be given in connection with a bodily function

must be some close and intimate service to the person of the claimant. The service is narrower than that of assistance. Assistance would cover activities done for the person. Attention implies services done to the person. The personal nature of what is comprised in attention prompts the observation made by Dunn LJ in the passage in his judgment in *Packer* [1981] 1 WLR 1017, 1023F that the attention must be a service involving personal contact carried out in the presence of the disabled person. But that should not be understood as being so absolute a requirement as to exclude the changing of bed linen which might be achieved without physical contact between the claimant and the person providing the service. Nor should it be understood to exclude an incidental activity which might occur outwith the presence of the claimant during the course of what is otherwise an attention given to and in the presence of the claimant. But the laundry work in the present case seems to me to fall outwith a service which is directed at the person of the claimant. It involves attention to the linen rather than attention to the claimant.

In Miss Fairey's case, the medical evidence was that she had been 'born deaf, she communicates mainly by signing and also can lip read but not very well, and speaks a little'. She 'may be in trouble if she gets lost and couldn't communicate to find her way. She is difficult to understand and doesn't lip read very well'. She could not hear a fire burning or hear traffic in the street. Physically and mentally she had no other disabilities than those arising from her deafness. Her mother wrote that she had to go out with her daughter as people did not understand what she was saying and she had to interpret for her.

Lord Slynn of Hadley gave the leading judgment in the House of Lords. He observed that:

There is no issue in Miss Fairey's case as to whether or not she is severely disabled by her deafness. She plainly is; she is not able to hear and that reduces or impedes her ability to speak. Nor is it challenged that, as a result of her disability, some attention throughout the day may be required in connection with her bodily functions. The question is the particular one as to whether such attention given to her '(consisting of the help given by an "interpreter" skilled in the use of sign language) as may enable the claimant to carry out a reasonable degree of social activity' falls within the scope of section 72(1)(b)(i). Is that help capable of being attention in connection with her bodily functions? Although movement of the limbs (including their use for walking and running) is a bodily function, so also in my view is the operation of the senses. The reception of sound, its communication to the brain and the brain's 'instruction' to the limbs or other parts of the body to act or refrain from acting are all as much bodily functions as the movement of the limbs and the actions of the digestive or excretory organs ... Providing someone who can explain or translate normal conversation, or radio or film speech, is different from providing physical guidance by an arm. It seems to me, however, that it is also capable of constituting 'attention'. It is the one, or the principal, way in which messages to the brain normally conveyed through hearing can be conveyed by alternate means. This obviously does not improve natural hearing. Nor does it produce a replacement method of hearing but it provides an alternative way of fulfilling the hearing function.

In *Commissioner's Decision CSDLA/133/2005* a tribunal of three Commissioners stressed that a bodily function primarily refers to the normal action of any organ of the body. For example, one normal function of the lower jaw is to move up and down. As one purpose of the lower jaw moving up and down is to masticate food, it could be said that mastication is a bodily function. But the tribunal stressed that activities such as eating, getting in and out of bed, dressing and undressing are not strictly bodily functions because it cannot properly be said that it is the normal action or purpose of any organ or sets of organs to perform these exercises. These are not functions of organs of the body, but merely things which a body can do if the relevant bodily functions (eg, movement of the lower jaw, arms and legs, etc) are working normally.

According to *CSDLA/133/2005* it is necessary first to identify the specific bodily function or functions that are deficient in a claimant's case and then to assess whether attention is reasonably required in respect of that deficiency. Such attention must, of course, have the active, close, caring and personal characteristics referred to above.

By the Social Security (Attendance Allowance and Disability Living Allowance) (Amendment) (No 2) Regulations 2000 (SI 2000/2313), a person does not satisfy the daytime or night-time attention tests 'unless the attention the severely disabled person requires from another person is required to be given in the physical presence of the severely disabled person'. This overturns such decisions as *Commissioner's Decision CDLA/1148/1997*, where the Commissioner had held that conversations over the telephone could constitute attention.

4.7.3 Degree of severity of disability and rate of pay

4.7.3.1 Lowest rate

(A) A significant portion of the day (s 72(1)(a)(i))

A person is entitled to the lowest rate if 'he requires in connection with his bodily functions [see **4.7.2**] attention from another person for a significant portion of the day (whether during a single period or a number of periods)'.

In *Commissioner's Decision CDLA/58/1993*, the Commissioner did not disagree with the generally held view that attention for a period of one hour or thereabouts is sufficient. He said, in this context, that 'significant' refers to the length, rather than the importance, of the time. Note that, in *Commissioner's Decision CSDLA/29/94*, the Commissioner doubted that approach and suggested that attention for less than one hour may be significant depending on the circumstances. So if, for example, the attention required from another person consists of many short periods, the total number of those periods may be significant even if it would not qualify on a pure time test.

(B) The cooking test (s 72(1)(a)(ii))

In the alternative, a person is entitled to the lowest rate if 'he cannot prepare a cooked main meal for himself if he has the ingredients'.

In *Moyna v Secretary of State for Work and Pensions* [2003] 4 All ER 162, the House of Lords held that the purpose of the cooking test is not to ascertain whether a claimant can survive, or enjoy a reasonable diet, without assistance. It is a notional test to calibrate the severity of the disability. It does not matter whether the claimant actually needs to cook. A person who cannot cook for himself is entitled to the benefit whether he solves the problem of eating by obtaining help, buying cooked food, or eating out. The Court of Appeal had been wrong to lay emphasis upon the fact that, unless the claimant in the case could cook more or less every day, she would not enjoy a reasonable quality of life. Moreover, the test says nothing about how often the person should be able to cook. Section 72(2) contemplates a claimant who throughout a nine-month period has a disability which causes him to be unable to cook a main meal. The cooking test involves looking at the whole period and saying whether, in a general sense, the person could fairly be described as a person who is unable to cook a meal. It is an exercise in judgment rather than an arithmetical calculation of frequency.

4.7.3.2   Middle rate

(A) Frequent daytime attention (s 72(1)(b)(i))

A person is entitled to the middle rate if 'he is so severely disabled physically or mentally that, by day, he requires from another person frequent attention throughout the day in connection with his bodily functions' (see **4.7.2**).

If attention to bodily functions for a significant portion of the day is about one hour (see **4.7.3.1(A)**), then how much more attention must be given throughout the day for it to be frequent? A person will have to show a pattern of need over the day (eg with help to get up, get dressed, eat meals, go to the toilet, get undressed, bathe, go to bed, etc). In *Commissioner's Decision CA/281/1989*, it was said that the attention must arise at intervals spread over the day. It therefore is not enough if it is rendered in the morning and evening, however frequent or intense that might be, as it must also be given at least once during the intervening period. In *Commissioner's Decision CA/140/1985*, it was said that a person might qualify even if the spread of need was uneven provided lengthy periods were involved. In *R v National Insurance Commissioner, ex p Secretary of State for Social Services (Packer's Case)* [1981] 1 WLR 1017, Lord Denning MR said (at p 1022) that, 'Frequently connotes several times – not once or twice'.

(B) Continual daytime supervision (s 72(1)(b)(ii))

In the alternative, a person is entitled to the middle rate if 'he is so severely disabled physically or mentally that, by day, he requires from another person continual supervision throughout the day in order to avoid substantial danger to himself or others'.

Continual, rather than continuous, supervision is required. So supervision may be continual even if a claimant can be left alone for short periods. In *Commissioner's Decision CDLA/468/2006* it was said that:

> The nature and degree of supervision which a claimant requires will vary from case to case, so that, for example, it may be possible to leave a claimant who has a propensity

to fall sitting in an armchair for short periods without any risk of the claimant causing danger to himself or others. The fact that a supervisor in such a case is able to leave the same room, or even house, as the claimant for a short period of time while the claimant is sitting in the armchair will not prevent the supervision which the claimant requires from being regarded as continual.

The 'characteristic nature of supervision is overseeing or watching over considered with reference to its frequency or regularity of occurrence' (*Commissioner's Decision R(A)2/75*). But the purpose of this continual supervision must be to avoid a substantial danger to the disabled person or another person. In *Commissioner's Decision R(A)1/83* it was said that:

> What is a substantial danger will, of course, depend upon the facts of each individual case. ... The substantial danger must not be too remote a possibility. The fact that it may take the form of an isolated incident does not in itself constitute remoteness. Moreover, the mere infrequency of a contemplated danger is immaterial. An isolated incident can have catastrophic effects.

(C) Prolonged or repeated night-time attention (s 72(1)(c)(i))

In the alternative, a person is entitled to the middle rate if 'he is so severely disabled physically or mentally that, at night, he requires from another person prolonged or repeated attention in connection with his bodily functions' (see **4.7.2**).

First, we need to consider for these purposes when the day ends and the night begins. In *R v National Insurance Commissioner, ex p Secretary of State for Social Services (Packer's Case)* [1981] 1 WLR 1017, Lord Widgery CJ, sitting in the Court of Appeal said:

> The argument before us has been at one in a number of respects; both [advocates] invite us to regard the night for the purpose of the section as being that period of inactivity, or that principal period of inactivity through which each household goes in the dark hours, and to measure the beginning of the night from the time at which the household, as it were, closed down for the night. I would commend to [tribunals] dealing with this difficult question in future that they should look at the matter in that way.

Secondly, we need to ask what prolonged or repeated attention means. In *R v National Insurance Commissioner, ex p Secretary of State for Social Services* [1981] 1 WLR 1017, Lord Denning MR said (at 1022) that, 'Prolonged means some little time. Repeated means more than once at any rate'. It is generally accepted that 20 minutes or more is a prolonged period. Note also that the test is repeated, not repeatedly, so twice a night is sufficient.

(D) Night-time watching over (s 72(1)(c)(ii))

In the alternative, a person is entitled to the middle rate if 'he is so severely disabled physically or mentally that, at night, in order to avoid a substantial danger to himself or others he requires another person to be awake for a prolonged period or at frequent intervals for the purpose of watching over him'.

'Prolonged', in this context, probably has the same meaning as in s 72(1)(c)(i) above. 'Frequent intervals' probably constitute more than two occasions following s 72(1)(b)(i) above.

4.7.3.3   Highest rate (s 72(4)(a))

If a person satisfies both a daytime *and* a night-time middle rate care condition (or is terminally ill), he is entitled to payment of the care component at the highest rate.

4.7.4 Terminally ill (s 66(2))

A person is 'terminally ill' at any time if at that time he suffers from a progressive disease and his death in consequence of that disease can reasonably be expected within six months. These claims are normally processed within 10 working days.

4.7.5 Additional test for children under 16

The cooking test does *not* apply to children under 16 years of age (s 72(6)(a)).

If a child is to be entitled to the care component at any rate his needs must be 'substantially in excess of the normal requirements of persons of his age' or substantial needs 'which younger persons in normal physical and mental health may also have but which persons of his age and in normal physical and mental health would not have' (s 72(6)(b)).

4.7.6 Test when needs vary

In *Commissioner's Decision CDLA/1252/1995*, the Commissioner said that if the needs of the disabled person for attention and/or supervision vary over a week, it is necessary to discover if there is such a thing as a 'normal' night (or day). If so, the question is whether the attention or supervision normally given, or on average, satisfies the appropriate test. The Commissioner said:

> For example, I do not consider that the attention requirements would be either prolonged or repeated if, in an average week, a claimant required attention for a short period once a night on six days but required attention three times a night on a single day. On the other hand the attention would satisfy the night-time condition if on average the claimant required attention once a night every other night but required attention three or four times a night on the remaining nights. I think this would be the case even if there were occasional nights when no attention at all was required.

Given the House of Lords decision in *Moyna* (see **4.7.3.1(B)**), the approach should be more general than mathematical.

4.7.7 Summary of key points for DLA care component

The claimant must be under 65 when he first claims and disabled for a continuous period of three months immediately before the claim and likely to continue to be so throughout the next six months (or terminally ill). He must pass an additional test if he is under 16 years of age.

The rate of pay is determined by the degree of disability. The rates for 2008/09 are set out below with a reminder of the qualifying tests:

(a)   Lowest rate: £17.75 if the claimant either:
   (i)   'requires in connection with his bodily functions attention from another person for a significant portion of the day (whether during a single period or a number of periods)'; or
   (ii) 'he cannot prepare a cooked main meal for himself if he has the ingredients'.

(b)   Middle rate: £44.85 if the claimant is either so severely disabled physically or mentally that:
   (i)   'by day, he requires from another person frequent attention throughout the day in connection with his bodily functions'; or
   (ii) 'by day, he requires from another person continual supervision throughout the day in order to avoid substantial danger to himself or others'; or

    (iii) 'at night, he requires from another person prolonged or repeated attention in connection with his bodily functions'; or

    (iv) 'at night, in order to avoid a substantial danger to himself or others he requires another person to be awake for a prolonged period or at frequent intervals for the purpose of watching over him'.

(c) Highest rate: £67.00 if the claimant satisfies both a day *and* a night-time middle rate test (or is terminally ill).

4.8 DLA mobility component

4.8.1 Conditions of entitlement (SSCBA 1992, s 73)

A person is entitled to the mobility component of DLA if he:

(a) is under 65 when first claims; and

(b) is severely disabled (see **4.8.2**); and

(c) has been so disabled for a continuous period of three months immediately before the claim and is likely to continue to be so throughout the next six months *or* is terminally ill (see **4.7.4**); and

(d) can benefit from enhanced facilities for locomotion (see **4.8.3**);

(e) has attained the relevant age (see **4.8.4**); and

(f) passes an additional test for the lower rate if under 16 years of age (see **4.8.5**); and

(g) is not subject to immigration control and satisfies the residence conditions (see **Chapter 10**).

4.8.2 Degree of severity of disability and rate of pay

4.8.2.1 Higher rate

(A) Unable or virtually unable to walk (s 73(1)(a))

A person is entitled to the higher rate if 'he is suffering from a physical disablement such that he is either unable to walk or virtually unable to walk'. The Disability Working Allowance (General) Regulations 1991 (SI 1991/2887) (DLA Regs 1991), reg 12 provides that a person meets these conditions only if:

(a) his physical condition as a whole is such that, without regard to circumstances peculiar to that person as to the place of residence or as to the place of, or nature of employment—

    (i) he is unable to walk (eg paraplegic, tetraplegic etc); or

    (ii) his ability to walk out of doors is so limited, as regards the distance over which or the speed at which or the length of time for which or the manner in which he can make progress on foot without severe discomfort, that he is virtually unable to walk; or

    (iii) the exertion required to walk would constitute a danger to his life or would be likely to lead to a serious deterioration in his health.

As to reg 12(a)(ii), each of the four factors must be considered. Note that there is no set distance in the regulation. This had led to conflicting cases; for example, in *Commissioner's Decision CM/47/86*, a person who could walk only 50 yards did not qualify, but in *Commissioner's Decision R(M) 5/86*, a person who could only walk the same distance did qualify. As to speed, again there is no guidance in the regulation. The starting point is to consider the disabled person's progress on foot against the average walking speed of an adult, which is approximately 3.4 miles per hour (or 100 yards per minute). The length of time involved takes into account the need to stop and rest. The manner of walking involves looking at the person's balance, gait, incidence of dizziness or falls etc. In *Commissioner's Decision CDLA/ 608/1994*, the Commissioner said that the test is how far the person can walk before severe discomfort occasioned by going further stops him. In *Commissioner's Decision CDLA/4388/1999*, the Commissioner said that even if a claimant is not virtually unable to walk by reason of limitations on distance, if there were, for example, periods when after walking a moderate distance he could not then walk for some time, it may be that he is virtually unable to walk by reason of limitations on the length of time for which he can walk. Any severe discomfort that might arise after walking has finished is irrelevant.

What does reg 12(a)(iii) mean? In *Commissioner's Decision R(M) 3/78*, it was said that the test may be satisfied if a condition, such as angina, might be induced or precipitated by walking. In *Commissioner's Decision CM/23/1995*, it was suggested that the serious deterioration need not be permanent nor last any great period of time. However, in *Commissioner's Decision CM/158/1994*, the Commissioner imposed a more strenuous test, ie there must be a worsening in the person's health from which he would never recover or only after a significant period (such as 12 months) or medical intervention.

By reg 12(4), a person fails to meet these conditions if he can walk with a prosthesis or artificial aid which he habitually wears or uses, or if he could walk were he to wear or use a suitable prosthesis or artificial aid.

Will a claimant qualify if he suffers from a mental disorder that manifests itself as a physical problem that satisfies the test? Yes, said Commissioner Jacobs in *Commissioner's Decision CDLA/4125/2000*. In that case the claimant's mental condition had caused muscle weakness in her legs such that she could not walk more than 50 yards.

(B) Blind and deaf (s 73(2))

By reg 12(2) and (3), a person is taken to satisfy this condition if he is 100% blind and not less than 80% deaf (on a scale where 100% deaf represents absolute deafness) and 'by reason of the combined effects of the person's blindness and deafness, he is unable, without the assistance of another person, to walk to any intended or required destination whilst out of doors'.

(C) Double amputee (DLA regs 1991, reg 12(1)(b))

In the alternative, a person is entitled to the higher rate if 'he has both legs amputated at levels which are either through or above the ankle, or he has one leg amputated and is without the other leg, or is without both legs to the same extent as if it, or they, had been so amputated'.

It is irrelevant that a person who satisfies this condition might be able to walk with artificial limbs.

(D) Severely mentally impaired with severe behavioural problems and receiving the care component at the highest rate (s 73(3))

By reg 12(5), a person is treated as severely mentally impaired if he 'suffers from a state of arrested development or incomplete physical development of the brain, which results in a severe impairment of intelligence and social functioning'.

Regulation 12(6) provides that a person suffers from severe behavioural problems if he exhibits disruptive behaviour which is '(a) extreme, (b) regularly requires another person to intervene and physically restrain [the disabled person] in order to prevent him causing physical injury to himself or another, or damage to property and (c) is so unpredictable that he requires another person to be present and watching over him whenever he is awake'.

In *Commissioner's Decision CDLA/156/1994*, the claimant was suffering from Alzheimer's disease. The medical evidence satisfied the Commissioner that the claimant's condition had taken effect after the brain had reached its maturity. Accordingly, there could be no question of the claimant's suffering from a state of arrested development or incomplete physical development of the brain. The sufferer in that case was well advanced in years, as indeed are normally all sufferers from Alzheimer's disease.

In *Commissioner's Decision CDLA/8353/95*, the claimant had suffered from schizophrenia since about the age of 16 and she applied for the benefit when she was aged 60. The Commissioner accepted the medical evidence that she suffered from an arrested development of the brain but held that this did not result in severe impairment of intelligence and social functioning.

As to an autistic child, see *Megarry v Chief Adjudication Officer* (1999) *The Times*, 11 November.

4.8.2.2   Lower rate (s 73(1)(d))

A person is entitled to the lower rate if:

> He is able to walk but is so severely disabled physically or mentally that, disregarding any ability he may have to use routes which are familiar to him on his own, he cannot take advantage of the faculty out of doors without guidance or supervision from another person most of the time.

What constitutes guidance or supervision in this context? In *Commissioner's Decision CDLA/042/94*, the Commissioner expressed the view that 'guidance' could involve physically leading or directing a claimant or oral suggestion or persuasion. In starred *Commissioner's Decision 29/00*, a tribunal of three Commissioners held that mere reassurance cannot constitute supervision. There has to be an element of monitoring or readiness to intervene.

Note that by the Social Security (Disability Living Allowance) (Amendment) Regulations 2002 (SI 2002/648), a person will not meet this test if the reason he does not take advantage of the faculty of walking out of doors unaccompanied is fear or anxiety. However, he will meet the test where the fear or anxiety is a symptom of a mental disability which is so severe as to prevent him from taking advantage of the faculty of walking out of doors unaccompanied.

4.8.3   Benefiting from enhanced facilities for locomotion

A person in a coma or who cannot be moved on medical grounds clearly will not benefit from enhanced facilities for locomotion. But does a claimant have to show that at some point in time, with guidance or supervision, he will actually, rather than theoretically, have an ability to take advantage of the faculty of walking? Unfortunately, there are conflicting views. See *Commissioner's Decisions CDLA/ 042/94* and *CDLA/2364/1995*.

4.8.4   The relevant age

By s 1A, the minimum age to qualify at the higher rate is three and for the lower rate is five.

4.8.5 Additional test for children under 16

If a child is to be entitled to the mobility component at the lower rate, he must require 'substantially more guidance or supervision from another person than persons of his age in normal physical and mental health would require' or 'persons of his age in normal physical and mental health would not require such guidance or supervision' (s 73(4)).

4.8.6 Summary of key points for DLA mobility component

The claimant must be under 65 when he first claims and have been disabled for a continuous period of three months immediately before the claim and that must be likely to continue to be so throughout the next six months (or he is terminally ill). The claimant must be able to benefit from enhanced facilities for locomotion. He must have attained the relevant age (ie three for the higher rate and five for the lower rate). He must pass an additional test if under 16 years of age.

The rate of pay is determined by the degree of disability. The rates for 2008/09 are set out below with a reminder of the qualifying tests:

(a)   higher rate: £46.75 if the claimant is:
   (i)   unable or virtually unable to walk; or
   (ii)   blind and deaf; or
   (iii) a double amputee; or
   (iv)   severely mentally impaired with severe behavioural problems and receiving the care component at the highest rate;

(b)   lower rate: £17.75 if 'he is able to walk but is so severely disabled physically or mentally that, disregarding any ability he may have to use routes which are familiar to him on his own, he cannot take advantage of the faculty out of doors without guidance or supervision from another person most of the time'.

4.9 Attendance allowance

4.9.1 Differences from DLA care component

Attendance allowance (AA) is very similar to DLA care component. The definitions of attention and supervision are identical. However, there are significant differences, namely:

(a)   if the claimant is aged 65 or over at first claim, he must claim AA, not DLA;

(b)   the qualifying period before the claim is six months, not three;

(c)   the AA has only two rates of pay, corresponding to the middle and highest rates of DLA care. The attention and supervision requirements are the same as those rates of DLA. There is no equivalent to the cooking test or the attention for a significant portion of the day test.

4.9.2 AA and other benefits

The AA is treated the same as DLA (see **4.6.2**).

4.10 Industrial disablement benefit

4.10.1 What is industrial disablement benefit?

Industrial disablement benefit (IDB), sometimes simply called 'disablement benefit', is the principal remaining component of the industrial injury benefit scheme. The other current component of the scheme is constant attendance allowance (see **4.11**).

The industrial injury scheme provides no-fault compensation to people who have become disabled at work. This may be as a result of an industrial accident (see **4.10.2**) or a prescribed industrial disease (see **4.10.9**).

Industrial disablement benefit is not an earnings replacement benefit. There are no national insurance contribution requirements. It is a non means-tested benefit.

Industrial disablement benefit does not overlap with any other benefit for limited capability for work. At the lower levels of disability it does not imply limited capability for work, and many claimants can and do work. This has no effect on their IDB. However, constant attendance allowance (CAA) (see **4.11**) does overlap with the DLA care component (see **4.7**).

An award of IDB may be for a limited period or for life depending on the nature of the injury or particular disease. If the former, then the claimant may need to apply for renewal of the benefit at the end of the period.

4.10.2   Industrial accident (SSCBA 1992, s 94)

Section 94(1) provides that industrial injuries benefit shall be payable 'where an employed earner suffers personal injury ... by accident arising out of and in the course of his employment, being employed earner's employment'.

To claim benefit as a result of an industrial accident, the claimant must have suffered:

(a)   personal injury;

(b)   arising out of and in the course of his employment;

(c)   as an employed earner;

(d)   by accident;

(e)   resulting in a loss of faculty and disablement.

As to the effect of the accident occurring outside Great Britain or the EEA, see **10.4.5**.

4.10.3   Personal injury

Most personal injuries are obvious (eg a broken arm or leg). However, psychological injuries such as post-traumatic stress disorder may also qualify. As the DfWP *Decision Maker's Guide* puts it, the claimant must show that he has suffered a physiological (or, as doctors prefer to call it, a pathological) 'change for the worse affecting the mind or body'. It does not include injury to reputation or to property eg clothing or glasses damaged in the accident, although dislocation of an artificial hip counts according to *Commissioner's Decision R(I) 7/56*.

4.10.4   'Arising out of and in the course of employment'

4.10.4.1   Case-law definition

In *Faulkner v Chief Adjudication Officer* [1994] PIQR 244, Hoffmann LJ said (at 256):

> An office or employment involves a legal relationship: it entails the existence of specific duties on the part of the employee. An act or event happens 'in the course of' employment if it constitutes the discharge of one of those duties or is reasonably incidental thereto: *Smith v Stages* [1989] AC 928. It follows that there are always two separate questions. The first involves deciding what the employee's duties were. As Lord Thankerton crisply put it in *Canadian Pacific Railway Co v Lockhart* [1942] AC 591, 600: 'the first consideration is the ascertainment of what the servant is employed to do.' The second question is whether the act or event was in the discharge of a duty of something reasonably incidental thereto.

4.10.4.2 Statutory deeming provisions

It can often be difficult to determine if an act or event happens in the course of employment. The SSCBA 1992 assists by providing that in certain circumstances an employee is deemed to have sustained an accident in the course of his employment. These are set out below.

(A) Where no evidence is available

By s 94(3), 'an accident arising in the course of an employed earner's employment shall be taken, in the absence of evidence to the contrary, also to have arisen out of that employment'. This provision applies *only* where no facts are known about the accident. For example, the claimant sustains a head injury whilst at work. There are no witnesses as he was working alone at the time. He cannot recall what happened as he lost his memory.

(B) Acting in contravention of regulations etc

By s 98:

> An accident shall be taken to arise out of and in the course of an employed earner's employment, notwithstanding that he is at the time of the accident acting in contravention of any statutory or other regulations applicable to his employment, or of any orders given by or on behalf of his employer, or that he is acting without instructions from his employer, if:
>
> (a)   the accident would have been taken so to have arisen had the act not been done in contravention of any such regulations or orders, or without such instructions, as the case may be; and
>
> (b)   the act is done for the purposes of and in connection with the employer's trade or business.

As the DfWP *Decision Maker's Guide* says, 'this deeming provision is often misunderstood'. It covers an employee who does something he is employed to do, albeit he does it negligently or in breach of regulations or instructions. However, the action must be done for and in connection with his employer's trade or business and not for the claimant's own personal purposes. The claimant must still show that his actions were of a kind that he was employed to do. For example, a miner is injured whilst riding on an underground tram. He falls off and sustains personal injury. Normally, he would not be covered. However, he says he saw the load was moving and he rode with it to stop it falling. As this was done for and in connection with his employer's trade or business he should be covered.

(C) Travelling

By s 99:

> An accident happening while an employed earner is, with the express or implied permission of his employer, travelling as a passenger by any vehicle to or from his place of work shall, notwithstanding that he is under no obligation to his employer to travel by that vehicle, be taken to arise out of and in the course of his employment if:
>
> (a)   the accident would have been taken so to have arisen had he been under such an obligation; and
>
> (b)   at the time of the accident, the vehicle—
>
> (i)   is being operated by or on behalf of his employer or some other person by whom it is provided in pursuance of arrangements made with his employer; and
>
> (ii)   is not being operated in the ordinary course of a public transport service.

In this context, 'travelling' has been held to include the act of getting on or off the vehicle and at times when the vehicle is stationary before, during and after a journey. For example, the claimant's employer rents a minibus to collect staff every morning and bring them to the factory. As the minibus is slowly stopping, the claimant gets off, falls and injures himself. This will be an industrial accident arising out of and in the course of his employment as the claimant has merely acted negligently. If the minibus had been going at speed then attempting to get off it in such circumstances would be so rash as to take the act wholly outside the scope of his employment (*Commissioner's Decision CL 182/49*).

What about journeys outside the scope of s 99? Many employees will make their own way to and from work. And what about trips made in the meantime? Lord Lowry, in the House of Lords in the case of *Smith v Stages* [1989] 2 WLR 529 at 551, suggested the following guidelines.

(a)   Travelling in the employer's time between workplaces (one of which may be the regular workplace) or in the course of a peripatetic occupation, whether accompanied by goods or tools or simply in order to reach a succession of workplaces (as an inspector of gas meters might do), will be in the course of the employment.

(b)   Receipt of wages (though not receipt of a travelling allowance) will indicate that the employee is travelling in the employer's time and for his benefit and is acting in the course of his employment, and in such a case the fact that the employee may have discretion as to the mode and time of travelling will not take the journey out of the course of his employment.

(c)   An employee travelling *in the employer's time* from his ordinary residence to a workplace other than his regular workplace or in the course of a peripatetic occupation or to the scene of an emergency (such as a fire, an accident or a mechanical breakdown of plant) will be acting in the course of his employment.

(d)   A deviation from or interruption of a journey undertaken in the course of employment (unless the deviation or interruption is merely incidental to the journey) will for the time being (which may include an overnight interruption) take the employee out of the course of his employment.

(e)   Return journeys are to be treated on the same footing as outward journeys.

It must be stressed that these are only guidelines and each case will turn on its own unique facts. For example, in *Commissioner's Decision R(I) 1/88*, a claimant had a road accident whilst driving home in his employer's van. It was a Monday evening and he had been working on his employer's site over the weekend. It was held that the accident arose in the course of his employment because he did not have a single place of work; the journey home by van rather than by the usual train was a direct result of his employer requiring him to work that weekend; he was using the van with his employer's consent and was subject to restrictions imposed by his employer as to his route and overnight parking.

(D) Emergencies

By s 100:

> An accident happening to an employed earner in or about any premises at which he is for the time being employed for the purposes of his employer's trade or business shall be taken to arise out of and in the course of his employment if it happens while he is taking steps, on an actual or supposed emergency at those premises, to rescue, succour or protect persons who are, or are thought to be or possibly to be, injured or imperilled, or to avert or minimise serious damage to property.

'Premises' have been given a fairly wide interpretation in this context and include a place where goods are being delivered to, a place being visited to obtain an order and a private house where an employee has been sent to work. However, the emergency must be 'in or about' the relevant premises. If there is, say, a fire in premises adjacent to the employer's property which threatens to spread to that property then an employee giving assistance to put out the fire and being injured as a result may fall within this provision.

What if s 100 does not apply? If the claimant is in the ordinary course of work when the emergency arises and takes action clearly arising from a duty of employment, any personal injury suffered whilst taking that action arises out of and in the course of employment. But if the action taken has nothing to do with any duty the claimant is employed to perform, the action is not in the course of employment (eg a railway worker travelling on a train to work injures himself in an accident caused when helping another passenger to free a stuck window (*Commissioner's Decision C135/50*)). However, a claim may succeed if despite the action being outside the scope of employment it can be said to have been reasonable and sensible to take in the interests of the employer. Moreover, a claimant's action in an emergency need not be essential nor the best course to have taken provided it was reasonable and sensible and not unnecessarily foolhardy in the circumstances.

(E) Misconduct

By s 101:

> An accident ... shall be treated for the purposes of industrial injuries benefit, where it would not apart from this section be so treated, as arising out of an employed earner's employment if—
> (a)   the accident arises in the course of employment; and
> (b)   the accident is caused—
>> (i)   by another's misconduct, skylarking or negligence, or
>> (ii)   by steps taken in consequence of any such misconduct, skylarking or negligence, or
>> (iii)   by the behaviour or presence of an animal (including a bird, fish or insect),
> or is caused by or consists in the employed earner being struck by any object or by lightning; and
> (c)   the employed earner did not directly or indirectly induce or contribute to the happening of the accident by his conduct outside the employment or by any act not incidental to the employment.

The DfWP *Decision Maker's Guide* says:

> This provision would not apply to a person who while at work teases and angers an animal and is attacked by it, unless that is what they are employed to do.

Fortunately, it also says that:

> the decision maker should interpret [the provision] in a broad common-sense way aiming to apply it in employees' favour to accidents at work for which they are the innocent victim of circumstances.

4.10.5   'Employed earner's employment'

An employed earner is 'a person who is gainfully employed in Great Britain either under a contract of service, or in an office (including an elective office) with emoluments chargeable to income tax under Schedule E' (s 2(1)).

In effect, an employed earner is someone who pays Class 1 NICs, or would pay them if his earnings were high enough (see **2.2.3.1**). The Social Security (Employed Earners' Employments for Industrial Injuries Purposes) Regulations 1975 (SI 1975/467) deem a limited number of people to be employed earners (eg apprentices, special constables and taxi drivers). However, they also exclude, for example, an employed earner who is employed by his or her spouse where the employment is either not for the purposes of the spouse's employment or the earnings are normally below the LEL. So a wife employed by her husband to manage his shop would be included.

The largest group of people excluded from the scheme is the self-employed.

4.10.6   'Accident'

An accident has most often been defined as a mishap or untoward event which has neither been planned nor wanted by the employed earner but happens by chance. It covers the obvious, like accidents with machinery, falling off a ladder, being burnt by a blow lamp, etc, but it also includes incidents where the only untoward event is the occurrence of the injury itself, such as heart conditions, hernia, prolapsed intervertebral discs and nervous shock.

Given this definition, a person sustains an accident even if his own negligence or foolhardiness causes it. Equally, an accidental injury may be caused by the deliberate performance of a dangerous act or exposure to a known risk or the deliberate act of another person by, say, a practical joke or assault. However, in these circumstances, as noted above, careful consideration must be given as to whether the accident arose out of and in the course of the claimant's employment.

An injury that arises from a continuous process going on substantially day to day (but not necessarily minute to minute or from hour to hour) where that process produces incapacity gradually over a period of years is not a personal injury caused by an industrial accident. A man who is deafened because he is too near an explosion suffers an accident. But a man who becomes deaf after working for many years in a noisy environment does not suffer personal injury by accident, although he may have a prescribed industrial disease (see **4.10.9**).

The DfWP *Decision Maker's Guide* provides that in deciding whether an injury is due to accident or process it is for the claimant to show that the condition was the result of an accident. It is not enough to show the condition was caused by work. The longer the period over which the events occur (particularly if they are in themselves trivial) the less likely it is that the resultant condition was accidentally caused. Whilst minor, untoward events over a space of hours or several days might be caused by accident, those happening over a period of weeks or months are more likely to be evidence of process.

4.10.7   Accident in Great Britain or EEA

As a general rule, the accident must occur in Great Britain or an EEA country. See further **Chapter 10**.

4.10.8   'Loss of faculty and resulting disablement'

As well as showing that he sustained a personal injury due to an accident arising out of and in the course of his employment, the claimant must also establish that as a consequence he suffered a loss of faculty leading to him being disabled. A loss of faculty was defined in *Jones (Receiver) (on behalf of Wilde) v The Insurance Officer*

[1972] AC 944 as damage or impairment of part of the body or mind. So, a person who loses an eye in an industrial accident suffers the loss of sight in that eye. A disability must arise as a result of the loss of faculty. In the example just given this would be partial blindness. By Sch 6, the degree of disablement is assessed by a medical examiner who compares the physical and mental condition of the claimant against that of a person of the same age and sex whose physical and mental condition is normal. No other particular circumstances of the claimant are relevant. See further 4.10.10.

4.10.9 Prescribed industrial diseases (ss 108 and 109)

A person who is exposed to hazards in the course of his work may contract a disease as a result. This may be the result of a long-term process which would not count as an accident, or sometimes as a result of one unidentifiable occasion. He can claim IDB if the disease is a 'prescribed industrial disease'. There is a list of 66 prescribed diseases set out in Sch 1 to the Social Security (Industrial Injuries) (Prescribed Diseases) Regulations 1985 (PD Regs 1985), together with the occupations for which they are recognised hazards. The list is constantly updated.

The prescribed diseases are in four categories, labelled A to D:

Category

A	Conditions due to physical agents (heat, pressure, radiation, noise, vibration): for example heat cataract, writer's cramp, some cancers, deafness, carpal tunnel syndrome.
B	Conditions due to biological agents (infections): for example leptospirosis, tuberculosis, hepatitis.
C	Conditions due to chemical agents (including solvents and heavy metals): for example lead poisoning, and assorted skin diseases and cancers.
D	Miscellaneous conditions. This includes the miners' disease pneumoconiosis, caused by inhaling dust; cancers caused by asbestos, and asthmas caused by allergies.

In each case, the claimant must show that he has the condition and that it arose from a prescribed employment. He may be helped by reg 4 of the PD Regs 1985, which provides a list of circumstances in which causation will be presumed until disproved.

4.10.10 Degree of disability (s 103(1))

All IDB claims are decided on medical grounds, and part of the decision relates to the degree of disability. As seen, the degree of disability is assessed by loss of physical or mental faculty. The result is expressed as a percentage. Certain degrees of disability are prescribed in Sch 2 to the Social Security (General Benefit) Regulations 1982 (SS(GB) Regs 1982); these relate only to physical loss of part of the body. See **Appendix 4** to this book.

If a claimant is unfortunate enough to suffer more than one industrial accident, the percentages of disablement can be added together. If a later relevant accident aggravates an earlier industrial injury, a percentage increase will also be awarded for the effect of the interaction.

What if a disability has more than one cause? The rules for assessment are quite complex. As a general rule, if a disability is congenital or otherwise arose before that sustained in the industrial accident, it is deducted from the total disability. For example, a claimant is born with no little finger on his right hand (for IDB purposes that would be assessed at 7% disablement). At work the claimant's right hand becomes trapped in machinery and has to be amputated. The loss of a hand for IDB purposes is assessed at 60% (although it may in fact be a little more or less than that depending on whether or not the claimant is right-handed) but the claimant's pre-existing non-industrial injury must be taken into account. The assessment will be at 53%, ie 60% less 7% and so paid at 50% (see **4.10.11**).

If a person is described as '100% disabled', he is not necessarily completely helpless. It includes loss of sight sufficient to make the claimant incapable of a job for which eyesight is essential, and loss of a hand and a foot. The lowest level at which benefit is payable for an injury is 14%, which is the amount of disability suffered by the loss of a forefinger or the whole of a big toe. For the prescribed diseases of pneumoconiosis, byssinosis and diffuse mesothelioma, for example, even 1% disability can give rise to a payment of benefit.

4.10.11 Rate of benefit (s 103(3))

Benefit is payable on a sliding scale related directly to the degree of disability. If the claimant is 100% disabled, he receives 100% benefit. Lower degrees of disability are rounded to the nearest 10% (5 or more being rounded up and 4 or less being rounded down), and benefit paid at the resulting rate. The exception to this is that an assessment of 14–19% is always rounded up to 20%.

4.10.12 Waiting period (s 103(6))

There is a waiting period before IDB is payable. Ninety days (excluding Sundays – so, in effect, 15 weeks) must have passed since the date of the accident or the onset of the prescribed disease (save in the case of mesothelioma).

4.10.13 IDB and other benefits

Industrial disablement benefit is not treated as income when calculating child tax credit or working tax credit (see **9.6**).

It is treated as income when calculating income support, income-related ESA, income-based JSA, housing benefit and council tax benefit (see **7.3**).

Industrial disablement benefit does not affect the payment of any other non means-tested benefit, except that constant attendance allowance (see **4.11**) overlaps with DLA care component (see **2.6** and **4.6.2**).

4.11 Constant attendance allowance

A person who is receiving IDB at *100%* and requires constant attendance as a result of the relevant loss of faculty, may also receive an additional amount of benefit by way of 'constant attendance allowance' (CAA). Note that this benefit overlaps with DLA care component (see **4.7**), and some claimants may be better off claiming one rather than the other because of the range of different rates and different tests applied.

The rate of pay of CAA depends on the amount of attendance given. The tests set out in the SS(GB) Regs 1982, reg 19 are rather ambiguous. The *exceptional* (highest) rate is payable if the claimant is 'so exceptionally severely disabled as to be entirely, or almost entirely, dependent on such attendance for the necessities of life, and is likely to remain so dependent for a prolonged period and the attendance so required is whole-time'. The *normal* rate is payable if the claimant is 'to a substantial extent dependent on such attendance for the necessities of life and is likely to remain so dependent for a prolonged period'. The *intermediate* rate is payable if 'the extent of such attendance is greater by reason of the [claimant's] exceptionally severe disablement'. The *part-time* (lowest) rate is payable if the claimant is 'to a substantial extent dependent on such attendance for the necessities of life and is likely to remain so dependent for a prolonged period' but 'the attendance so required is part-time only'.

Constant attendance allowance is ignored when calculating any tax credit or other means-tested benefit.

4.12   New Deal for disabled people

The New Deal for disabled people provides one-to-one advice and assistance to help people with disabilities to find work. It is not compulsory and there are no penalties for failing to attend or take part.

4.13   Claimant profiles

4.13.1   Statutory sick pay

This is payable to an employee who is incapable of carrying out the work for which he is employed (the 'own occupation test'). It is payable for a maximum of 28 weeks. If the claimant is still incapable of work he may qualify for the earnings replacement benefit of CESA (for which he will be subject to a work capability assessment, unless exempt).

4.13.2   Contributory ESA

This is an earnings replacement benefit for any worker with limited capability for work (for which he will be subject to the work capability assessment, unless exempt) and who has the appropriate history of Class 1 or 2 National Insurance payments.

4.13.3   Non-contributory ESA

This is for young people aged 16 or over whose limited capability for work starts before they reach the age of 20 (or in limited circumstances, 25 years of age).

4.13.4   DLA care component

This is payable to a claimant under 65 who needs help with his bodily functions or supervision to avoid being a danger. The minimum period of need is normally nine months.

4.13.5   DLA mobility component

This is payable to a claimant under 65 whose severe physical or mental disability affects his ability to walk. The minimum period of need is normally nine months.

4.13.6   Attendance allowance

This is payable to a claimant aged 65 or over who needs a substantial amount of help with his bodily functions or supervision to avoid being a danger. The minimum period of need is normally 12 months.

4.13.7 Industrial disablement benefit

This is payable to an employee who has an accident at work that arises out of and in the course of his employment, which results in a loss of faculty and usually at least 14% disablement.

4.13.8 Constant attendance allowance

This is payable to a recipient of IDB at the rate of 100% and who requires care. It is an alternative to the DLA care component.

Chapter 5

Retirement and Bereavement

5.1 Introduction

This chapter is concerned with two groups of benefits: those for people who have reached retirement age, and those for people who have been bereaved by the death of a spouse or civil partner at any age.

These benefits are relatively straightforward in their application. The most complex aspects of State Pension and bereavement benefits are those which are described in **Chapter 2**:

(a) the contribution conditions (see **2.3.6**); and

(b) the availability of an increase (see **2.4**).

It may be helpful to refer to these sections, especially the first, before continuing with this chapter.

In addition, this chapter also deals with the State pension credit.

5.2 Retirement benefits

5.2.1 State Pension (SSCBA 1992, s 44)

The slang name 'old age pension', is actually more accurate than the correct 'State or retirement pension'. What matters is the claimant's age. He does not need to stop work to claim.

There are three conditions for receipt of the benefit. The claimant must:

(a) have reached retirement age;

(b) not have given notice to defer retirement; and

(c) have the appropriate contribution record (see **2.3.6**).

5.2.1.1 Retirement age

At present, 'retirement age' means 65 for a man, and 60 for a woman. The Pensions Act 1995 provides for the ages for both sexes to be equalised at 65 by 2020. The change is due to be phased in incrementally with effect from 6 April 2010, and will not affect any woman who reaches the age of 60 before that date. This is because the Act provides that a woman who was born before 6 April 1950 will reach pensionable age on her sixtieth birthday. A woman born after 5 April 1955 will reach pensionable age on her sixty-fifth birthday. Women born between 6 April 1950 and 5 April 1955 will reach pensionable age between 60 and 65 depending on their birthdates. For example, a woman who was born between 6 December 1950 and 5 January 1951 will reach pensionable age on 6 September

2011 at age 61. A woman born between 6 July 1953 and 5 August 1953 will reach pensionable age on 6 November 2016 when she is 63.

5.2.1.2 Deferring retirement

Under SSCBA 1992, s 55, a claimant may elect to defer his claim for State Pension for up to five years from normal retirement age. He will not be liable to pay any NICs in the meantime but, when he does claim, will receive a higher rate of pension than he would have had if he had claimed at the normal time.

A person who has reached retirement age must claim his pension; it is not paid automatically. As he approaches retirement age, he should receive notification from HMRC of his contribution record and information about the likely rate. He should not assume that he need do nothing more.

5.2.2 Couples and State Pension

Where one or both members of a couple are of pensionable age, there are several different ways in which their combined pension rights could work. The factors going into the equation include:

(a)   the increases rules (see **2.4**);

(b)   the contribution records of both partners;

(c)   their ages; and

(d)   whether they are married or in a civil partnership.

A pensioner may receive an adult dependant's increase, under the normal rules, for a partner who is a dependant (whether married or not). If they are both of retirement age, they may each receive a pension on their own contributions (a Category A pension).

There is a special rule for married couples or those in a civil partnership, where both are over retirement age and one has a seriously defective contribution record. This is very common among older married couples, where the wife has not worked since marriage but is too old to have benefited from home responsibilities protection (see **2.2.5.4**). A married person in this situation can claim a pension in her own right, on her husband's contributions (a category B pension: men can claim it too, but this is very rare).

This pension is paid at exactly the same rate as the adult dependant's increase. Since women very often reach 60 before their husbands are 65, this can result in a special application of the overlapping benefit rules, which is illustrated below.

Example

Eileen and her husband Patrick are both 60. Eileen has a short contribution record since she worked for only nine years after she left school. Since her marriage in 1965, she has not worked, and she has home responsibilities protection for the period from 1978 to 1986, when her last child left school.

Applying the rules for pension entitlement with home responsibilities protection (see **2.3.6.3**), she would need 31 years' contributions for a full category A pension, and she only has 9. She will therefore immediately receive a pension of 9/31 (roughly 30%) of the full State Pension. But when Patrick reaches 65 she could claim a category B pension on his contributions, which would be 60% of the full pension if he has a complete record. This is obviously higher than her own category A pension, so under the overlapping benefit rules she would receive that and forfeit the other.

5.2.3   Additional State Pension scheme

Although the basic State Pension is paid at a flat rate, many pensioners receive much higher payments because they are in the additional State Pension scheme. Any employee who has not joined an occupational pension scheme or taken out a personal pension will be a member of this scheme. This means that he pays his primary Class 1 contributions at a rate slightly higher than those who have contracted out of the scheme (see **2.2.3**). These extra contributions build up an earnings-related element on top of the basic pension.

5.2.4   Other retirement benefits

The State Pension is by no means the only form of pension payable to people who have retired or reached retirement age. Many pensioners receive one of the following, either in addition to or instead of the State Pension.

5.2.4.1   Occupational or personal pension

Employees, particularly at senior level, have long been able to join occupational pension schemes operated by their employers. Self-employed people have also long been able to make personal provision for pensions. Since the 1980s, personal pensions have also been available to employees whose employer had no occupational scheme, or who chose to make their own arrangements.

5.2.4.2   Stakeholder pensions

The new stakeholder pensions were introduced in 2001 by the Welfare Reform and Pensions Act 1999 provide a simple, low-cost alternative to occupational pension schemes, particularly suited to people on incomes as low as £6,000 per year.

5.2.4.3   Category D retirement pension

A person who has reached the age of 80 and has no other retirement pension may claim a Category D non-contributory State Pension. This pension can also be paid to a person who has only a very low Category A or B pension, which is below the level of the Category D pension, as an alternative. It is paid at the same rate as the married person's Category B pension (see **5.2.2**).

5.2.5   State Pensions for bereaved persons (SSCBA 1992, s 48BB)

If a person who has been bereaved then reaches retirement age, and is not entitled to a pension on his own contributions, his rights depend on his benefit history.

5.2.5.1   Dependent children

If the claimant was receiving widowed parent's allowance (see **5.4.3**) at the time of reaching retirement age, he will receive a Category B State Pension at the same rate.

5.2.5.2   No dependent children

If the claimant had received widowed parent's allowance in the past, or bereavement allowance (see **5.4.4**), he will receive a Category B State Pension calculated by reference to his spouse's National Insurance record at the date of death. The detailed provisions of the calculation of this pension are beyond the scope of this book.

5.2.5.3   Bereavement after retirement age

If the claimant is bereaved after reaching retirement age, he will receive a full State Pension at the rate his spouse would have received it as a single person.

5.3   State pension credit

5.3.1   Conditions of entitlement

(a)   *Age:* to qualify for the pension credit the claimant (man or woman) must have reached 60 years of age. Additionally, the claimant or any partner must be 65 or over in order to qualify for the savings credit element (see **5.3.2.2**).

(b)   *Low income:* the credit is a top up for low income pensioners and some reward for making any provision beyond the basic State Pension.

(c)   *Immigration requirements:* the claimant must not be subject to immigration control and must satisfy the residence requirements (see **Chapter 10**).

5.3.2   The credit elements

The main element of pension credit is the guarantee credit. It is designed to ensure that pensioners have a minimum standard of living. So the amount of the guarantee credit that is payable is the difference between the weekly needs of the claimant (and any partner) and his (or their joint) income. Factors affecting needs include whether the claimant or any partner suffers from a disability, or has caring responsibilities or incurs eligible housing costs. As to what counts as income see **5.3.4**.

The second potential element of pension credit is the savings credit. This is an additional amount designed to reward those pensioners who have made some provision for their retirement beyond the basic State Pension. It can be paid only if the claimant or any partner is at least 65 years of age. It is subject to a cap and will not be paid if the claimant has too much income.

All the figures below are for 2008/09.

5.3.2.1   Guarantee credit

By s 2 of the State Pension Credit Act 2002, a claimant is entitled to this credit if he has no income, or if his income (see **5.3.3**) does not exceed the appropriate minimum guarantee. The latter is the total of the standard minimum guarantee and such prescribed additional amounts as may be appropriate.

The standard minimum guarantee for a single person is £124.05 per week and for a couple it is £189.35 weekly.

The following additional amounts may be claimed:

(a)   Severe disability guarantee: for a single person this is £50.35 per week and for a couple (if both qualify) it is £100.70 weekly. The qualifying conditions for this guarantee are the same as for the severe disability premium for the mainstream means-tested benefits (see **7.7.2**).

(b)   Carer guarantee: this is £27.75 per week if the claimant or any partner qualifies, but £55.50 weekly if both qualify. The qualifying conditions for this guarantee are the same as for the carer's premium for the mainstream means-tested benefits (see **7.7.4**).

(c)   Eligible housing costs: these are the same as for IS, income-related ESA and income-based JSA (see **8.3**).

5.3.2.2   The savings credit

By s 3 of the State Pension Credit Act 2002, a claimant is entitled to this credit if his qualifying income (see **5.3.4**) exceeds the savings credit threshold, namely £91.20 per week for a single person and £145.80 weekly for a couple.

The amount of savings credit payable is subject to a cap known as the maximum savings credit. This is 60% of the difference between the standard minimum guarantee (see **5.3.2.1**) and the savings credit threshold. This means that the maximum savings credit is for:

(a)   a single person the sum of £19.71 (ie £124.05 – £91.20 = £32.85 × 60%); and

(b)   a couple, £26.13 (ie £189.35 – £145.80 = £43.55 × 60%).

The maximum savings credit must be reduced, where appropriate, on a sliding scale of 40% for every £1 of qualifying income above the appropriate guaranteed minimum level. See the third worked example at **5.3.5**.

5.3.3 Income

There is no upper capital limit for the pension credit. As to what constitutes capital, see **7.2**. However, if the claimant has capital above £6,000 he is treated as having a weekly income of £1 for every £500 or part of £500 by which his capital exceeds £6,000. This is known as 'tariff income'. It is similar to that deemed to arise for the four mainstream means-tested benefits (see **7.3.6**).

Income from an occupational or a personal pension scheme counts. Child maintenance is ignored. Spousal maintenance counts as income for the guarantee credit only.

The following benefits count as income when calculating pension credit:

(a)   contribution-based JSA (see **3.4**);

(b)   CESA (see **4.3**);

(c)   maternity allowance (see **6.4**);

(d)   carer's allowance (see **6.7**);

(e)   bereavement allowance (see **5.4.4**);

(f)   State Pensions (see **5.2**);

(g)   industrial disablement benefit (see **4.10**);

(h)   working tax credit (see **9.6**).

The following benefits are not treated as income but are ignored when calculating pension credit:

(a)   child benefit (see **6.6**);

(b)   child tax credit (see **9.6**);

(c)   disability living allowance and attendance allowance (see **4.7**);

(d)   constant attendance allowance (see **4.11**);

(e)   widowed parent's allowance (see **5.4.3**).

Note that a bereavement payment is ignored only if the claimant or any partner is aged 60 or over and not claiming IS or IBJSA.

5.3.4 Qualifying income for the savings credit

For the purposes of the savings credit, the position is as described at **5.3.3** above but the following benefits are ignored:

(a)   contribution-based JSA;

(b)   CESA;

(c)   maternity allowance;

(d)   working tax credit.

5.3.5 Worked examples

(1) Gavin and his partner, Annette are both aged 66. Their weekly income consists of £145.05 basic State Pension.

    (a) *Guarantee credit*

        They are entitled to the couple standard minimum guarantee of £189.35. If we deduct their weekly income (£145.05) from this figure, they will receive £44.30 each week.

    (b) *Savings credit*

        As their qualifying income does not exceed the savings threshold (£145.80), none is payable.

(2) Liam is a single man, aged 68. He receives the basic State Pension of £90.70 per week. He has savings of £7,500.

    (a) *Guarantee credit*

        He is entitled to the single standard minimum guarantee of £124.05. If we deduct his weekly income of £93.70 from this figure, he will receive £30.35 each week. Do not forget that his income consists of his State Pension and tariff income on his savings above £6,000 at the rate of £1 for every £500 or part (ie £3 here).

    (b) *Savings credit*

        His total qualifying income is £93.70. As a single man his savings credit threshold is £91.20. So he is entitled to the credit. 60% of the excess (£93.70 – £91.20), namely £2.50, is £1.50 and so he will receive £1.50 as savings credit in addition to the guarantee credit each week.

(3) Harry and his wife, Irene are both aged 70. Their weekly income consists of £145.05 basic State Pension and £50 personal pension payments.

    (a) *Guarantee credit*

        They are entitled to the couple standard minimum guarantee of £189.35. However, their weekly income (£195.05) exceeds this figure and so none is payable.

    (b) *Savings credit*

        Their total qualifying income of £195.05 exceeds the savings credit threshold of £145.80 and also the standard minimum guarantee of £189.35.

        So they can only receive 60% of the excess between the savings credit threshold of £145.80 and the standard minimum guarantee of £189.35 and this must be reduced by 40% for every £1 of qualifying income above the standard minimum guarantee of £189.35.

        First let us remind ourselves that the maximum savings credit is 60% of the difference between the standard minimum guarantee and the savings credit threshold. This means that the maximum savings credit for Harry and Irene is, as a couple, £26.13 ie (£189.35 – £145.80 = £43.55 × 60%).

        But as their qualifying income exceeds the standard minimum guarantee by £5.70 (£195.05 – £189.35) the maximum savings credit must be reduced by 40% of that excess.

        £5.70 × 40% = £2.28.

        Therefore, Harry and Irene are paid a savings credit of £23.85 per week (£26.13 – £2.28).

5.3.6 Payments of pension credit

The scheme is administered by the DfWP. The benefit is payable weekly. It can be paid by order book, giro or direct credit transfer to a bank, building society or post office account.

5.4 Bereavement benefits

5.4.1 What are bereavement benefits?

Bereavement benefits, which are governed by ss 36–39 of the SSCBA 1992, are those benefits which are paid to a widow or a widower as a result of the death of his or her spouse or civil partner. In order to claim bereavement benefits, the claimant must have been lawfully married or in a valid civil partnership, at the date of death, to the person who has died.

When a claimant registers the death of his or her spouse or civil partner with the local registrar, he or she will be given a registration or notification of death certificate. The claimant must complete this and send it to Jobcentre Plus. He or she will then receive a claim form for bereavement benefits.

5.4.2 Contributory benefits

The three primary benefits within this group – widowed parent's allowance, bereavement allowance and a bereavement payment – are National Insurance contributory benefits, but the relevant contribution record is that of the deceased spouse or civil partner, not the claimant. See **2.3.6.4** for the contribution conditions.

5.4.3 Widowed parent's allowance (SSCBA 1992, s 39A)

To qualify for widowed parent's allowance, the claimant must:

(a) be under retirement age at the date of the spouse's or civil partner's death; and

(b) be caring for a child or qualifying young person for whom either the claimant or the deceased spouse or civil partner was receiving child benefit immediately before their death; or

(c) be pregnant with her husband's child; and

(d) satisfy the NIC requirements (see **2.3.6.4**).

The allowance may be paid until child benefit for a qualifying child or young person comes to an end. See further **6.6**. Payment stops when the claimant reaches pension age.

The flat weekly rate of pay is reduced if the deceased spouse or civil partner did not pay sufficient NICs (see **2.3.6.4**).

The benefit ceases if the claimant remarries, and is suspended during any period in which the claimant cohabits (for the law on cohabitation, see **7.4.2**).

5.4.4 Bereavement allowance (SSCBA 1992, s 39B)

To qualify for a bereavement allowance, the claimant must:

(a) be under retirement age and over 45 at the date of the death of the spouse or civil partner or when any entitlement to widowed parent's allowance ends; and

(b) not be entitled to widowed parent's allowance; and

(c) satisfy the NIC requirements (see **2.3.6.4**).

The flat weekly rate of pay is reduced by 7% for every year or part of a year by which the claimant was under 55 at the time of the claim. It will be further reduced if the deceased spouse or civil partner did not pay sufficient NICs (see **2.3.6.4**).

This allowance is payable for 52 weeks.

The benefit ceases if the claimant remarries, and is suspended during any period in which the claimant cohabits (for the law on cohabitation, see **7.4.2**).

5.4.5   Bereavement payment (SSCBA 1992, s 36)

A bereaved person will qualify for a tax-free lump sum bereavement payment of £2,000 if:

(a)   the claimant is under retirement age when his or her spouse or civil partner dies or that person was not on death entitled to a Category A State Pension; and

(b)   the deceased spouse or civil partner satisfies the NICs requirements (see **2.3.6.4**).

There is no requirement that the couple had to be cohabiting at the time of the death of the spouse or civil partner. However, if they had separated, no payment can be made if the claimant was cohabiting at the time of his or her partner's death (see **7.10**).

The claim must be made within 12 months of the death of the spouse or civil partner.

5.4.6   Summary of key points

Client's age and status when spouse or civil partner dies	Benefit(s)
Under 45 with no child(ren) or qualifying young person(s)	Bereavement payment only
45 or over, under retirement age, with no child(ren) or qualifying young person(s)	Bereavement payment and bereavement allowance
Under retirement age, expecting late husband's child	Bereavement payment and widowed parent's allowance
Under retirement age, with child(ren) or qualifying young person(s)	Bereavement payment and widowed parent's allowance

5.4.7   Bereavement benefits and other benefits

Widowed parent's allowance and bereavement allowance are treated as income when calculating entitlement to the child tax credit and working tax credit. A bereavement payment is not treated as income (see **9.6**).

A bereavement payment counts as capital when considering eligibility for and the amount of any tariff income in respect of income support, income-related ESA, income-based JSA, housing benefit and council tax benefit (see **7.3**).

Only some of widowed parent's allowance is treated as income when calculating the means-tested benefits. The first £10 is ignored for the purposes of income support, income-related ESA and income-based JSA; £15 is ignored when calculating housing benefit and council tax benefit.

Widowed parent's allowance is not treated as income when calculating the pension credit (see **5.3**).

Bereavement allowance is treated as income when calculating income support, income-related ESA, income-based JSA, housing benefit, council tax benefit and the pension credit.

Widowed parent's allowance and bereavement allowance are earnings replacement benefits (see **1.2.5**).

5.5 Claimant profiles

5.5.1 State Pension

This earnings replacement benefit is payable to a claimant who has reached retirement age and has the appropriate National Insurance record.

5.5.2 State pension credit

This is payable to a claimant who has reached 60 years of age and who has a low income. Any capital is irrelevant save for any tariff income that it generates.

5.5.3 Widowed parent's allowance

This is an earnings replacement benefit that is payable to a widow or widower who is under retirement age when his or her spouse or civil partner dies and who is caring for a child or qualifying young person for whom child benefit is paid, or the claimant is a woman who is pregnant with her husband's child.

5.5.4 Bereavement allowance

This is an earnings replacement benefit that is payable to a widow or widower who is over 45 but under retirement age when his or her spouse or civil partner dies or his or her entitlement to widowed parent's allowance ends, and who is not entitled to widowed parent's allowance.

5.5.5 Bereavement payment

This is an one-off capital payment to a widow or widower or civil partner who is under retirement age when his or her spouse or civil partner dies and whose spouse or civil partner has the appropriate Class 1, 2 or 3 National Insurance payment history.

Chapter 6
Maternity, Children and Carers

6.1 Contents of this chapter

This chapter deals with benefits for three groups of claimants who are not covered by the benefits described in earlier chapters: women who give up work to have a baby, people with young children, and carers. The benefits are:

(a) statutory maternity pay (see **6.3**), for most long-term employees who have stopped work to have a baby;

(b) maternity allowance (see **6.4**) for other women with the appropriate work history who have stopped work to have a baby;

(c) Sure Start maternity grant (see **6.5**) for pregnant women on low incomes;

(d) child benefit (see **6.6**) for people looking after a child or a young person aged under 20 in full-time, non-advanced education or Government approved training;

(e) carer's allowance (see **6.7**) for people acting as full-time voluntary carers for people with disabilities.

6.2 Maternity benefits: an overview

6.2.1 What are the maternity benefits?

The maternity benefits are statutory maternity pay (SMP) (see **6.3**) and maternity allowance (MA) (see **6.4**). Maternity allowance can be paid only to a woman who does not qualify for SMP. Most employees will qualify for SMP.

6.2.2 Terminology

The jargon common to maternity benefits is set out below:

(a) 'A week' is a period of seven days, beginning on a Sunday.

(b) 'The expected week of childbirth' is the week in which the pregnant woman's medical advisers have told her that her baby is likely to be born. Neither benefit can be paid more than 11 weeks before the expected week of childbirth. If the baby arrives earlier or later than the expected week of childbirth, this has no effect on the right to benefits. The benefits are payable even if the baby is born dead, provided that the pregnancy has lasted at least 24 weeks.

(c) 'The qualifying week' is the fifteenth week before the beginning of the expected week of childbirth.

(d)   'The maternity allowance threshold' is the minimum average weekly earnings limit which is needed to qualify for maternity allowance. It was £30 a week in 2008/09.

6.2.3   Calculating key dates for SMP and MA

Assume that the claimant's baby is due on Friday, 5 June 2009. The relevant dates are:

(a)   her expected week of childbirth starts on the previous Sunday, namely 31 May;

(b)   the earliest she can claim is the eleventh week before the expected week of childbirth (ie 15 March 2009);

(c)   her qualifying week is the fifteenth week before the expected week of childbirth. It therefore starts on Sunday, 15 February 2009 and ends on Saturday, 21 February 2009.

6.3   Statutory maternity pay

There is no general right for an employee to be paid while she is absent on maternity leave unless there is an express provision to the contrary in her contract. However, many employees have the right to SMP, which is quite independent of their rights in employment law to maternity leave itself, and to return to work after the birth of the baby. The right cannot be excluded by contract, or the rate of payment reduced.

6.3.1   Qualifying conditions (SSCBA 1992, s 164)

To qualify for SMP, the claimant must:

(a)   be an employee; and

(b)   be employed for at least one day in the qualifying week and have been employed by the same employer for a continuous period of at least 26 weeks ending with employment in at least part of the qualifying week;

(c)   earn gross not less than the LEL (see **2.2.2.1**) during a normal working week over the period of eight weeks prior to the qualifying week; and

(d)   be pregnant and reached, or had the baby prior to, the start of the eleventh week before the expected week of childbirth; and

(e)   given notice (in writing if so requested) to her employer of her intended absence at least 21 days prior to the start of the absence or as soon as is reasonably practicable; and

(f)   have stopped work.

6.3.2   The continuous employment rule

The woman must have worked for a continuous period of 26 weeks for the same employer, including at least one day in the qualifying week. Temporary absences from work, such as periods of illness or holiday, count towards the 26 weeks. A strike does not break continuity of employment but it does not count towards the 26 weeks unless the woman can show that at no time did she have a direct interest in the trade dispute (Statutory Maternity Pay Regulations 1986 (SMP Regs 1986) (SI 1986/1960) , reg 13).

6.3.3 The earnings condition

Although a claim for SMP does not depend on the woman's National Insurance contribution record, she must have earned a gross weekly average wage of no less than the LEL during the eight-week period before the qualifying week. If the baby is born before the qualifying week, the woman's earnings are averaged over the last eight weeks before the week of birth. What counts as earnings? Any bonuses, overtime and SSP are included but tips and money paid through a profit sharing scheme are excluded.

6.3.4 The maternity pay period

The woman may choose the date upon which to give up work and claim SMP during the maternity pay period as long as it is in or after the eleventh week before the expected week of childbirth and no later than the week after birth. Once begun, it can continue for up to a maximum of 39 consecutive weeks. The period cannot be extended to take account of a late birth.

6.3.5 The amount of benefit

Although SMP may currently be paid for up to a maximum of 39 consecutive weeks, it is paid at two different rates. For the first six weeks of the claim it is paid at the rate of 90% of the woman's average weekly earnings as calculated in **6.3.3**. For the remaining 33 weeks it is paid either at the rate of £117.18 per week (in 2008/09) or it continues at the earnings-related rate if that rate of pay is less than £117.18 per week.

What if the claimant is awarded a pay rise during her maternity leave? By the Statutory Maternity Pay (General) (Amendment) Regulations 2005 (SI 2005/729) the amount of SMP must be recalculated.

6.3.6 Summary of key dates

The diagram below shows the key dates for SMP purposes. The starting point is, of course, the week the baby is due and then looking backwards at earlier weeks to see if the conditions of entitlement have been met. The following abbreviations are used.

(a)   EWC: expected week of childbirth;

(b)   QW: qualifying week;

(c)   SCP: the start of the required 26-week period of continuous employment before, and including at least one day in, the QW (see **6.3.1(b)**).

Week 40 before EWC	Weeks 16 to 39 before EWC	Week 15 before EWC	Weeks 1 to 14 before EWC	Week baby due
SCP		QW		EWC

6.3.7 SMP and other benefits

The first £100 of SMP is ignored when calculating child tax credit or working tax credit and any SMP over £100 is treated as employment income (see **9.6**).

Statutory maternity pay is treated as income when calculating income support, income-related ESA or income-based JSA. It is treated as earnings when calculating housing benefit or council tax benefit and so any appropriate earnings disregard can be made (see **7.3**).

Statutory maternity pay is taken into account when calculating entitlement to the pension credit (see **5.3**).

It is incompatible with, and so cannot be claimed at the same time as, CESA, MA, SSP or contribution-based JSA (see **2.5**).

6.4 Maternity allowance (SSCBA 1992, s 35)

Maternity allowance is an alternative to SMP. It is available to a woman who does not qualify for SMP, perhaps because she has been self-employed or has changed her job during the pregnancy, or given up work just before or during her pregnancy.

6.4.1 Conditions of entitlement for maternity allowance

Maternity allowance is payable if the woman:

(a)   has become pregnant and has reached, or given birth before reaching, the start of the eleventh week before the expected week of childbirth; and

(b)   she has been engaged in employment as an employed or self-employed earner for any part of a week in respect of at least 26 of the 66 weeks immediately preceding the expected week of childbirth (see **6.4.2**); and

(c)   her average weekly earnings are not less than the maternity allowance threshold (see **6.4.3**); and

(d)   she is not entitled to statutory maternity pay for the same week in respect of the same pregnancy.

6.4.2 The employment and earnings conditions

The period of employment or self-employment for at least 26 of the 66 weeks immediately preceding the expected week of childbirth need not be continuous.

Maternity allowance is payable provided the woman earned at least the MA threshold (see **6.4.3**), or paid Class 2 NICs for any of the 13 weeks in the 66 weeks immediately preceding the expected week of childbirth.

6.4.3 The maternity allowance threshold

This is the figure set by the Government as the minimum average weekly earnings which must have been received in order to be eligible for MA. For the year 2008/09, it was £30.

6.4.4 Amount of benefit

The weekly rate is the lesser of the fixed standard rate (it was £117.18 in 2008/09) or 90% of the woman's average weekly earnings.

Maternity allowance carries a possible adult dependant increase. Remember that there are two questions to be answered, namely: Does the spouse for whom the increase is claimable receive an earnings replacement benefit in his own right? Does he have any earnings from work? See further **2.4**.

Maternity allowance is payable for a maximum of 39 weeks.

6.4.5 Maternity allowance period

A woman may claim MA at any time between the eleventh week prior to the expected week of childbirth and the week following birth.

6.4.6 MA and other benefits

Maternity allowance is ignored when calculating child tax credit or working tax credit (see **9.6**).

It is treated as income when calculating income support, income-related ESA, income-based JSA, housing benefit or council tax benefit (see **7.3**).

It is taken into account when calculating entitlement to the pension credit, but ignored when calculating the claimant's qualifying income for the savings credit element (see **5.3**).

It is an earnings replacement benefit (see **1.2.5**) and so may affect the entitlement of a spouse to any adult dependant increase in an appropriate benefit (see **2.4**). It is incompatible with, and so cannot be claimed at the same time as, SSP or SMP or contribution-based JSA (see **2.5**).

6.5 Other benefits for pregnant and recently delivered women

Many women will not be eligible for either SMP or MA because they are not currently employed or do not satisfy the earning conditions. A woman is deemed to have limited capability for work for the last four weeks of her pregnancy and for 14 days after the birth of her baby. This means that she could claim CESA (see **4.3**) for those weeks provided she satisfies the contribution conditions (see **2.3.3.2**); otherwise she might be eligible for income-based ESA (see **Chapter 7**).

Pregnant women from low-income families may also qualify for a £500 maternity grant under the Sure Start scheme. The claimant or claimant's partner must be receiving either income support, or income-related ESA or income-based JSA (see **Chapter 7**); or working tax credit where a disability or severe disability element is included, or child tax credit at a higher rate than the family element (see **Chapter 9**). Payment can be claimed at any time from 11 weeks before the expected week of childbirth until three months after the birth occurs. Note that although called a grant, this is a non-repayable lump sum paid out of the social fund (see **9.16**).

6.6 Child benefit (SSCBA 1992, s 143)

6.6.1 What is child benefit?

Child benefit can be paid to any person who has a child or young person in his or her care (note that the great majority of the claimants are women and traditionally payment is made to a child's mother). For full details see the Child Benefit Act 2005 and the Child Benefit (General) Regulations 2006 (SI 2006/223).

Benefit is payable for each 'qualifying child or young person' for whom the claimant is 'responsible' during a week.

The claimant must not be subject to immigration controls and must meet the residence requirements (see **Chapter 10**).

6.6.2 A qualifying child

A person is treated as a qualifying child for any week in which he is under the age of 16.

6.6.3   Qualifying young person

A qualifying young person is:

(a)   a person aged 16 years, from the date on which he attains that age until and including the 31 August which next follows that date; or

(b)   a person aged 16 years and over who is undertaking a course of full-time education at a school or college which is not advanced education; or

(c)   a person aged 16 years and over who is undertaking approved training that is not provided through a contract of employment.

For the purposes of (b) and (c) above, the person must have commenced the course of full-time education or approved training before reaching the age of 19 and must not have attained the age of 20 years.

What is full-time education? This is a course of at least 12 hours per week during term time that is spent receiving tuition, engaged in practical work or supervised study, or taking examinations.

What is advanced education? This is a course in preparation for a degree, a diploma of higher education, a higher national diploma, or a teaching qualification; or any other course which is of a standard above an ordinary national diploma, a national diploma, a national certificate of Edexcel or a general certificate of education (advanced level).

Courses which do not count as advanced education include GCSEs, 'A' levels, NVQ levels 1, 2 or 3, BTEC National Diploma, National Certificate and 1st Diploma.

What is approved training? In England the Government schemes covered are 'Entry to Employment' and 'Programme Led Pathways into Apprenticeships'; in Wales they are 'Skillbuild', 'Skillbuild+' and 'Foundation Modern Apprenticeships'.

6.6.4   Responsibility for a qualifying child or young person

A person is responsible for a child or young person who is part of his benefits household in the week of the claim, or if he contributes to the weekly cost of supporting the child or young person at a rate not less than that payable for child benefit.

6.6.5   Competing claims (SSCBA 1992, Sch 10)

Only one person may receive child benefit for any one child. If the parents of the child are living in the same household, the benefit will usually be paid to the mother. If a child spends equal time in two households because his parents are living apart, they must decide who will have the benefit. There is no provision in social security law to split child benefit in these circumstances. What if there is more than one child and their care is shared between the separated parents? See *R (Graham Ford) v Board of Inland Revenue* [2005] EWHC 1109 (Admin).

6.6.6   Administration and payment

There are two possible levels of payment of child benefit.

(a)   For the only or eldest qualifying child or young person a higher rate is paid. If the eldest qualifying child or young person is one of twins, the higher rate is paid for the elder twin. If a new family unit is formed by a couple, both of whom already have qualifying children or young persons from previous relationships, then it will become payable for the qualifying child or young person who is the eldest overall.

(b)   For all subsequent qualifying children or young persons a standard rate applies.

6.6.7   Child benefit and other benefits

Child benefit is ignored when calculating entitlement to the child tax credit and working tax credit (see **9.6**).

Child benefit is ignored when calculating entitlement to income support, income-related ESA and income-based JSA (see **7.3**).

Child benefit is treated as income when calculating entitlement to housing benefit and council tax benefit (see **7.3**).

Child benefit is not payable if the child in question receives non-contributory ESA (see **4.3.2**).

6.7   Carer's allowance (SSCBA 1992, s 70)

6.7.1   What is carer's allowance?

Carer's allowance (CA) is paid to people who are not professional carers, but are spending a significant amount of their time without payment attending to the needs of a person who is seriously disabled. Although CA is classified as a non means-tested benefit, the claimant's earnings can disqualify him from receiving it (see **6.7.6**). Carer's allowance carries an adult dependant increase (see **2.4**). It is an earnings replacement benefit (see **1.2.5**).

To qualify for CA, the claimant must:

(a)   be 16 years of age or over; and

(b)   be regularly and substantially engaged in caring (see **6.7.3**) for a severely disabled person (see **6.7.4**); and

(c)   not be in full-time education (see **6.7.5**);

(d)   not be gainfully employed (see **6.7.6**); and

(e)   not be subject to immigration controls and must meet the residence requirements (see **Chapter 10**).

6.7.2   Age requirement

The minimum age to qualify is 16. There is no maximum age.

6.7.3   Regularly and substantially engaged in caring

To satisfy this condition, the claimant must spend at least 35 hours per week in caring for the disabled person. A 'caring week' is a period of seven days beginning with a Sunday. However, the care may be given over a shorter period, for example, seven hours per day during a five-day period, or 17.5 hours per day over a weekend. The carer, however, must be engaged for 35 hours in *every* week for which the claim is made so that any average amount of hours over a number of weeks will not satisfy the condition.

There is no legal definition of 'caring'. Guidance from DfWP is that it is reasonable to expect that the carer and severely disabled person are together for most of the time. However, this is not limited to the time that constitutes attention to bodily functions (see **4.7.2**) for the purposes of DLA or AA. There may be occasions when the carer spends some time apart from the severely disabled person, for example preparing for and clearing up after their stay. Any reasonable time spent in these ways can be counted as a period of caring for CA purposes.

If two people care regularly and substantially for the same severely disabled person, only one of them will be entitled to receive CA.

Most claimants are close relatives of the person for whom they are caring, and live in the same accommodation. There is, however, no reason why a friend or neighbour should not claim this benefit.

6.7.4   Severely disabled person

This is a person who is receiving either attendance allowance (see **4.9**), or the care component of disability living allowance (see **4.7**) at the highest or middle rates, or constant attendance allowance in respect of industrial disablement benefit (see **4.11**).

6.7.5   Full-time education

A person is treated as receiving full-time education for any period during which he attends a course of education at a university, college, school or other educational establishment for 21 hours or more a week.

In calculating the hours of attendance, there is included the time spent receiving instruction or tuition, undertaking supervised study, examination or practical work or taking part in any exercise, experiment or project for which provision is made in the curriculum of the course: see *Flemming v Social Security Commissioners* [2002] EWCA Civ 641.

6.7.6   Gainfully employed

If the carer earns net more than a prescribed amount per week (in 2008/09 it was £95), he is gainfully employed and will not be entitled to CA. Voluntary work or an occupational pension will not make the claimant fall foul of the earnings rule.

6.7.7   Administration and payment

Carer's allowance is paid at a flat rate, subject to the availability of an adult dependant increase. Remember that there are two questions to be answered, namely: Does the spouse for whom the increase is claimable receive an earnings replacement benefit in his own right? Does he have any earnings from work? See further **2.4**.

An award of CA can be made for a fixed period or indefinitely. It will usually last for the same duration as the severely disabled person's benefit (see **6.7.4**).

6.7.8   CA and other benefits

A person entitled to CA may also be entitled to income support, housing benefit and council tax benefit with a carer's premium (see **7.7.4**). However, note that if the disabled person is also entitled to income support, housing benefit or council tax benefit, then he will not be able to claim the severe disability premium if his carer receives CA. Therefore, a check should be made to see whether it is more advantageous for the carer to forgo any entitlement to CA where the disabled person is entitled to the severe disability premium.

Carer's allowance is treated as income when calculating child tax credit and working tax credit (see **9.6**), income support, income-related ESA, income-based JSA, housing benefit and council tax benefit (see **7.3**).

It is taken into account when calculating entitlement to the pension credit and when calculating the claimant's qualifying income for the savings credit element (see **5.3**).

It is an earnings replacement benefit (see **1.2.5**) and so may affect the entitlement of a spouse to any adult dependant increase in an appropriate benefit (see **2.4**).

6.8 Claimant profiles

6.8.1 Statutory maternity pay

Paid by employers to an employee who has been with that employer throughout her pregnancy.

6.8.2 Maternity allowance

This is an earnings replacement benefit that is paid by the DfWP to a short-term employee or self-employed woman.

6.8.3 Child benefit

Paid to a person who is responsible for a qualifying child or young person.

6.8.4 Carer's allowance

This is an earnings replacement benefit that is paid to someone who cares for at least 35 hours every week for a severely disabled person. The claimant must not be in full-time education or in remunerative employment.

Chapter 7

Introduction to the Means-Tested Benefits

7.1 The scope of this chapter

7.1.1 Contents of this chapter

In this chapter, we shall consider the following topics:

(a) a reminder of the main means-tested benefits;

(b) the meaning of the expression 'means test';

(c) capital and income;

(d) the family and the benefits household;

(e) the applicable amount;

(f) cohabitation;

(g) overpayments of benefit and their recovery.

Most of these topics are common to all the means-tested benefits and it is more sensible to consider them together. Variations applicable to the individual benefits are considered in the main discussion of the benefits in **Chapters 8** and **9**.

7.1.2 The benefits discussed in this chapter

7.1.2.1 Income support; income-related employment and support allowance and income-based jobseeker's allowance

Income support (IS), income-related employment and support allowance (IRESA) and income-based jobseeker's allowance (IBJSA) (see **Chapter 8**) are the ultimate top-up benefits for anyone who has a very low income, from whatever source, and is not in remunerative work. These are the benefits which are meant when people talk about 'being on social security'. It is only with these benefits that an owner-occupier may get assistance with his housing costs, particularly mortgage interest payments or service charges under a long lease.

7.1.2.2 Local authority benefits

The local authority benefits are housing benefit (HB) and council tax benefit (CTB) (see **Chapter 9**). Housing benefit gives help to those under a legal liability to pay rent for the place they occupy (but do not own) as their home; CTB reduces the amount that the occupiers of residential property pay in local taxes.

7.1.3 What is the means test?

In order to qualify for any of these benefits, the claimant must satisfy a means test, in addition to satisfying any qualifying conditions specific to the benefit he wishes to claim. The means test is an arithmetical calculation which compares the claimant's means, or resources, with a specified level of need. The resulting figure shows whether the client is entitled to benefit on the basis of the means test, and if so how much benefit he will receive.

The details of how the means test is carried out differ according to which benefit is being claimed. There are, however, a number of common factors which we shall deal with here. We shall consider the factors specific to each benefit as a preliminary to discussing the other aspects of that benefit in the appropriate chapter.

7.2 Resources: capital

7.2.1 What is capital?

For all these benefits, there are three types of capital which may be taken into account.

7.2.1.1 Actual capital

Any form of asset or investment is capable of being capital for benefit purposes. This includes savings, lump sum or one-off payments, shares, life insurance policies, real property and trust monies. Even the rights to capital are regarded as capital because such rights can be sold (eg endowment policies) or enforced (eg by legal action).

For benefit purposes, only capital in which the person has a beneficial interest can be included in the calculation. If a person is the legal owner of a capital resource, an assumption will be made that he is also the beneficial owner unless he can prove to the contrary. Beneficial ownership may arise in a variety of circumstances wherein the person is not the legal owner. For example, he has invested in a limited company; his solicitor holds personal injury damages; he is a beneficiary in an estate still in probate or he has an interest in a trust fund.

7.2.1.2 Income which is treated as capital

Certain types of income are treated as capital. These include an advance of earnings or a loan from an employer; income tax refunds and irregular (one-off) charitable payments. However, these do not count if the claimant is involved in returning to work after a trade dispute.

7.2.1.3 Notional capital

This is capital in which the claimant has a beneficial interest but which is not in his possession at the date of the claim. It most often arises in the following circumstances:

(a)   Where the claimant has deliberately deprived himself of the capital resource in order either to claim a benefit or a greater amount of benefit. This is largely a matter of common sense. Using capital to pay debts or to buy personal possessions will often be regarded as deprivation of capital, but the

DfWP will still have to show that it was the claimant's intent in doing so to secure the benefit or more of it. If it is found that the claimant has deprived himself of capital then the value of the capital or whatever it purchased will be counted as notional capital. For example, if the claimant buys a car in order to reduce his capital so that he will be eligible for benefits, then the value of the car will be considered as notional capital.

The onus of proving that a claimant has deliberately deprived himself of capital to improve his benefits position is on the DfWP. It does not have to show that the claimant's or his partner's sole or predominant purpose was to get benefit or to get more benefit but must show that it was a significant one. The following factors will be taken into consideration:

(i)   the mental capabilities of the claimant and/or his partner at the time of disposing of the capital;

(ii)   the options open to the claimant and/or his partner. If there was a choice as to how the capital should be used, then it is more likely that it will be considered as having been spent in order to get benefit. If money is spent extravagantly (eg on an expensive holiday); or to pay off a debt early; or simply given away then the amount in question will be notional capital included in the benefit calculation. If, on the other hand, the money was used to pay for necessities of life such as food or fuel, or immediately repayable debts, then it will probably not be considered as notional capital;

(iii) the knowledge of the claimant and/or his partner. If they did not know that the amount of capital they owned would affect their benefit entitlement then they would not be considered to have deliberately deprived themselves of capital in order to gain benefit. The amount of knowledge they are deemed to have will depend on their familiarity with the benefits system, the contents of any forms they may have been given when applying for benefit and their general standard of education.

A claimant who has received a personal injury payment which is put into a discretionary trust on his behalf will not be considered as having notional capital.

(b)   What about the situation where a claimant is able to get capital if he were to apply for it? This is known as 'capital which is available on application' and includes money which may be owed to the claimant and/or his partner in the form of say an unclaimed win on the national lottery or premium bonds or a returnable deposit.

(c)   There may be capital in which the claimant has a beneficial interest and this has been paid to a third party or the claimant may have received money on behalf of a third party. Where money is paid to a third party (eg a household utility supplier or a bank or building society) on behalf of the claimant or a member of his benefits household (excluding payments made by certain specified trust funds), then that may be treated as notional capital in the possession of the claimant. It counts as capital if the payment is to cover certain of the claimant's or his family's normal living expenses. These include such items as food, household fuel, ordinary clothing and footwear. As to the last two items, school uniforms and sportswear are excluded. Payments for other kinds of expenses (eg a television licence fee) do not count. Conversely, where the claimant or a member of his benefits household receives money on behalf of a third party but retains this or uses it for his own purposes, this will count as capital.

7.2.2 Capital that is disregarded

Not all capital will be included when calculating the amount of capital held by the claimant. Certain types of capital can be disregarded for an indefinite period of time; other types will be disregarded for two years; others for one year and still others for six months. The onus is on the claimant to show that the capital should be disregarded.

Capital which is disregarded indefinitely includes:

(a)   the surrender value of any life assurance policy or endowment policy or annuity;

(b)   business assets of a self-employed earner whilst he continues in self-employment;

(c)   the dwelling which is occupied as the claimant's home (this includes any garage, garden, outbuildings and land, together with any premises not occupied as a home which it is impracticable or unreasonable to sell separately);

(d)   all personal possessions such as jewellery, cars, furniture, etc;

(e)   the value of the right to an occupational pension;

(f)   personal injury damages held in a trust fund or a fund administered by the court;

(g)   the value of a personal pension;

(h)   social fund payments;

(i)   most charitable trust lump sum payments;

(j)   money deposited with a housing association by tenants as a condition of occupying the home.

Capital which can be disregarded for up to two years includes certain specified trust fund payments which are beyond the scope of this book.

Capital which can be disregarded for one year includes arrears of the majority of benefits.

Capital disregarded for six months includes:

(a)   loans or gifts made for the express purpose of essential repairs and improvements to the claimant's home;

(b)   grants made to local authority tenants for the purchase, repair or alteration of a home;

(c)   proceeds of sale of a home if a replacement home is to be purchased;

(d)   insurance payments or compensation paid for the replacement or repair of the home or personal possessions.

There is a discretionary extension of time available for all these matters.

7.2.3 Value of the capital

The value of actual capital will be determined by the DfWP. Each type of asset will be valued according to a set of rules specific to it but generally speaking the current market value is used (ie the price that a willing buyer would pay a willing seller in that market on the date of the claim). Ten per cent of the proceeds will be deducted from the capital to cover the relevant costs of the sale. Stocks and shares will first be valued by looking at the figures given in most of the daily newspapers. If the value is close to the capital limit, then a complicated calculation using the figures given by the Stock Exchange Daily Official List is used. Shares in a private company need to be valued by an expert.

7.2.4 Capital limits

For each benefit, there is an upper and a lower capital limit. The upper limit is the amount of capital which acts as an absolute bar to receiving the benefit. The lower limit is an amount which is completely disregarded and has no effect whatsoever on the amount of benefit. Between the limits, the capital is deemed to produce income which is described as 'tariff income' (see **7.3.6**).

The lower limit for these benefits is £6,000.

The upper limit for these benefits is £16,000.

7.2.5 The diminishing notional capital rule

The amount of notional capital is calculated in the same way as actual capital and the same disregards apply (see above). It is then added to actual capital and any income which is treated as capital to determine eligibility for these benefits. If, as a result, the maximum is exceeded (see above), the claimant will not be entitled to the benefit. In the alternative, if the capital adds up to more than the lower capital limit then the tariff income rule (see **7.3.6**) applies and the claimant's benefit will reduce by £1 for every £250 or part that is above £6,000. However, if the notional capital figure affects the claimant's entitlement to the benefit, the diminishing notional capital rule comes to his aid by reducing the value of the notional capital to which he is presumed to have access. The amount of notional capital is reduced gradually by the extra the claimant would have received in benefits each week if the notional capital had not been included in his capital figure. As soon as the capital figure drops beneath the maximum the claimant will be eligible for the benefit. Where a claimant is receiving benefit at a reduced rate because of the tariff income rule, then the benefit will increase as the notional capital figure decreases.

> #### Example
> Humphrey is 38 years of age and he has no actual capital or income that is treated as capital but he is found to have notional capital of £7,000 and that yields a tariff income of £4 and so reduces his weekly benefit by £4. If his benefit were otherwise, say £56.20 a week, he will be paid only £52.20 per week as a result. The notional capital which he is deemed to have will decrease by £4 each week until the notional capital reaches £6,750 (after approximately 62 weeks) when the tariff income will fall to £3 a week and so on.

7.3 Resources: income

7.3.1 What is income?

For all these benefits, income from all sources has to be taken into account. Some income may be disregarded (see, for example, Sch 9 to the IS Regs 1987 for a list). The principal types of reckonable income that a claimant may have are:

(a)   earnings from employment (see **7.3.2**) or self-employment (see **7.3.3**);

(b)   maintenance (see **7.3.4**);

(c)   other benefits and pensions (see **7.3.5**);

(d)   other income, eg from boarders or lodgers (see **7.4**); and

(e)   tariff income (see **7.3.6**).

Each of the types of income has its own rules, but only some are the same for all the benefits. Here we shall consider the rules which are common to all or most of the benefits.

7.3.2   Earnings from employment and earnings disregard

Earnings from employment are taken net of tax and National Insurance contributions, and half of any contribution to a pension scheme. There are complex provisions for working out earnings that fluctuate from week to week. Usually, some sort of average over a period of several weeks is used. There is a system of disregards for the first slice of net earnings, varying from £5 to a maximum of £25 per week.

7.3.3   Earnings from self-employment and earnings disregard

Earnings from self-employment are based on profits after tax, National Insurance contributions, half of pension contributions, and allowable expenses. These expenses are the same that would be allowed for tax purposes. The same system of disregards applies as with earnings from employment. Earnings from self-employment are normally calculated from the annual profits of the business. There is a system of disregards for the first slice of net earnings, varying from £5 to a maximum of £25 per week.

7.3.4   Maintenance

As a general rule, £20 of maintenance paid in respect of a child of the family is ignored when calculating entitlement to IS, IRESA or IBJSA.

For HB and CTB purposes, child maintenance payments are ignored.

Spousal maintenance counts as income for all the benefits.

7.3.5   Other benefits and pensions

Other social security benefits and occupational or personal pensions usually count as income in full, without any disregards. However, here the differences between the pairs of benefits are most marked.

With all the benefits, the following always count in full as income:

(a)   the contributory benefits but, as to widowed parent's allowance, see **5.4.6**;
(b)   carer's allowance;
(c)   industrial disablement benefit;
(d)   all private and occupational pensions;
(e)   maternity allowance.

The following never count as income:

(a)   disability living allowance and attendance allowance;
(b)   IS, IRESA and IBJSA for HB and CTB.

This leaves the following benefits, which are treated differently for different benefits.

(a)   *Working tax credit:* whilst this counts as income for all the benefits, note that when calculating entitlement to HB and CTB any 30-hour element of working tax credit and/or relevant child care costs up to a maximum permitted figure (see **9.10.2.2**) may be ignored.

(b) *Child tax credit and child benefit:* these are ignored when calculating entitlement to IS, IRESA and IBJSA, but taken into account as income when calculating entitlement to HB and CTB.

(c) *SSP and SMP:* these are treated as income when calculating IS, IRESA or IBJSA. They are treated as earnings when calculating HB or CTB so any appropriate earnings disregard can be made. Note that if the claimant of HB or CTB, or any partner is aged 60 or over and not claiming IS, IRESA or IBJSA, then SSP and SMP are ignored.

7.3.6 Tariff income

For all the benefits, capital between the upper and lower limits is deemed to produce 'tariff income'. This is a complete fantasy: many forms of capital produce no income at all, while those that do rarely produce it at the level that is assumed for tariff income. Any actual income that an investment does produce is completely disregarded.

To calculate tariff income, the amount up to the lower capital limit (see **7.2.4**) is deducted from all relevant capital.

For all the benefits the general rule is that the claimant is assumed to have an income of £1 for every £250, or part of £250, by which capital exceeds £6,000 (up to the maximum of £16,000).

For HB and CTB purposes, if the claimant and any partner are aged 60 or over and not claiming IS, IRESA or IBJSA the following tariff income rules apply instead:

(a) if the guarantee credit element of pension credit (see **5.3**) is being paid then all capital is ignored;

(b) otherwise, the lower limit is £6,000 but the claimant is assumed to have an income of £1 for every £500, or part of £500, by which capital exceeds £6,000 (up to the maximum of £16,000).

Examples

(1) Enrico is 45 years of age and his capital consists of some shares in a private company, which are valued by the DfWP at £6,186. How much tariff income will they be deemed to produce?

Deduct the first £6,000 to leave £186. This is 'part of £250' so is deemed to be producing £1 per week. The total tariff income is therefore £1 per week.

(2) Florence is 55 years of age. She applies for IRESA as she has limited capability for work. Her partner is on a low income and not in remunerative work. They have savings of £9,645. What is her tariff income?

Deduct the first £6,000 to leave £3,645. £3,000 would produce a tariff income of £12 and the next £250 another £1 and the next £250 a further £1, leaving just £145. This is 'part of £250' and so is deemed to produce another £1 tariff income per week. So her total weekly tariff income is £15.

7.4 The family and the benefits household

7.4.1 What does 'family' mean in benefits law?

The members of the claimant's family are those people for whom he may be able to claim additional benefit, and whose resources may affect the amount of benefit he can claim (SSCBA 1992, s 137).

7.4.2 The claimant's partner

The first member of the claimant's family is his 'partner'. This means either:

(a)   a husband or wife, or any person of the opposite sex with whom he is 'living together as husband and wife'; or

(b)   a couple of the same sex in a civil partnership or who are living together as if they were civil partners.

The question of whether two people are indeed living in such a relationship is considered at **7.10**.

7.4.3   Children of the family

The children of the family are any children or qualifying young persons for whom the claimant or his partner is receiving child benefit (see **6.6**).

For IS, IRESA and IBJSA purposes, the existence of children or qualifying young persons in the benefits household does not play any part in the calculation. A check needs to be made to see if the claimant is entitled to child tax credit (see **9.6**). For HB and CTB purposes, the existence of children or qualifying young persons in the benefits household does play a part in the calculation.

7.4.4   The claimant's benefits household

When considering to how much of a means-tested benefit a claimant may be entitled, it is best to work out first who makes up his benefits household, as this will determine what personal allowances and premiums can be claimed for IS, IRESA, IBJSA, HB and CTB and housing costs for IS and IBJSA.

The claimant's benefits household may consist of the claimant, his or her partner and, for HB and CTB purposes, the children or young persons of the family, as defined above. Anyone else sharing the accommodation will have a different status that may well affect the amount of benefit payable (see **7.4.6**).

7.4.5   Aggregation of resources

The resources of a claimant and any partner are generally aggregated for means-tested benefit purposes, and treated as the resources of the claimant. Capital and income belonging to the claimant's partner are treated exactly as if they were capital or income of the claimant.

But what about the resources of a dependent child or young person for HB and CTB purposes? The rules are:

(a)   If the claimant or any partner is aged 60 or over and not claiming IS, IRESA or IBJSA, the child will form part of the benefits household regardless of the amount of capital held by that child. All appropriate allowances and premiums are payable, except that the lone parent rate of family premium is not payable if the child has more than £3,000.

(b)   If the claimant and any partner are both aged under 60 or claiming IS, IRESA or IBJSA, then if a child has capital exceeding £3,000 that child is ignored when calculating the applicable amount, except that any standard family premium or its lone parent rate is still payable.

7.4.6   What about people who are not in the claimant's benefits household?

Other people besides the claimant's family may share the family home. They are likely to have an effect on his benefit, because of the contributions that they make or are treated as making to household expenses.

There are three categories of people who may share the family home: non-dependants, subtenants (lodgers) and boarders. They are not members of the claimant's family and their resources are never aggregated with those of the claimant.

7.4.7   Non-dependants

A non-dependant is an adult who lives with the claimant on an informal basis. Most non-dependants are relatives, such as grown-up children or elderly parents.

Any actual payments that a non-dependant makes towards his keep are disregarded in full. However, if the claimant is receiving HB or CTB, or help with housing costs under IS, IRESA or IBJSA, his benefit will usually be reduced to reflect the expected contribution from the non-dependant. The deductions vary from benefit to benefit and with the gross earnings of the non-dependant. Examples of non-dependant deductions are shown at **8.7.2** and **9.5.3**.

7.4.8   Subtenants (lodgers) and boarders

A subtenant need not have a formal lease, but lives within the claimant's home under a contract, paying rent or a licence fee.

> #### Example
> John lives with his partner, Catherine and their child, Thomas, aged 4. They recently found a lodger, Robert, for their spare room after placing an advertisement in the local newspaper. John's benefits household consists of himself, Catherine and Thomas. Robert is a subtenant (lodger).

The difference between boarders and subtenants is that a boarder is provided with regular meals.

> #### Example
> Bryan lives with his partner, Anne and their children, Wayne, aged 14, and Chris, aged 9. They recently found a boarder, Janet, for their spare room after placing an advertisement in the window of a local shop. Janet is provided with an evening meal. Bryan's benefits household consists of himself, Anne, Wayne and Chris. Janet is a boarder.

7.4.9   How much rent or licence fee counts as the claimant's income?

Not all the rent or licence fee paid to a claimant by a subtenant, lodger or boarder counts as income. The first £20 of the weekly payment is ignored and only one-half of the remainder counts.

So, assume Robert, the subtenant in the above example at **7.4.8**, pays John £70 in rent each week. How much counts? First, ignore £20, which reduces the sum to £50. Secondly, divide the balance in half (£25). Thus, £25 is treated as John's income.

What about the other example, where Janet is a boarder? Assume she pays Bryan £105 rent a week. How much counts? First, ignore £20, which reduces the sum to £85. Secondly, divide the balance in half (£42.50). Thus, £42.50 is treated as Bryan's income.

7.5   Needs: the applicable amount

7.5.1   What is the applicable amount?

Once the claimant's resources have been worked out, they must be compared with his needs. For all the benefits, the figure that is used in the needs side of the equation is called the 'applicable amount', because this is the amount of income which is applicable in each benefit to a person in the claimant's circumstances.

For IS, IRESA and IBJSA, the applicable amount is the income which the Government says the claimant and any partner need to live on. Prescribed rates apply according to the status of the claimant eg single, disabled, etc. There are no elements for children as these form part of the child tax credit (see 9.6) and a check should be made to see if that is payable.

For HB and CTB, the applicable amount is the income the claimant's benefits household (ie including any partner and/or children or qualifying young persons) needs to meet such liability according to the Government's prescribed rates. Also, for HB and CTB the calculation has an additional element. It is necessary first to work out the maximum amount of benefit the claimant could get. If income exceeds the applicable amount, a prescribed percentage of the excess is then deducted from the maximum benefit to find out how much the claimant will actually get. This is called 'tapering', and is illustrated in **Chapter 9**.

7.5.2   How is the applicable amount calculated?

The applicable amount has two principal elements, common to all of these benefits, which are called 'allowances' and 'premiums'. For IS, IRESA and IBJSA only, a third element goes into the calculation if the claimant is an owner-occupier and responsible, for example, for paying a mortgage on his home. This is explained at 8.3. Here we shall confine ourselves to the common elements.

7.6   Personal allowances

The first element of the applicable amount is any personal allowances that reflect the composition of the claimant's benefits household: whether he is single or living with a partner, and for HB and CTB purposes whether he has qualifying children and/or young children and the ages of those children.

The personal allowances are categorised by age and by whether the claimant has a partner and, for HB and CTB purposes, any qualifying children or young persons. The child tax credit (see 9.8) has replaced the child allowances for IS, IRESA and IBJSA.

The categories are as follows:

(a)   single person aged 16 to 17;

(b)   single person aged 18 to 24;

(c)   single person aged 25 and over;

(d)   single person for HB or CTB only, aged 60 to 64 and not claiming IS, IRESA or IBJSA;

(e)   single person for HB or CTB only, aged 65 or over and not claiming IS, IRESA or IBJSA;

(f)   lone parent aged under 18;

(g)   lone parent aged over 18;

(h)   couple, where both aged under 18;

(i)   couple, where both or one aged over 18;

(j)   couple for HB or CTB only, where one or both are aged 60 to 64 and not claiming IS, IRESA or IBJSA;

(k)   couple for HB or CTB only, where one or both are aged 65 or over and not claiming IS, IRESA or IBJSA;

(l)   child under 16 (note that a child is not treated as being aged 16 until the first Monday in September of the year in which he is 16 (see **7.4.3**));

(m)   qualifying young person over 16.

At the very least, every claimant's applicable amount includes an allowance for himself. A single claimant with no children or young persons, in good health and under 60, has an applicable amount made up of his personal allowance only, according to his age.

7.7 Premiums

Many claimants also qualify for premiums in addition to their allowances. Premiums reflect special circumstances, which indicate that the claimant, or a member of his benefits household, if any, need a higher income than other people.

7.7.1 Standard rate family premium (HB and CTB only)

This will be paid if the claimant's benefits household includes at least one qualifying child or young person for child benefit purposes (see **6.6**). It is paid at a flat rate regardless of the number of qualifying children or young persons. It is still paid, even if there is only one qualifying child or young person. It is paid at a higher rate if at least one qualifying child is under one year old.

7.7.2 Severe disability premium (IS, IRESA, IBJSA, HB, CTB)

Single claimants and lone parents are entitled to this premium at the lower single rate if:

(a)   the claimant is in receipt of a 'qualifying benefit' ie attendance allowance; or DLA care component at the middle or highest rate; and

(b)   no non-dependant (see **7.4.7**) aged 18 or over normally resides with the claimant; and

(c)   carer's allowance is not payable to anyone for caring for the claimant.

Members of a couple are entitled to the higher couple rate if:

(a)   each of them is in receipt of a 'qualifying benefit'; and

(b)   no non-dependant (see **7.4.7**) aged 18 or over normally resides with them, and

(c)   carer's allowance is not payable in respect of both of them.

Note that provided (a) and (b) above for a couple are met, then the lower single rate is payable where carer's allowance is payable for one of the couple.

7.7.3 Disabled child premium (HB and CTB only)

This will be paid for each qualifying child or young person in the claimant's benefits household who receives DLA (either component at any rate of pay) or is registered blind.

7.7.4 Carer's premium (IS, IBJSA, HB and CTB)

This will be paid if the claimant or any partner are receiving or are treated as being entitled to carer's allowance. A double premium is payable if both the claimant and his partner qualify for the premium.

In what circumstances will the claimant or any partner be 'treated as being entitled to carer's allowance'? It must be remembered that carer's allowance is an earnings replacement benefit (see **1.2.5**). Where the claimant or a partner are entitled in their own right to another earnings replacement benefit, both benefits cannot be paid due to the overlapping benefits rule (see **2.6**). If the claimant or partner, as the case may be, elects to receive the other earnings replacement benefit instead of carer's allowance, he or she will still be treated as being entitled to carer's allowance and so will be entitled to carer's premium.

Example

Jo is entitled to carer's allowance as a result of caring for her husband. She is awarded income support which includes the carer's premium. She becomes incapable of work and fulfils the qualifying conditions for CESA. However, she still struggles to do her caring duties and remains entitled to carer's allowance. Although she meets the qualifying conditions for both benefits she will be paid for only one, and she should elect CESA as it is paid at a higher rate. She is said to have an 'underlying entitlement' to carer's allowance and as such is treated as entitled to it, and so will continue to receive the carer's premium as part of her income support.

7.7.5 Enhanced disability premium (IS, IRESA, IBJSA, HB, CTB)

The Social Security Amendment (Enhanced Disability Premium) Regulations 2000 (SI 2000/2629) introduced this premium. The qualifying conditions are:

(a)   the highest rate of DLA care component is paid to the claimant or a partner; or

(b)   for IRESA purposes only, the claimant receives the support component; or

(c)   for HB and CTB purposes only, any child or qualifying young person in the claimant's benefits household receives the highest rate of DLA care component.

For HB and CTB purposes, if a claimant is in receipt of the work-related component or support component for CESA (see **4.5.1.2**) then this premium is payable.

Note that for HB and CTB purposes, if the claimant or any partner is aged 60 or over and not claiming IS, IRESA or IBJSA, this premium cannot be paid for the claimant or any partner. The pensioner premium will be payable instead (see **7.7.8**).

It is payable at three rates: for a single claimant or qualifying child, or a couple where one or both qualify.

7.7.6 Lone parent family premium increase (HB and CTB only)

Prior to 6 April 1998, a higher rate of the family premium was payable to a lone parent. Some claimants remain entitled to this additional amount. The regulations are complex, but as a general rule the increase is payable if the claimant was entitled as a lone parent to the premium on 5 April 1998 and has continued since to be a lone parent.

The premium is not payable if the claimant or any partner is aged 60 or over.

It should be remembered that this premium cannot be claimed along with those that follow below.

7.7.7 Disability premium (IS, IBJSA, HB, CTB)

The circumstances in which this premium is payable depend upon whether or not the claimant has a partner. The premium is payable only where the claimant or any partner is under 60 and satisfies the qualifying conditions.

The qualifying conditions for the premium are that the claimant or any partner receives disability living allowance (either component at any rate of pay), or incapacity benefit at either the long-term rate or the special short-term rate payable to a terminally ill person, or is registered blind.

If the claimant has a partner, it is paid at the couple rate, provided one of them meets the qualifying conditions.

This premium is not payable for IRESA purposes.

For HB and CTB purposes, this premium is not payable if the claimant or any partner is aged 60 or over and not claiming IS or IBJSA.

Also for HB and CTB purposes, this premium is not payable if the claimant receives either type of ESA.

7.7.8 Pensioner premium (IS, IRESA, IBJSA, HB, CTB)

Age is the only qualifying condition for this premium, which is paid, for IS and IBJSA, if the claimant or any partner is aged 60 or over. This is the only relevant pensioner premium for IRESA. The only condition is that the claimant or the claimant's partner has reached the qualifying age for State pension credit (currently 60 years of age: see **5.3.1**). For HB and CTB purposes, this premium is payable only if the claimant or any partner is aged 60 or over and claiming IS, IRESA or IBJSA. There are two rates, one for single people and one for couples, where one or both of them is aged 60 or over.

7.7.9 Enhanced pensioner premium (IS, IBJSA, HB, CTB)

Age is the only qualifying condition for this premium which will be paid, for IS and IBJSA, if the claimant or partner is between the ages of 75 and 79 inclusive. For HB and CTB purposes, this premium is payable only if the claimant or any partner is aged 75 to 79 and claiming IS, IRESA or IBJSA. There are two rates, one for single people and one for couples where either or both qualify.

7.7.10 Higher pensioner premium (IS, IBJSA, HB, CTB)

The premium is payable if:

(a)   the HB or CTB claimant or any partner is aged 80 or over; or
(b)   the claimant was receiving a disability premium for at least eight weeks prior to his sixtieth birthday and has been receiving the premium ever since; or
(c)   the HB or CTB claimant or any partner is aged between 60 and 79, and at least one of them is either registered blind or in receipt of disability living allowance (either component at any rate of pay) or CESA.

There are two rates, one for single people and one for couples where either or both qualify.

7.7.11 Which premiums can be claimed together?

Of the premiums listed above, **7.7.1** to **7.7.5** inclusive can be claimed at the same time.

Example

A HB or CTB benefits household which consists of the claimant, his partner and a disabled qualifying child or young person who is cared for by the claimant will be able to claim the standard rate family premium but in addition to that may also be entitled to a disabled child's premium and a carer's premium.

However, only one of the premiums listed in **7.7.6** to **7.7.10** inclusive can be claimed at the same time, the highest in value being paid.

Example

A HB or CTB benefits household which consists of a disabled claimant who is also a lone parent will be able to claim the standard rate family premium but, in addition to that, the claimant may also be entitled to the lone parent family premium increase and to a disability premium. However, the lone parent family premium increase and a disability premium cannot be paid at the same time. If entitled to the disability premium, the claimant would receive that as it is paid at a higher rate than the lone parent family premium increase.

7.7.12   Premiums: a summary

For IS, IRESA and IBJSA purposes, none of the premiums concerning children or young persons are relevant. These form part of child tax credit.

For HB and CTB purposes, all the premiums should be considered if the claimant and any partner are aged under 60, or if over 60 and claiming IS, IRESA or IBJSA. However, if the claimant and any partner are aged 60 or over and are not claiming IS, IRESA or IBJSA then only the family, disabled child, enhanced disability, severe disability and carer's premium can potentially be claimed.

7.7.13   Support or work-related activity component for ESA

This is detailed at **4.5.1.2**. Note that for a claimant of IRESA, HB or CTB, the component should be added to the applicable amount.

7.8   The comparison

The last stage in the means test is a comparison of the applicable amount, as calculated, with the claimant's income, as calculated. This is the most important difference between IS and IBJSA on the one hand and HB and CTB. For IS and IBJSA, the comparison is extremely simple. If the claimant's income is less than the applicable amount, he receives benefit to top up the income to the level of the applicable amount. If his income equals or exceeds the applicable amount, he gets nothing.

For IRESA the same comparison occurs. However, it is important to remember that if a claimant is entitled to both IRESA and CESA, then he receives whichever is the greater (see **8.2.3.2**).

For HB and CTB there is another layer of calculation, and it is possible for a claimant to receive benefit even if his income is higher than the applicable amount. For details of how this last stage in the calculation works, see **Chapter 9**.

7.9   Common problems of means-tested benefits

Means-tested benefits are particularly likely to cause problems for claimants. The means test itself is so complicated that it is very easy for a mistake to be made. Claimants do not understand the law and frequently fail to pass on information which affects their right to benefit.

The problems covered in this section usually arise from unreported changes in the claimant's circumstances. The failure to report may be deliberate (and thus fraudulent), but is more often merely negligent, ignorant or misinformed. The consequence for the claimant may well depend on establishing which of these it is.

7.10 Living together as 'husband and wife' or 'civil partners'

To ensure fair treatment between those couples who are married or in a civil partnership and those who are not, couples who are living together as 'husband and wife' or 'civil partners' are treated for welfare benefit purposes in the same way as a married couple or a same-sex couple in a civil partnership.

The expression living together as 'husband and wife' or 'civil partners' is benefits jargon for the cohabitation of an opposite-sex or same-sex couple. We have already seen, at **7.4.5**, that when such a couple are living together their assets are aggregated.

If a person who is claiming a means-tested benefit starts to live with a partner, his entitlement to benefit will change. For all the benefits the applicable amount for a couple is less than the total for two single people. If the new partner is in remunerative work, the claimant's rights to IS, IRESA and IBJSA will cease immediately (see **8.2.1**).

7.10.1 The *Crake* guidelines

It is often very difficult to decide whether two people are living together as husband and wife or civil partners. The question is one of fact, not of law. There is an almost infinite range of possibilities, from true cohabitation to friends who just happen to share a house or flat. The crucial test is whether they live in the same household rather than in the same home. They may live in the same home without living together as husband and wife or civil partners, but if they live in the same household then they may well be considered as living together as husband and wife or civil partners. To avoid being considered as such, the two people must show that they live in entirely separate households within the home. Independent financial, eating and cooking arrangements, and exclusive occupation of an area within the home are evidence of separate households.

Difficulties may arise where there has been a previous relationship between the two people, such as a divorced couple, both of whom continue to live in the marital home. This may happen while one awaits new accommodation or, perhaps, through sheer obstinacy. When confronted with a situation in which two people may be living together as husband and wife or civil partner, the DfWP and appeal tribunals use guidelines approved by Woolf J in *Crake v Supplementary Benefits Commission; Butterworth v Supplementary Benefits Commission* [1982] 1 All ER 498 at 502, to make the determination. This case involved the judicial review of two tribunal decisions made under the old Supplementary Benefits Act 1976. In the first, Mrs Crake had claimed Supplementary Benefit (the forerunner of IS) for herself and her two children whilst living in the home of Mr Watts following the breakdown of her marriage. She claimed that she was his housekeeper and that she received no money for the services she provided as they were done in exchange for board and lodging. She further claimed that they led entirely independent lives and that Mr Watts could not support her and her two children. Her claim for Supplementary Benefit was rejected on the grounds that she and Mr Watts were living in the same household as husband and wife: 'There were no exceptional circumstances to justify not aggregating requirements and resources'.

The court held that, although the Tribunal had failed to give adequate reasons for its decision (the reason for the judicial review), it had considered the case on its merits and had taken into account the correct issues to determine the matter.

In the second case, the court upheld Mrs Butterworth's appeal. She had been badly injured in a road traffic accident and needed assistance in the house. She lived alone and was initially helped by her daughter-in-law until she was unable to assist. The daughter-in-law arranged for Mr Jones to come and live in Mrs Butterworth's house to assist her whilst she recuperated. There had been a relationship between Mrs Butterworth and Mr Jones in the past. Both she and Mr Jones had their own bedrooms with locks on the doors. Despite the fact that the tribunal accepted Mrs Butterworth's description of the situation, it still rejected her claim on the grounds that she was living with Mr Jones as husband and wife in the same household. It had come to this conclusion for two reasons: first, because he was 'performing the same duties and providing the same care and attention as a husband would give to his wife' and, secondly, because he and Mrs Butterworth were not maintaining entirely separate households within the same accommodation. The court held that neither of these facts were sufficient to establish that Mrs Butterworth and Mr Jones were living in the same household as husband and wife because they could not outweigh the fact that neither party intended to live as husband and wife.

No single factor can determine the issue as to whether two people are living together as husband and wife or civil partner and the authority making the decision should consider evidence relating to the existence of financial support; a sexual relationship; membership of the same household; stability in the relationship; any children of the relationship and the public image presented by the two people.

7.10.1.1   Financial support

Financial support is indicated by the pooling of resources; joint purchases, the responsibility of each person for payment of bills or the actual support by one of the other.

7.10.1.2   Sexual relationship

If a sexual relationship exists then it is more likely that two people are living as husband and wife or civil partners, but it is not conclusive evidence. Equally the non-existence of a sexual relationship is not conclusive evidence that the two people are not living together as husband and wife or civil partners.

7.10.1.3   Membership of the same household

Two people cannot be considered to be living together as man and wife or civil partners unless they occupy the same household. The terms 'household' and 'home' are not the same. The reason for sharing the same home and the circumstances which exist whilst they do so are of utmost importance when deciding the question of whether they are members of the same household.

7.10.1.4   Stability of the relationship

The activities undertaken by the two people together or for one another such as cooking, cleaning, caring for children, decorating and gardening may be indicative of a stable relationship. The amount of time the two people have been together is not regarded as conclusive evidence of stability. A lack of commitment and refusal to accept responsibility for jointly required activities might show a lack of stability.

7.10.1.5 Children of the relationship

Where there are children or young persons in the household who are the children of both the man and the woman, or where each person takes on the role of step-parent to the other's children, this will be regarded as strong evidence that the two people live together as husband and wife or civil partners.

7.10.1.6 Public image

The question here is how a couple are seen in their business and/or private lives. If the two people have given others the impression of being husband and wife or civil partners, by perhaps one taking the other's surname, then this is indicative of living together as husband and wife or civil partners.

7.11 Overpayment of benefits

Overpayments may arise with any benefit, where either a claimant has received a benefit to which he was not entitled at all, or has received more than he should have received. Because of the complexity of the means test, overpayment problems are most common with the four benefits.

Overpayments become a problem only if the paying department tries to make the claimant repay the money that has been wrongly paid to him. By definition, a person who is properly in receipt of a means-tested benefit, even if he has been receiving too much, has few spare resources to repay an overpayment. Overpayments can run for many years before they are discovered and repayment demanded. They may run into four or even five figures: the largest repayment demand the writer has ever seen was over £32,000. The Limitation Act 1980 does not apply to recovery of overpaid benefits, and it is common for overpayments only to come to light many years after they occurred.

7.11.1 How do overpayments arise?

Most overpayments of any benefit arise for one reason only: the paying department acts in ignorance of some circumstance of the claimant which affects his right to benefit. The technical term for such a circumstance is 'material fact'.

For all the benefits, typical examples of material facts might be:

(a) capital assets owned by the claimant or his family;
(b) benefits or earnings received by other members of the claimant's family;
(c) children leaving school and young persons ceasing to qualify for child benefit;
(d) pay increases or changes in working hours leading to increased earnings.

Some of these facts may have been in existence throughout the period of claim, while others may represent changes since the claim began. What is most important is why the paying authority acted in ignorance of the material fact, since that affects their right to recover.

7.11.2 Local authority benefits (HB and CTB)

7.11.2.1 No automatic right of recovery

Recovery of overpayments of HB and CTB is covered by Pt 13 of the HB Regs 2006 and Pt 11 of the CTB Regs 2006 respectively. The principle is that overpayments are recoverable, unless the claimant could not reasonably have been expected to recognise that he was being overpaid. This is so, even if the cause of the overpayment was 'official error', an administrative mistake for which the claimant was not in any way responsible.

This appears harsh, but in practice it is likely that a claimant would be able to succeed in arguing that he had done nothing wrong, had not misled the local authority in any way, and had no way of knowing that he was getting too much benefit. If he notified them of an important change in his circumstances, and his benefit did not change at all, he might have difficulty with this argument. However, an unrelated change in the amount of his benefit might mislead him into thinking that the right adjustment had been made.

7.11.2.2   Automatic right of recovery

Local authorities are supposed to process applications for HB for private tenants within two weeks, but rarely do. Any delay in paying benefit may put the tenant at risk of repossession, so, if there is a delay, the local authority must make interim payments. When the application is eventually processed, the amount paid in interim payments may prove to be too much. The excess is always recoverable.

7.11.3   Social security benefits and tax credits

The law on recovery of overpayments of all social security benefits and the two tax credits is contained in SSAA 1992, s 71. Here the presumption is that the overpayment is not recoverable unless it results from either misrepresentation of, or failure to disclose, a material fact. Causation is an essential part of this presumption. Unless there has been a failure to disclose or a misrepresentation, s 71 does not provide a remedy. Parliament did not provide a statutory right to repayment if the payment was due to an administrative error. The implications for the claimant are different depending on which of the two causes is alleged.

7.11.3.1   Misrepresentation

This means a statement of fact which is false, including innocent misrepresentation, for example, because the fact was not known to the claimant. A claimant risks making a misrepresentation whenever he signs a document that includes a declaration that he has declared all material facts. Such declarations are routinely found:

(a)   on all claim forms for any benefit;

(b)   on the orders in a payment book, which he signs when he cashes them; and

(c)   on the form he signs every time he signs on at the Jobcentre.

A misrepresentation can be either an act or omission by the claimant. A misrepresentation may occur, therefore, where a statement written by a claimant is incorrect or incomplete; where information supplied orally by the claimant is incorrect or incomplete; where someone else has written a statement based on incomplete or incorrect information supplied by the claimant; or where part of a form is left blank.

There are few defences to an allegation of misrepresentation. A claimant may argue that he did not know the fact and that he had signed a declaration which included the words 'known to me' or similar wording. This is rare, although some older claim forms had this form of wording, such as the old postal claim forms, which read: 'Declaration: as far as I know, the information on this form is true and complete'. If, on the other hand, the form read: 'Declaration: the information on this form is true and complete', then the claimant's knowledge of a material fact is irrelevant. If a man were to declare that he had no sources of income while, unbeknownst to him, his wife had earnings of her own, then he would still have made a misrepresentation. The only defence to this type of misrepresentation is non est factum (ie 'it is not my deed'). This defence will apply if the claimant did not know what he was signing. A claimant may have made a representation if he has signed a form which has been filled in by someone else. The only defence to misrepresentation in this instance would be if the claimant is blind, illiterate or lacks an understanding of the form because of poor education, illness or inborn incapacity. To rely upon this defence, however, the claimant must show that he made some attempt to understand what he had signed. If that person merely signs the form without thought, then he will be considered as having made a misrepresentation.

Some payments are made without any declaration. An example is a giro cheque in excess of £250. It is the act of trying to cash the giro cheque which amounts to the misrepresentation. For a giro cheque of less than £250, the claimant signs a declaration stating: 'I acknowledge receipt of the above sum to which I am entitled' and so a misrepresentation occurs only if the claimant is not entitled to benefit.

It is possible to raise a defence based on causation; that the misrepresentation did not cause the overpayment because the fact had been disclosed separately to the paying authority, outside the signed document (see below).

7.11.3.2 Failure to disclose

Claimants are under a continuing duty to disclose any material facts that are known to them, or that they ought to have known had they made reasonable enquiries, which might affect their claims. Further, the claimant is attributed to have knowledge of the types of circumstances which might affect his claim because of the warning notices on forms, etc, but also because such knowledge is within the public domain. It is not sufficient for a claimant to say that he did not realise the fact was material.

Does the disclosure have to be 'reasonably expected'? Is the meaning of 'failed to disclose' in s 71(1) qualified in favour of claimants who did not appreciate that they had an obligation to disclose a material fact once it became known? 'No', held the Court of Appeal in *B v Secretary of State for Work and Pensions* [2005] EWCA Civ 929. The appellant, B, appealed against the decision of the social security commissioners allowing the Secretary of State to recover an overpayment of child benefit. B suffered from severe learning disabilities. She received child benefit for her three children but they were taken into care. The DfWP was not informed of this fact and continued to pay B child-related benefits. The Secretary of State sought to recover the overpaid benefits on the basis that B was required to disclose the fact that her children were no longer living with her. It was argued for B that she was unable to understand that the placing of her children in care was a material fact that she needed to disclose. The Court of Appeal held that on the face of the legislation, a claimant was under a legal obligation to report more than she could reasonably be expected to report. There was no allowance in the legislation for the moral argument against fixing B with the financial consequences of not reporting something which she did not appreciate she needed to report. It was irrelevant that B did not understand the materiality of the fact.

If one Government department knows that a claimant is no longer entitled to a particular benefit, is it still a material non-disclosure if the claimant fails to inform another department of that fact? 'Yes', held the House of Lords in *Hinchy v Secretary of State for Work and Pensions* [2005] UKHL 16, [2005] 1 WLR 967.

Again, the Secretary of State must prove that the failure to disclose caused the overpayment to be made.

7.11.3.3 HMRC and tax credits

HMRC apply a slightly different test in respect of overpayments of tax credits, by considering how they and the claimant have discharged their responsibilities. Full details are in HMRC's Code of Practice (COP26) on their website (see **1.6.3**).

7.11.3.4 Proof

If an overpayment decision is taken to appeal, all elements of the burden of proof are on the Secretary of State: that there was an overpayment, that it is recoverable because it resulted from one of the specified causes, and how much was overpaid. The DfWP loses many cases on appeal because some element of this proof is missing.

A tribunal can decide, on the balance of probabilities, only whether the overpayment is recoverable, and has no power over the terms on which a recoverable benefit is recovered. However, it is always worth appealing an overpayment decision: if the calculation is complex, it may not be correct, and the DfWP may not discharge all elements of the burden of proof.

7.11.4 Automatic right of recovery (IS, IRESA, IBJSA, SPC)

The SSAA 1992, s 74 gives an automatic right of recovery if a claimant is overpaid IS, IRESA, IBJSA or State pension credit on receiving arrears of another benefit to which he is entitled. Sometimes a claimant will be paid too much of one of these benefits because money that is due to him (and which constitutes income when calculating any such benefit) is late in being paid and so the benefit is paid in full rather than taking the money due into account. Section 74 therefore seeks to avoid duplication of payment. When the income that affects the amount of the benefit is finally paid (and very often this may be another benefit or maintenance: see **5.3.3**, **7.3.4** and **7.3.5**), repayment of the overpayment will normally be requested.

7.12 Mechanics of recovery

7.12.1 How are overpayments recovered?

Even where recovery is possible, it is always in the discretion of the paying department. It may see little point in pursuing recovery, or compassionate grounds for not doing so. If it decides to recover, the commonest method is by deduction from current benefits. Most benefits may be used for this purpose, but there are ceilings on maximum deductions, especially where no fraud has been proved.

If the claimant is no longer on benefits, the overpayment decision is treated as a judgment debt and can be enforced through the civil courts.

7.12.2 From whom may the overpayment be recovered?

The overpayment will usually be recovered from the claimant himself, but may be recovered from anyone else who is responsible for causing it. This may be a person who has stolen a benefit order book or Girocheque and misrepresented himself as the payee on cashing it. More often, the problem arises if someone has been appointed to deal with the affairs of a person with diminished mental capacity, and misrepresents the claimant's affairs. Exceptionally, if the appointee has acted culpably, he may be made personally liable to repay the overpayment.

There are special rules allowing the recovery of overpaid mortgage interest from the lender, and HB from the tenant or landlord.

7.13 Deductions from benefit

We have already seen two types of deduction from benefits, where part of a claimant's benefit is withheld. The first is where the benefit is being paid direct to the ultimate intended recipient: the mortgage lender or the landlord. The second is to pay a liability of the claimant: repayment of an overpayment of benefit.

There are other repayments which may also be made from benefits, especially IS, IRESA and IBJSA. They fall into one or other of the two categories.

(a) Payment to intended recipient: payments may be made by deduction to gas and electricity suppliers, if the claimant has got into debt and needs the fuel supply to continue. In return, the fuel company agrees not to disconnect the service. Deductions cover arrears and current needs.

(b) Payment of liabilities: as well as payment of arrears of fuel charges, deductions may be made for:

    (i)   arrears of council tax and water charges;
    (ii) child support maintenance;
    (iii) magistrates' court fines, costs and compensation orders; and
    (iv) repayment of social fund loans (see **9.16.5**).

Chapter 8

Income Support, Income-Related Employment and Support Allowance, and Income-Based Jobseeker's Allowance

8.1 Background

This chapter is concerned with the three most important means-tested benefits, income support (IS), income-related employment and support allowance (IRESA), and income-based jobseeker's allowance (IBJSA). The means test for these benefits is virtually identical. Jobseeker's allowance (JSA) was introduced in October 1996, and the income-based form of the benefit replaced IS for one category of claimants, the unemployed. Employment and support allowance (ESA) was introduced in October 2008, and the income-related form of the benefit replaced IS for one category of claimants, those with limited capability for work.

8.2 Which benefit?

8.2.1 Conditions of entitlement

Almost any person who satisfies the means test, because his capital and income fall below the prescribed limits, is potentially able to claim IS, IRESA or IBJSA. They may be claimed as the claimant's sole source of income, or as a top-up to other benefits, part-time earnings, maintenance or other sources of income. But it is impossible for one person to be entitled to more than one at any time because the statutory conditions of entitlement are mutually exclusive. So which does the claimant claim?

8.2.1.1 Income-based jobseeker's allowance

A person will qualify for IBJSA if:

(a) he has an income which does not exceed the applicable amount, or has no income;

(b) his capital when aggregated with that of any partner does not exceed £16,000;

(c)   he is not receiving IS;

(d)   any partner is not receiving IS or IBJSA already;

(e)   he is not a young person for whom someone else already claims IS or IBJSA for him as part of their benefits household;

(f)   he is aged 18 or over (some 16- and 17-year-olds may get IBJSA in exceptional circumstances but they are outside the scope of this book);

(g)   he is below pensionable age;

(h)   he is not in full-time education (some students may get IBJSA in exceptional circumstances but they are outside the scope of this book);

(i)   he and any partner are not in remunerative work;

(j)   he has signed a jobseeker's agreement;

(k)   he meets the labour market conditions;

(l)   he is not disqualified from the benefit for any reason;

(m)   he is capable of work;

(n)   he is not subject to immigration control and is habitually resident (see **Chapter 10**).

As to conditions (a) and (b), see **Chapter 7**, and in respect of conditions (h) to (l), see **Chapter 3**. However, note that, for IBJSA, 'remunerative work', in respect of the claimant, means that he or she must not be working 16 hours or more a week and, as to any partner, he or she must not be working 24 hours or more a week. As to condition (g), as a man's pensionable age is currently 65, a man aged between 60 and 65 can choose to claim either the pension credit (see **5.3**) or IBJSA. A woman aged 60 or more cannot claim IBJSA and must claim the pension credit.

8.2.1.2   Income-related employment and support allowance

First, a quick reminder (the detail is in **Chapter 4**) of the general conditions of entitlement for ESA. The basic conditions are that the claimant:

(a)   has limited capability for work (see **4.4**);

(b)   is at least 16 years old;

(c)   has not reached pensionable age;

(d)   is in Great Britain (see **Chapter 10**);

(e)   is not entitled to IS; and

(f)   is not entitled to either type of jobseeker's allowance and is not a member of a couple who are entitled to a joint claim for IBJSA.

Secondly, in addition to the above, the conditions specific to IRESA are that the claimant:

(g)   has an income which does not exceed the applicable amount, or has no income;

(h)   does not have capital which, aggregated with that of any partner, exceeds £16,000;

(i)   is not entitled to State pension credit;

(j)   is not a member of a couple the other member of which is entitled to State pension credit, IS or IBJSA;

(k)   is not engaged in remunerative work;

(l)   is not a member of a couple the other member of which is engaged in remunerative work;

(m)   is not receiving full-time education;

(n)   is not subject to immigration control and is habitually resident (see **Chapter 10**).

As to conditions (g) and (h), see **Chapter 7**. Note that as to condition (j), the claimant's partner might be unemployed and in receipt of CBJSA. If so, that benefit will count as income when calculating entitlement to IRESA (see **7.3.5**). For condition (k), the general rule is that any work done by the claimant will disentitle him from both types of ESA: but see **4.5.4** for the exceptions. As to condition (l), remunerative work by a claimant's partner means work on average for not less than 24 hours a week.

8.2.1.3   Income support

A person will qualify for IS if:

(a)   he has an income which does not exceed the applicable amount, or has no income;

(b)   his capital when aggregated with that of any partner does not exceed £16,000;

(c)   he and any partner are not in remunerative work;

(d)   he is not receiving IBJSA or CBJSA;

(e)   any partner is not receiving IBJSA or pension credit;

(f)   he is at least 16 years of age;

(g)   as a general rule he is not studying full time (but see **8.2.2**);

(h)   he is in a prescribed category of permitted claimants (see **8.2.2**);

(i)   he is not subject to immigration control and is habitually resident (see **Chapter 10**).

As to conditions (a) and (b), see **Chapter 7**. In respect of condition (c), note that, for IS, 'remunerative work', in respect of the claimant, means that he or she must not be working 16 hours or more a week and, as to any partner, he or she must not be working 24 hours or more a week. As to condition (e), note that a claimant's partner may receive CBJSA but that will be taken into account when calculating the amount of IS (see **7.3.5**).

8.2.2   Who may claim income support? (IS Regs 1987, reg 4ZA)

Only certain people are entitled to claim IS. The most important categories are as follows.

(a)   Any person who is a single parent, with qualifying children under the age of 16, but not older than that. Note that at the time of writing (August 2008) the Government intends to reduce the age to 12 unless the claimant has a child in receipt of disability living allowance, care component, paid at the middle or highest rate. Hence, a lone parent whose youngest child is aged 12 or over will usually be transferred to JSA. Further note that the Government proposes to reduce the age to 10 years and 7 years of age in subsequent years.

(b)   Any person who receives or would be entitled to claim carer's allowance.

(c)   Some disabled people in work whose earning capacity is reduced by at least 25% because of their disability.

(d)   Full-time students who are deaf or entitled to a disability premium.

If neither the claimant nor his partner falls into any of the prescribed categories, he must claim IRESA if neither has limited capability for work, or otherwise IBJSA and be subject to the standard JSA regime (see **Chapter 3**).

8.2.3   Relationship between the two forms of JSA and ESA

8.2.3.1   Jobseeker's allowance

An unemployed person will claim IBJSA for one or more of the following three reasons:

(a)   he does not have the contribution record necessary to claim CBJSA; or

(b)   he has been unemployed for more than 26 weeks, and his entitlement to CBJSA has expired; or

(c)   his income from all sources, including any CBJSA, is below his applicable amount.

The following conditions, described in **Chapter 3**, for the award of JSA apply to IBJSA as well as CBJSA:

(a)   that the claimant has entered into a jobseeker's agreement (see **3.2.3**);

(b)   that he is not in remunerative work (see **3.2.4**);

(c)   that he is available for work and actively seeking employment, with full-time students excluded on the grounds of non-availability (see **3.2.5** to **3.2.8**);

(d)   that he is not disqualified from benefit for any reason (see **3.3**); and

(e)   that he is capable of work and under retirement age.

Sanctions, as described at **3.3.5**, apply to IBJSA as well as CBJSA. Sanctions may last for up to 26 weeks, which could mean that the claimant is faced with the possibility of no income at all for that period. Some claimants who are barred from claiming any form of JSA will be able to claim hardship payments, at a lower level than IBJSA in its normal form (see **8.11**).

8.2.3.2   Employment and support allowance

A person with limited capability for work may claim IRESA for one or more of the following three reasons:

(a)   he does not have the contribution record necessary to claim CESA;

(b)   he has been off work for more than 28 weeks and so his entitlement to SSP (see **4.2**) has ended; or

(c)   his income from all sources, including any SSP or CESA, is below his applicable amount.

What counts as CESA and as IRESA when a claimant is entitled to both? The answer is in s 6 of the Welfare Reform Act 2007. If the amount payable to the claimant is the same as or less than the assessment period and/or main phase period rate payable for CESA (see **4.5.1**), it is all treated as the contributory allowance. But where the amount payable to the claimant exceeds that, the excess is treated as the income-related allowance. Why do we need to know the answer? If a claimant fails to attend a work-focused health-related assessment or a work-related activity interview without good cause, his CESA will be reduced first (see **4.5.2**). Also, deductions may occur only from CESA if the claimant receives a personal or an occupational pension (see **4.5.2**).

8.2.4   Joint claims for income-based jobseeker's allowance

In certain circumstances a couple must make a joint claim for IBJSA. Those circumstances are as follows:

(a)   one or both members of a couple are born after 28 October 1947;

(b)   one is aged 18 or over;

(c)   they have no children in their household and neither works 16 hours or more a week.

This means that it is not possible for one member of the couple to claim IBJSA for them as a couple, and the other to make no effort to find work. There are complex rules to deal with disqualification from benefit for industrial disputes or sanctions applicable to one member of a joint-claim couple. Effectively in each case the other is allowed to claim as a single person.

8.2.5   Key claimant profiling points for IS, IRESA and IBJSA

What are the common conditions of entitlement for all three of these benefits? They are that the claimant:

(a)   has an income which does not exceed the applicable amount, or has no income;

(b)   does not have capital which, aggregated with that of any partner, exceeds £16,000;

(c)   is not engaged in remunerative work;

(d)   is not a member of a couple the other member of which is engaged in remunerative work.

So we have a profile of a claimant and any partner who are on a low income, with capital of less than £16,000, and who are not working or, at most, working only 'part time'.

What distinguishes one from the others? What are the key profiling points for each?

A lone parent and a carer will claim IS because they are in a prescribed category of permitted claimants.

A person with limited capability for work will claim IRESA. That person may or may not be in receipt of SSP (see **4.2**) or CESA (see **4.3**).

That leaves all other claimants – those who are not in a prescribed category of permitted IS claimants and who are capable of work. These people will 'sign on' for IBJSA.

8.3   Housing costs

8.3.1   Meaning of 'housing costs'

As well as allowances and premiums, there is a third element which may be included in the applicable amount for IS, IRESA and IBJSA only, for the claimant's housing costs.

The housing costs element is payable only with respect to owner-occupied accommodation. Where a claimant is a tenant who rents his accommodation, he will not receive assistance as part of IS, IRESA or IBJSA entitlement to pay the rent and any associated charges, but he must make a separate application to his local authority for housing benefit (see **Chapter 9**).

The usual types of housing costs included as part of IS, IRESA or IBJSA are:

(a)   interest on mortgages and other loans used to buy a home;

(b) interest on loans used to fund certain repairs and improvements or to pay a service charge on a leasehold property in respect of repairs and improvements;

(c) ground rent and certain qualifying service charges in respect of a leasehold property (the so-called 'other housing costs').

8.3.2   Who is entitled to claim assistance with housing costs?

Regulations provide that a claimant is entitled to assistance only with housing costs which 'he or, where he is a member of a family, he or any member of that family, is ... liable to meet in respect of the dwelling occupied as the home'. This means that, as a general rule:

(a) a person is liable to meet housing costs where the liability falls upon him or his partner. If the claimant or any partner share the liability with anyone else they may be able to get assistance with their share;

(b) housing costs are payable only for the home in which the claimant normally lives.

8.3.3   Mortgage and loan payments

Mortgage payments may comprise two elements, the capital and the interest of a loan, which is normally secured against a property. However, there is no requirement for the loan to be secured to qualify for assistance. It is possible, for example, for a claimant who lives in a mobile home to claim for interest in respect of a hire-purchase agreement if it was used to fund the purchase of his home.

The claimant will be entitled only to assistance to pay the interest element of his mortgage. There are different types of mortgages which affect this. The most common are endowment mortgages and repayment mortgages. If a person takes out an endowment mortgage then he will need to make interest payments each month on the entire capital sum throughout the duration of the mortgage. In addition to the interest payments, he must pay the premiums on an endowment policy, which is a method of investment. When the endowment policy matures, there should be sufficient money to repay the capital. As we have seen, the benefits legislation disregards the value of the endowment policy when considering the amount of the claimant's capital (see 7.2.2). A repayment mortgage operates differently. The person makes one payment per month which is divided between interest and capital. This means that the outstanding capital is reduced each year.

Allowable housing costs will not cover any capital repayment, nor any endowment policy premiums. The claimant should do his best to continue to pay these from available resources, but few claimants can afford to do so. Most mortgagees, however, will come to an arrangement with the claimant in respect of the capital and endowment policy instalments, particularly since the mortgage interest payments are made directly to them by the DfWP and therefore become a regular source of repayment.

So what types of mortgages and loans qualify? The conditions are that the mortgage or loan must have been taken out:

(a) to buy the home in which the claimant normally lives. If any part of the loan was taken out for any other purpose, that part will not qualify (see the example in 8.4); or

(b)   to buy an additional interest in that home (eg to buy out an ex-partner's share or to purchase the freehold on a leasehold property); or

(c)   to repay a loan which itself would have qualified.

8.3.4   Loans for repairs and improvements

A loan qualifies for assistance where it is taken out, with or without security, for and used for the purpose of:

(a)   carrying out repairs and improvements to the dwelling occupied as the home; or

(b)   paying any service charge imposed to meet the cost of repairs and improvements to the dwelling occupied as the home; or

(c)   paying off another loan to the extent that it would have qualified had it not been paid off.

What are qualifying 'repairs and improvements'? These are any of the following measures undertaken with a view to maintaining the fitness of the dwelling for human habitation or, where the dwelling forms part of a building, any part of the building containing that dwelling:

(a)   Provision of a fixed bath, shower, wash basin, sink or lavatory, and necessary associated plumbing, including the provision of hot water not connected to a central heating system.

(b)   Repairs to existing heating systems.

(c)   Damp-proof measures.

(d)   Provision of any of the following:

  (i)   ventilation and natural lighting;

  (ii)   draining facilities;

  (iii)   facilities for preparing and cooking food;

  (iv)   insulation of the dwelling occupied as the home;

  (v)   electric lighting and sockets;

  (vi)   storage facilities for fuel or refuse.

(e)   Repairs of unsafe structural defects.

(f)   Adapting a dwelling for the special needs of a disabled person.

(g)   The provision of separate sleeping accommodation for children of different sexes aged 10 or over who are part of the same family as the claimant.

Note that the provision of any of the above matters, like a fixed bath in (a), may include its repair or replacement.

Where a loan is applied only in part for any of the above purposes, only that portion of the loan which is actually applied for that purpose qualifies for assistance.

8.3.5   Assistance with 'other housing costs'

Allowable housing costs include the normally weekly charge for ground rent under a long lease (ie of more than 21 years) and certain service charges payable in respect of leasehold property (eg buildings insurance payable under the terms of the lease). If the charge relates to a repair or improvement, as defined above, the claimant is expected to take out a loan to meet the cost (and can then claim assistance with the interest repayments). Certain charges are expressly excluded, for example:

(a)   charges in respect of day-to-day living expenses including, in particular, any provision of laundry services (other than the provision of premises or equipment to enable a person to do his own laundry);

(b)   leisure items such as sports facilities (except a children's play area);

(c)   the cleaning of rooms and windows except the exterior of any windows in accommodation where neither the claimant nor any member of his household is able to clean those windows and those in communal areas.

8.4   Restrictions on housing costs

Example

You take instructions from David and learn that he and his wife bought a one-bedroom flat in 1992 while they were both working. They purchased the home for £70,000 and paid a deposit of £5,000 out of their own savings. They took out an endowment mortgage of £80,000, partly to fund the balance of the purchase price of £65,000, but the rest was to fund the purchase of a car costing £15,000. They make payments of £600 per month in interest and pay £75 per month for the endowment policy. In 1998, they took out a second mortgage, this time a repayment mortgage of £15,000 to fund an extension to their home in preparation for the arrival of their first child. They pay a single amount of £150 per month, £25 in respect of the repayment element of the mortgage and £125 in respect of the interest payments.

At the time David claims IBJSA, the amount outstanding on the first mortgage is £80,000 (it has yet to decrease because the endowment policy has not matured). There is £12,500 outstanding on the second mortgage.

What is David's entitlement with regards to housing costs?

There are two loans relating to the home but only the first mortgage is definitely a qualifying loan to the extent that he and his partner who are liable for it used it to finance the purchase of the property. They used £65,000 towards the house purchase, therefore, only £65,000 qualifies for assistance. The contractual interest they pay is irrelevant and the mortgagee will receive the prescribed rate of interest calculated on the outstanding capital (see **8.5.5**). David and his wife will have to meet any shortfall in interest payments and the cost of the endowment policy premiums themselves or come to some arrangement with the mortgagee. The second mortgage will not qualify unless they can show the extension was necessary to maintain the home's fitness for human habitation because of the arrival of the baby. This argument may not succeed if it is felt that the accommodation was already adequate for two adults and a child. If it does succeed, David could claim payment of the prescribed interest on the outstanding part of the loan but he and his wife would need to fund the capital repayments themselves.

8.4.1   Is there a maximum amount on qualifying loans?

The maximum amount on which housing costs will be paid is £100,000.

8.4.2   Excessive housing costs

Here we are not concerned with the amount of the qualifying loan but more with the size and location of the claimant's home. The starting point is to consider who lives there. Excluding any part which is let, the question is whether the home is larger than is required by the claimant, any partner, any person under the age of 20 and any non-dependants, having regard, in particular, to suitable alternative accommodation occupied by a household of the same size. The next question is whether the immediate area in which the home is located is more expensive than other areas in which suitable alternative accommodation exists. The final question is whether any allowable housing costs are higher than those for suitable alternative accommodation in the area. If the answer to one or more of these questions is 'Yes', then normally the excess is not allowed.

In other words, a claimant living in a luxury home is expected to move or pay the difference between his contractual housing costs and those allowable. When applying the restriction, however, account will be taken of other non-financial factors, such as the age and health of the benefits household, the employment prospects of the claimant, interruptions to children's education, negative equity, the ability to sell the home and any inability to raise new funds.

8.4.3 What is the effect of a claimant taking out a loan or increasing it whilst in receipt of IS, IRESA or IBJSA?

The answer is that, generally, no assistance is given for the increased amount. There are two main exceptions to that rule.

(a)   If the loan, or increased amount, is used to buy a home which is better suited to the needs of a disabled person than the previous property. A disabled person in this context is someone for whom any of the following premiums are payable: disabled child, disability, enhanced pensioner or higher pensioner.

(b)   If the claimant has a boy and a girl aged 10 or over and the loan was increased to move to a home where they could have separate bedrooms.

8.5 Calculation and payment

The law on interest payments changed substantially on 1 October 1995. A loan taken out before that date is known as 'existing housing costs': if it was taken out on or after that date, it is 'new housing costs'. There is an important difference in the way the two are treated.

8.5.1 Existing housing costs

If the claimant's loan is classified as 'existing housing costs', he is not eligible for any assistance with housing costs as part of his applicable amount for the first 8 weeks after his claim. He is then eligible for 50% of his maximum allowable housing costs for 18 weeks. Only after a total of 26 weeks are his maximum allowable housing costs paid in full. This is often called the '26 weeks rule'. For an exception to it, see **8.5.4**.

8.5.2 New housing costs

If the loan is classified as 'new housing costs', the claimant is expected to have taken out insurance to cover himself for the first 39 weeks of his period of claim. Only after 39 weeks will he receive any help with housing costs. These are then paid in full as part of the applicable amount. This is often called the '39 weeks rule'.

8.5.3 New housing costs which are treated as existing housing costs

In certain prescribed circumstances new housing costs are treated as existing housing costs (ie the claimant is subject to the more generous 26 weeks rule (see **8.5.1**) rather than having to wait 39 weeks for housing costs to form part of his applicable amount). The main exceptions are:

(a)   the claimant is a carer receiving carer's allowance; or

(b)   the claimant is caring for someone receiving attendance allowance or disability living allowance care component at the middle or highest rate; or

(c)   the claimant claims the benefit as a lone parent either because of the death of his partner or due to being 'abandoned'. In *Secretary of State for Work and Pensions v W* [2005] EWCA Civ 570, the Court of Appeal held that 'abandonment' has the same meaning as 'desertion' in matrimonial law. Desertion requires both physical separation and an intention on the part of the deserting party to desert the other party. This exception will cease to apply if the claimant starts to cohabit during the relevant period.

For a general exception to the 39 weeks rule, see **8.5.4**.

8.5.4   An exception to both rules

The distinction between existing or new housing costs does not apply to a claimant of IS or IRESA whose partner is aged 60 or over, nor to an IBJSA claimant where he or his partner is aged 60 or over. In those circumstances the claimant will qualify for maximum housing costs as part of his applicable amount immediately.

8.5.5   Prescribed interest rate

A standard prescribed rate is used for all loans, rather than the actual contractual rate. The prescribed rate is based on the Bank of England base rate plus 1.58% from dates determined by the Secretary of State.

To calculate the amount payable:

(a)   calculate the allowable capital after any restrictions;

(b)   multiply that capital by the prescribed rate to find the annual rate;

(c)   divide by 52 to find the weekly rate; and

(d)   round up to the next whole penny.

The claimant's actual interest payments are simply irrelevant.

All housing costs are paid direct to the lender, to avoid any risk of the claimant being tempted to use the money for other purposes. Because of the restrictions and delays in paying full benefit, most claimants get into arrears with their payments when they are on benefits. Advisers should keep the lender fully informed of what is happening to avert any attempt to get possession. Lenders can usually be persuaded to accept whatever the DfWP pays in full satisfaction of the borrower's liability, at least for the short term, as long as they are kept fully informed.

8.5.6   Summary: mortgage interest

When checking whether a loan under which the client pays interest will form part of the client's applicable amount as allowable housing, and if so, how much, you should ask the following questions.

(a)   Is it all a qualifying loan?

(b)   Is it subject to the £100,000 cap?

(c)   Is it excessive?

(d)   Was it taken out when the applicant was already on IS, IRESA or IBJSA?

(e)   Was the loan taken out on or before 1 October 1995? Does the loan constitute existing or new housing costs? If new, is there any exception making it existing? In either case will the allowable housing costs immediately form part of the applicable amount because the claimant or partner is aged 60 or over?

(f)   What is the prescribed mortgage interest rate?

(g)   Will any non-dependant deduction have to be made?

8.5.7   Changes to mortgage interest from April 2009

At the time of writing (August 2008) the Government has announced that it intends to make temporary changes to the mortgage interest provisions from April 2009 as follows:

(a)   The maximum limit will be raised to £175,000 for new claimants of working age.

(b)   The waiting period for all new claimants of working age will be reduced to 13 weeks.

(c)   There will be a time limit on mortgage interest assistance of two years for new IBJSA claimants. This will not apply to existing claimants or to new claims of IS, IRESA or pension credit.

The Government states that it will keep this system of support under review.

8.6   Non-dependants and housing costs

Generally, the resources of a person who is not a member of the claimant's family are irrelevant to the claimant's right to benefits. The exception is if that person is a non-dependant (see 7.4), usually an adult relative who is sharing the accommodation and making an informal contribution to the cost of his keep. If there is a non-dependant and the claimant is receiving housing costs, the maximum allowable housing costs will usually have to be reduced to take account of the contribution the non-dependant is expected to make. There is no effect at all if the claimant is not receiving housing costs. Moreover, if the non-dependant does pay anything towards his keep, that is disregarded.

If there is a non-dependant sharing the claimant's accommodation, the maximum allowable housing costs will be reduced by a prescribed amount determined by the gross earnings of the non-dependant. However, deductions from allowable housing costs will not be made in respect of non-dependants if:

(a)   the claimant or his partner is blind or receiving attendance allowance or the care component of disability living allowance;

(b)   the non-dependant is a full-time student in a period of study or not in remunerative work during the recognised summer vacation relevant to their course;

(c)   the non-dependant is not normally resident with the claimant (see *Commissioner's Decision CIS 14850/96*);

(d)   the non-dependant is a person aged 16 to 17;

(e)   the non-dependant is a person who is aged 18 to 24 who is receiving IS, IRESA or IBJSA in his own right,

(f)   the non-dependant is a co-owner or joint tenant.

8.7   Worked examples

8.7.1   Purpose of this section

To understand how to calculate means-tested benefits, it is useful to have some examples. We shall therefore look at three short case studies. These examples are worked using the benefit rates in force for the period 6 April 2008 to 5 April 2009.

Before presenting each calculation, we shall analyse the key facts of each case study.

8.7.2 Lone parent's income support: no capital or earnings, renting accommodation

8.7.2.1 Facts

Elizabeth, aged 20, is a lone parent. Her daughter, Rose, is aged 3. Neither Elizabeth nor Rose suffers from any disability. Elizabeth lives in rented accommodation (for which she claims housing benefit: see **Chapter 9**). Elizabeth's only source of income is child benefit (see **6.6**). She has no savings.

8.7.2.2 Analysis

Step 1: calculate the applicable amount

Elizabeth receives a single parent allowance. That will be her applicable amount. Remember that Rose, a child, does not count for IS purposes. Elizabeth should claim the child tax credit (see **Chapter 9**).

Step 2: calculate Elizabeth's income from all sources

Child benefit does not count as income.

Step 3: comparison

Elizabeth has no income that counts. Her IS is therefore £60.50, her single parent's allowance, each week.

As Elizabeth receives IS, she will also be entitled to her maximum housing benefit and maximum child tax credit (see **Chapter 9**).

8.7.3 Married jobseeker with capital, a mortgage and a non-dependant sharing the accomodation

8.7.3.1 Facts

Mark (aged 49) was made redundant last month. He is married to Janet (aged 42). She does not work. They have one child, Laura, who is 19 and earns £120 per week gross. They live in a house which they bought in 1994 with the help of a £75,000 endowment mortgage. Laura gives her mother £30 per week for her keep. Mark receives CBJSA. The couple have savings of £7,680 including what is left over from his redundancy payment. Assume a standard mortgage interest rate of 5%. How much IBJSA should he receive now?

8.7.3.2 Analysis

Step 1: calculate the applicable amount

(a)   The couple allowance for a couple with both members at least 18.
       Note: only this allowance will form the applicable amount for the first eight weeks of the claim as during that time no allowable housing costs are payable (see immediately below). Once allowable housing costs are payable then such will be added to this amount.

(b)   Interest on his mortgage. The original loan was £75,000, and as it is an endowment mortgage no capital will have been repaid, so that will remain the figure to use in the calculation. A check should be made to ensure it is a qualifying loan and that it is not excessive. It does not exceed £100,000. Find the weekly rate at a prescribed rate of 5%. The mortgage was taken out in 1994 so this is 'existing housing costs'. As neither Mark nor Janet is aged 60 or over, the '26 weeks rule' applies and nothing will be paid by way of allowable housing costs for the first eight weeks of the claim, then only 50% of such can be paid from the ninth to the twenty-sixth week and the full amount is payable after 26 weeks. However, both of those amounts that are payable will be reduced because there is a non-dependant, Laura, sharing the accommodation. The amount of the deduction will be determined by her gross earnings. The £30 she pays towards her keep is disregarded.

Step 2: calculate Mark's income from all sources

(a)   CBJSA at the standard flat rate for a person of at least 25. This will end after 26 weeks and so his income will be reduced by that amount.

(b)   Tariff income on savings of £7,680. Deduct the first £6,000 and calculate £1 for each £250 or part of £250.

Step 3: calculate the benefit payable by deducting the income from the applicable amount

Step 1: calculate applicable amount	£	£	£
Couple allowance		94.90	
Housing costs (£75,000 × 5% ÷ 52) (72.12) at 50% from 9th to 26th week, rounded up to next penny	(72.12) 36.06		
Less deduction for non-dependant with gross earnings of £120	17.00	19.06	
Housing costs at 100% after 26 weeks	72.12		
Less non-dependant deduction	17.00	55.12	
Applicable amount			
For first 8 weeks			94.90
For next 18 weeks			113.96
After 26 weeks			150.02
Step 2: calculate income from all sources			
CBJSA	60.50		
Tariff income on £7,680	7.00		
Income			67.50
Step 3: deduct income from applicable amount			
Applicable amount for first eight weeks			94.90
Deduct income			67.50
Amount of benefit payable			27.40
Applicable amount from 9th to 26th week			113.96
Deduct income			67.50
Amount of benefit payable			46.46
Applicable amount after 26 weeks			150.02
Deduct income (CBJSA no longer received)			7.00
Amount of benefit payable			143.02

8.7.4   Income-related ESA several premiums

8.7.4.1   Facts

Elon, aged 38, has had limited capability for work following a road accident 14 weeks ago. He is not paid CESA as he does not meet the NIC requirements. He is part of the support group and is paid DLA care component at the higher rate. He is married to Sharon (aged 33), and she looks after him and receives carer's allowance. They live in a ground-floor maisonette rented from the local council, and have no savings. How much IRESA should Elon now receive during the main phase of his claim? Note that whilst Sharon could have claimed IS, the couple decided that Elon would claim IRESA. Although Elon is in the support group, he is very keen to try to find some sort of work and is voluntarily attending work-related activity interviews.

8.7.4.2   Analysis

Elon is entitled to claim IRESA because he has limited capacity for work.

Step 1: calculate the applicable amount

(a)   Couple allowance at the rate applicable to a couple aged at least 18.

(b)   Support component because he is part of the support group.

(c)   Enhanced disability premium at the couple rate, as he receives the support component.

Step 2: calculate Elon's income from all sources

(a)   Sharon's carer's allowance counts. She will receive an adult dependant increase for Elon because he is not receiving an earnings replacement benefit and he has no earnings. The amount of the increase is £30.20.

(b)   His DLA is not taken into account as income.

Step 3: calculate the benefit payable by deducting the income from the applicable amount.

Step 1: calculate applicable amount	£	£
Couple allowance	94.95	
Carer's premium	27.75	
Support component	29.00	
Enhanced disability premium (couple rate)	18.15	
Applicable amount		169.85
Step 2: calculate income from all sources		
Carer's allowance	50.55	
Adult dependant increase	30.20	
Income		80.75
Step 3: calculate amount of benefit payable		
Applicable amount less		169.85
Income		80.75
Benefit payable		89.10

8.7.4.3   What if Elon had been entitled to both types of ESA?

If Elon satisfied the conditions for both CESA and IRESA, you would calculate each separately in the usual way. As Elon is in the main phase, his CESA (see **4.5.1.2**) would be (for 2008/09) the flat rate of £60.50 plus the support group component of £29, giving a total CESA of £89.50. We have seen at **8.7.4.2** that his IRESA for the main phase (in 2008/09) is £89.10. By s 6 of the WRA 2007, as the amount of CESA exceeds that of IRESA then CESA of £89.50 per week is payable.

If, however, Elon's IRESA had been more than his CESA, say, £100, that amount would have been payable instead. It would then have consisted of £89.50 CESA and £10.50 IRESA.

8.8 Change of circumstances and reviews

A claimant must report any material change in his circumstances that might affect his entitlement to, or the amount of, his benefit. Any failure to report may lead to an overpayment (see **7.11**). A decision-maker considers the facts and makes a new decision on the claim – this is known as 'supersession' (see **1.4.3.3**). Provided the report was made within one month of the change in circumstances, the new decision takes effect from the payment week in which the change occurred.

8.9 The passport effect

8.9.1 What is the passport effect?

Income support, IRESA and IBJSA provide a basic subsistence-level income. A person whose income is at this level has no spare income left over to pay for anything other than the basic necessities of life.

We shall see at **9.16** that there are a number of means-tested benefits outside the social security system, for which people on low incomes qualify. These include free prescriptions, eye tests and dental treatment. Entitlement to public funding is also dependent upon resources. Most people have to undergo a means test in order to ascertain their entitlement to these extra benefits, but a person who is in receipt of IS, IRESA or IBJSA will be able to claim many of them without further means testing. These benefits are called 'passport benefits' because the entitlement to IS, IRESA or IBJSA is an automatic passport to them.

One benefit is available only to families in receipt of IS, IRESA or IBJSA. That is the right to free school meals. For a family struggling to bring up several children on a very low income, free school meals can be of great value.

8.9.2 Rent and council tax

The housing costs which can be paid as part of IS, IRESA or IBJSA are limited to the interest on qualifying loans and leaseholders' service charges and ground rents. Tenants must rely on housing benefit to cover the cost of their rent, and all householders must pay council tax or receive council tax benefit.

In **Chapter 9**, we shall look at the means test for these two benefits, which is more generous than the IS, IRESA or IBJSA means test. This means that a person who qualifies for IS, IRESA or IBJSA will automatically qualify for the maximum amount of housing benefit or council tax benefit that could be paid, subject only to deductions for non-dependants. All the local authority needs is a certificate from the DfWP or Jobcentre Plus that the claimant is receiving one of these benefits, and he will immediately be awarded the maximum amount of housing benefit or council tax benefit.

8.10   Hardship payments and urgent cases payments

8.10.1   What are hardship and urgent cases payments?

A person who is not entitled to IS, IRESA or IBJSA under the normal rules may be able to make a successful claim under either the hardship or the urgent cases rules, if he has no other means of support.

The test is more realistic than the standard means test. Tariff income is ignored, as are some forms of income which the claimant may be treated as possessing, even though he does not. For IS, IRESA and IBJSA, the claimant is usually treated as receiving income which is due to him, even though he may never receive it. This does not apply to payments due from an employer on redundancy. For hardship payments and urgent cases, only resources actually available to the claimant go into the calculation.

8.11   Hardship payments

Your client is unemployed and has made a claim for JSA, but has not received it yet, or it has been stopped. He has no income and he and his family have nothing to live on. What is he to do?

8.11.1   Who may claim hardship payments?

He may be able to make an immediate claim for hardship payments, but only if his failure to receive benefit is for one of the following reasons.

(a)   He has not signed a jobseeker's agreement (see **3.2.3**), or the Secretary of State has decided the agreement is not valid.

(b)   There is a problem with the labour market conditions (see **3.2.5** to **3.2.8**): either the Secretary of State has not yet decided whether the claimant satisfies them, or has decided that he does not, or has suspended payment of benefit because the matter is in doubt.

(c)   He has been sanctioned (see **3.3.5**).

If the failure is for some other reason, such as disputes about his capital, his partner's working hours or whether he is involved in industrial action, there is no right to claim hardship payments.

No hardship payment can be made if the claimant's partner would be entitled to claim IS or IRESA.

8.11.2   Assessment of hardship

When the claimant has applied for hardship payments, the Secretary of State will decide whether he and his family will be in hardship if no payment is made. The following factors must be taken into account:

(a)   whether any member of the family is sick or disabled;

(b)   all actual resources available to the family; and

(c)   whether there is a substantial risk that the family will be without essentials, such as food, clothes, heating and accommodation, if no payment is made.

This list is not exhaustive.

8.11.3 Effect of being in a 'vulnerable group'

If the claimant is in a vulnerable group, he will be able to receive hardship payments immediately. Those who are not in a vulnerable group will have to wait two weeks for any payment. The claimant is in a vulnerable group if:

(a)   his family includes a qualifying child or a sick or disabled member, and that family member (not the claimant) would suffer hardship if no payment was made; or

(b)   the claimant or his partner is a carer and could not go on caring without a payment.

The amount of a hardship payment is calculated in the normal way, but the applicable amount is reduced by 40% of the single person's allowance, or 20% if any member of the family is pregnant or seriously ill.

8.12 Urgent cases payments

8.12.1 Eligibility

Urgent cases payment may be paid as part of IS, IRESA or IBJSA. They are most likely to be paid to people who have been admitted to the UK with a condition against resorting to public funds (see **10.3.1**). Members of this group are allowed to claim if a source of income on which they were relying has temporarily ceased.

Similarly, a British resident may be debarred from claiming benefit under the normal rules because he is treated as having income that he does not in fact have, such as rent from a tenant. In these circumstances, he may be able to claim urgent cases payments.

8.12.2 Calculation of benefit

Urgent cases payments are more generous than hardship payments. Although some forms of capital disregard applicable to standard IS, IRESA or IBJSA are not available, the usual capital limits still apply. The applicable amount is reduced by 10% of the personal allowance for the claimant himself if he is single, or 10% of the couple allowance if he has a partner.

8.13 Passporting

Hardship payments are part of IBJSA and urgent cases payments are part of IS, IRESA or IBJSA as appropriate. All the consequences described at **8.9** therefore apply just as if the claimant was receiving the standard benefit.

8.14 IS, IRESA, IBJSA and other benefits

Working tax credit counts as income when calculating these benefits (see **9.6**). Child tax credit is ignored.

A person entitled to one of these benefits is immediately entitled to the maximum amount of housing benefit and council tax benefit that can be paid (see **Chapter 9**).

As to which non-means tested benefits are ignored or taken into account when calculating these benefits, see **7.3.5**.

8.15 Claimant profiles

8.15.1 Income-based JSA

This is payable to a person capable of and available for work but who is not in remunerative work. The claimant must sign a jobseeker's agreement and have a low income with a limited amount of capital.

8.15.2 Income support

This is payable to a person who does not have to be available for work (such as a lone parent or carer), who is not in remunerative work and who has a low income and limited amount of capital.

8.15.3 Income-related employment and support allowance

This is payable to a person who has limited capability for work, who is not in remunerative work, and who has a low income and a limited amount of capital.

Chapter 9

Other Means-Tested Benefits

9.1 The scope of this chapter

In this chapter, we are mainly concerned with the means-tested benefits, except for IS, IRESA and IBJSA which were covered in **Chapter 8**. These are:

(a) the local authority benefits, housing benefit (HB) and council tax benefit (CTB);

(b) working tax credit and child tax credit;

(c) the social fund; and

(d) passport benefits.

9.1.1 Local authority benefits

There are two local authority-administered benefits, HB and CTB. Housing benefit covers those housing costs which are irrelevant to IS, IRESA and IBJSA, ie a tenant's rent and a licensee's licence fees in all their variety; CTB is to help with paying council tax.

9.1.2 The tax credits

Working tax credits and child tax credits were introduced in April 2003 following the Tax Credits Act 2002. The Government said that the tax credits were to

> separate support for adults in a family from support for the children, and for the first time integrate all income-related support for children, to provide a clearer focus on the two aims of: supporting families and tackling poverty through the Child Tax Credit and making work pay through the Working Tax Credit. The Child Tax Credit will create a single, seamless support system for families with children, irrespective of the work status of the adults in the household ... The Working Tax Credit will tackle poor work incentives and persistent poverty among working people.

(See the Treasury Paper, *The Child and Working Tax Credits: The Modernisation of Britain's Tax and Benefits System, Number Ten.*)

9.1.3 Other means-tested benefits

We shall conclude the chapter by looking briefly at the social fund, which makes means-tested grants and loans for various purposes, and at the National Health Service benefits, which may be provided free or at very low cost to people on low incomes.

9.2 Local authority benefits: common features

9.2.1 Administration

The two local authority benefits have many features in common, not least that they are administered at local level by the local housing authority: district or borough council, unitary authority, or London borough.

9.2.2 Non-dependants

If the claimant has a non-dependant sharing his accommodation, this may affect his entitlement to both benefits. The figures used differ for the two benefits: HB uses the same deductions as IS, IRESA and IBJSA, but the deductions for CTB are lower because the weekly amount of council tax is itself much lower.

For both benefits, any non-dependant deduction that is to be made occurs when calculating the maximum benefit. However, no non-dependant deduction is made in the following circumstances:

(a)   if the claimant or any partner is registered blind or receives AA, CAA for IDB purposes or the care component of DLA (at any rate of pay);

(b)   if the non-dependant is any of the following: a full-time student during his period of study (or the summer vacation, unless he is in full-time work); a person under 18; or a person under 25 receiving IS, IRESA or IBJSA. Note that, for CTB purposes only, no non-dependant deduction is made if:

    (i)   the non-dependant is a full-time student even if he is in full-time work during the summer vacation; or

    (ii)   the non-dependant is aged 25 or over but in receipt of IS, IRESA or IBJSA.

9.2.3 Income

The calculation of the claimant's income is identical for the two benefits. See **Chapter 7** for a reminder of the basic means test, and the special rules for these two benefits. The major differences from the income calculation for IS, IRESA and IBJSA are:

(a)   earnings disregards tend to be higher;

(b)   all child maintenance is ignored;

(c)   the treatment of maternity benefits and SSP is more generous;

(d)   there is an earnings disregard for the costs of qualifying childcare. The qualifying conditions are:

    (i)   the claimant must be either:

        (A)   a lone parent; or

        (B)   a member of a couple where both work at least 16 hours a week or one of them works at least 16 hours a week and the other is either

(1) 'incapacitated', ie in receipt of any of the following benefits: CESA; AA; DLA (either component at any rate of pay); HB or CTB that includes a disability premium or higher pensioner premium based on disability; HB or CTB that includes a disregard for childcare costs; or (2) a hospital in-patient; or (3) in prison;

and

(ii)   the care must be provided for a child in the claimant's benefits household who is under the qualifying age, ie from birth up to but not including the first Monday in September that follows the child's fifteenth birthday (or sixteenth birthday if the child receives DLA (either component at any rate of pay) or is registered blind);

and

(iii)   each child of qualifying age must be receiving 'relevant childcare', ie care provided by any of the following: a registered childminder in the childminder's home; a registered childcare provider such as a nursery, playscheme or after school club; an out of hours club on school premises run by a school or local authority.

If the claimant qualifies, the childcare costs will be disregarded from his and any partner's earnings up to a prescribed maximum amount. In 2008/09 this was £175 for one child of qualifying age receiving relevant childcare and £300 for two or more qualifying children each receiving relevant childcare.

Examples

Bruce pays £160 a week for his four-year-old daughter to attend a nursery. As that does not exceed the prescribed maximum of £175, the whole £160 will be disregarded from his and any partner's earnings.

Claire pays £385 a week in total for her three qualifying children who each receive relevant childcare. The amount exceeds the maximum of £300 and so Claire is limited to that, namely £300 will be disregarded from her and any partner's earnings.

Note that special rules apply to recipients of the pension credit (see generally **5.3**) where the claimant or any partner is aged 60 or over and not claiming IS, IRESA or IBJSA. In outline these mean that, if the guarantee credit element is being paid, then all income is ignored. However, where only the savings credit element is being paid, then income for the purposes of HB and CTB is the income figure used by the DfWP to assess the pension credit plus the amount of the savings credit element, any child benefit, any child tax credit and any partner's income not taken into account for the pension credit.

9.2.4   Applicable amount

The applicable amount is calculated using allowances and premiums (see **Chapter 7**).

9.2.5   Tapering

For all the means-tested benefits, the final stage of the means test involves a comparison between the claimant's income and his applicable amount. For all except IS, IRESA and IBJSA, the calculation also involves a third figure, the 'maximum benefit'. For HB, the maximum benefit is the 'eligible rent' (see **9.3.2.1**) or local housing allowance (see **9.3.2.2**); and for CTB it is the amount of council tax payable (see **9.4.4**). Both are subject to any deduction for non-dependants.

If the claimant's income does not exceed his applicable amount, he will receive the maximum benefit. If the income does exceed the applicable amount, the maximum benefit is reduced by a fixed percentage of the excess income. This process is called 'tapering', and we shall meet it again when we consider tax credits. For HB the percentage used for tapering is 65%, and it is 20% for CTB.

9.2.6 Claimants receiving IS, IRESA or IBJSA, or the guarantee credit element of pension credit

For both benefits, there is no need to carry out a full means test calculation if the claimant is in receipt of IS, IRESA or IBJSA, or the guarantee credit element of pension credit. He will automatically receive the maximum amount of benefit, subject to any non-dependant deduction(s).

9.3 Housing benefit

9.3.1 Who is entitled to housing benefit?

Housing benefit may be paid to a person who has a legal liability to pay rent for the place where he lives (ie his 'dwelling') (SSCBA 1992, s 130). The term 'dwelling' includes caravans, mobile homes and houseboats.

To be eligible for HB, the claimant (or any partner) must be liable to pay the rent for accommodation that is normally occupied as a home. The term 'rent' is used loosely to cover:

(a)   rent paid by local authority tenants to the local authority;

(b)   rent paid by private tenants of residential property to their landlords;

(c)   service charges paid by tenants to private landlords or local authorities for such things as cleaning and maintaining common parts of the building;

(d)   licence fees paid by boarders and lodgers to the person in whose household they live (see **7.4.8**);

(e)   charges for hostels and bed-and-breakfast accommodation.

It does not include:

(a)   payments of ground rent or service charges by owner-occupiers under a long lease. These may be paid as part of IS, IRESA, pension credit or IBJSA (see **8.3**);

(b)   payments made under an informal arrangement by a non-dependant (see **7.4.7**);

(c)   payments for anything other than the accommodation itself – food, heating, lighting, hot water and so on (see **9.3.2**).

To be eligible for HB, the claimant must be liable to pay the rent for accommodation that is normally occupied as a home or any partner must be so liable. If a couple is jointly liable for rent, only one can claim. 'Liable', in this context, means an agreement that is legally enforceable. In certain limited circumstances, a person who is not legally liable to pay rent is treated as liable to pay it for HB purposes (eg the claimant's former partner is liable to make the payments on the dwelling but is not doing so, and the claimant is paying the rent in order to remain living in that property as a home).

An agreement that is not on a commercial basis does not give rise to a liability to pay rent. So, for example, an adult child who continues to live with his parents whilst in full-time work is not their tenant or lodger but for benefit purposes is treated as their non-dependant (see **7.4.7**).

9.3.2 Maximum housing benefit

What is the maximum housing benefit that a claimant might receive? The starting point is determined by the type of landlord.

If the claimant's landlord is a local authority or a registered social landlord, which includes most housing associations and local housing companies, then his maximum housing benefit is known as his 'eligible rent' (see **9.3.3**). A list of registered social landlords can be found at www.housingcorp.gov.uk.

If the claimant is a tenant of a private landlord then the local housing allowance will apply (see **9.3.4**).

In either case, if a non-dependant is sharing the accommodation, a deduction may have to be made (see **9.2.2** and the worked example at **9.5.3**).

Note that special rules apply to tenants of caravans, mobile homes and houseboats, which are outside the scope of this book.

9.3.3 Eligible rent

As noted at **9.3.2**, the starting point for determining a claimant's maximum housing benefit is whether or not he rents from a private landlord. If he does, see **9.3.4**. If he rents from a local authority or a registered social landlord (which includes most housing associations and local housing companies) then his maximum housing benefit is known as his 'eligible rent'. Once you have worked that out, do not forget that you may have to reduce it by the amount of any relevant non-dependant deduction (see **9.2.2** and the worked example at **9.5.3**).

The 'eligible rent' is that part of the contractual payment which covers the housing element and includes most service charges. However, Sch 1 to the HB Regs 2006 provides that the following service charges are ineligible, namely those that are in respect of day-to-day living expenses including, in particular, all provision of meals (including the preparation of meals or provision of unprepared food); laundry (other than the provision of premises or equipment to enable a person to do his own laundry); leisure items, such as either sports facilities (except a children's play area), or television rental, television subscription charges and licence fees; cleaning of rooms and windows (except the exterior of any windows in accommodation where neither the claimant nor any member of his household is able to clean those windows himself) and in communal areas; and transport. Also excluded are charges in respect of the acquisition of furniture or household equipment, the use of such furniture or equipment where that furniture or household equipment will become the property of the claimant by virtue of an agreement with the landlord, charges in respect of the provision of an emergency alarm system.

Where a charge for meals is ineligible to be met by housing benefit, the amount that is ineligible in respect of each week is that specified in the HB Regs 2006 and not the claimant's tenancy agreement. As to any other ineligible service charge, such as fuel costs, if this is not separated from or separately identified within other payments made by the claimant under his tenancy agreement, the local authority 'apportion such charge as is fairly attributable to the provision of that service having regard to the cost of comparable services' (Sch 1).

If the local authority considers that the amount of any ineligible service charge which is separately identified within other payments made by the occupier in respect of the dwelling is unreasonably low having regard to the service provided, it will substitute a sum for the charge in question which, it considers, represents the value of the services concerned and the amount so substituted is ineligible to be met by housing benefit. Further, if the local authority considers that the amount of an eligible service charge is excessive in relation to the service provided for the claimant or his family, having regard to the cost of comparable services, it will deduct from that charge the excess and the amount so deducted is ineligible to be met by housing benefit.

9.3.4   Local housing allowance

9.3.4.1   Flat rate allowance set locally

The LHA is a flat rate allowance based on the number of people occupying the claimant's property, the age of the claimant if single, and the location in which he lives. The amount is not directly related to the rent the private landlord charges. The LHA is determined locally by rent officers and is based on the median rent charged by private landlords for properties of various sizes. This means that a claimant's LHA may be lower than, the same as or sometimes even higher than the contractual rent he pays.

To work out a claimant's LHA you need to determine how many bedrooms he is entitled to under the so-called 'room size test'; then you need to look up the appropriate LHA for the area in which he lives or wishes to move to.

9.3.4.2   The room size test

The total number of bedrooms to which a claimant is entitled determines his LHA rate. So who counts? The answer is the claimant, those in his benefit household (that is a partner and any children: see **7.4.4**) and also any non-dependants (see **7.4.7**). Sub-tenants, lodgers and boarders (see **7.4.8**) do not count.

As a general rule a claimant is entitled to one bedroom for each of the following people who count:

- Every adult couple.
- Any other adult aged 16 or over.
- Any 2 children of the same sex.
- Any 2 children under 10.
- Any other child.

Note that each person is counted only once and in the first category that applies to that person. For example, if Alan and Barbara are married, they count as an adult couple. If they have triplets, Clive, Derek and Edward, aged 9, then Clive and Derek fall within the '2 children of the same sex' category and Edward falls within the 'any other child' category.

Table 9.1   Examples of the room size test

Occupiers	Number of bedrooms
Alan and Barbara, Clive, Derek and Edward (as above).	1 for Alan and Barbara, 1 for Clive and Derek 1 for Edward TOTAL: 3

Occupiers	Number of bedrooms
Frank and Grace are a couple. Frank's father, Henry, lives with them. Their 3 children, Irene (21), Janet (15) and Keith (13) also live with them.	1 for Frank and Grace 1 for Henry (adult aged 16 or over) 1 for Irene (adult aged 16 or over) 1 for Janet (any other child) 1 for Keith (any other child) TOTAL: 5
Louise is a single parent. She has 3 children, Martin (15), Norman (11) and Oliver (7).	1 for Louise (an adult) 1 for Martin and Norman (2 children of same sex) 1 for Oliver (any other child). TOTAL: 3
Paul and Rose are married. They have 5 children, Steven (17), Vanessa (14), Alice (12), Tom (8) and Brenda (6).	1 for Paul and Rose (adult couple) 1 for Steven (adult aged 16 or over) 1 for Vanessa and Alice (2 children of same sex) 1 for Tom and Brenda (2 children under 10). TOTAL: 4

What happens when a child reaches 10 or 16? The local authority should check to see if this affects the LHA award and apply any new rate from the Monday following the child's birthday.

9.3.4.3 The room size test: special cases

A single claimant living on his own and under the age of 25 is not normally entitled to LHA at the one-bedroom rate unless the severe disabilty premium (see **7.7.2**) forms part of his applicable amount. A special reduced rate, based on the LHA for the locality for one bedroom in shared accommodation, will apply instead.

A single claimant aged 25 or over living on his own, and a couple with no children are entitled to LHA at the one-bedroom rate, but only if they are renting property of at least that size, eg a one-bedroom flat or studio, or other kind of self-contained accommodation. If they choose to live in shared accommodation then they will receive only the LHA for the locality for one bedroom in shared accommodation.

9.3.4.4 LHA rates

As we have seen, a claimant's LHA is determined by how many bedrooms he is entitled to under the room size test. Once you know that, you need to look up the appropriate LHA for the area in which the claimant lives or wishes to move to. The rates are determined monthly by each local authority and can be found at www.lha-direct.therentservice.gov.uk.

By way of example only, at the time of writing (July 2008) the LHA weekly rates for Brighton and Hove, East Sussex, were as follows:

1 bedroom shared	1 bedroom self contained	2 bedrooms	3 bedrooms	4 bedrooms	5 bedrooms
£83.54	£150	£184.62	£225	£300	£392.31

9.3.4.5 Contractual rent and LHA rates

If a claimant's contractual rent exceeds his LHA, he is expected to make up the shortfall and may ultimately have to seek cheaper rented accommodation. So, for example, if the claimant pays £170 rent but his LHA is £150, he is immediately £20 short. But do not forget that the LHA is only the maximum housing benefit he might get, and you will still have to make any non-dependant deduction (see **9.2.2** and the worked example at **9.5.3**) and apply the usual income means test.

But what if a claimant's LHA exceeds the amount of his contractual rent? In these circumstances the LHA is 'capped' at a maximum of £15 over the contractual rent paid.

Examples

Anne's contractual rent is £140 but her LHA is £150. Her maximum housing benefit will include a LHA of £150 (that is her contractual rent of £140 plus £10, bringing it up to the LHA).

Brian's contractual rent is £130 but his LHA is £150. His maximum housing benefit will include a LHA of £145 (that is his contractual rent of £130 plus the maximum addition of £15).

Note that in these circumstances you must work out the capped amount of LHA before taking into account any non-dependant deduction (see **9.2.2** and the worked example at **9.5.3**).

9.3.5 Administration and payment

If the landlord is the local authority itself, no actual payments of benefit are made. The benefit takes effect as a rebate, that is a reduction of the amount of rent which is payable.

A LHA determination usually applies from the date of the claim for a year. Changes in the amount of the rent during that time are normally irrelevant. However, if the claimant's room entitlement or address changes, the LHA will be updated.

Payments of HB under the LHA scheme are usually made to the claimant. Local authorites have a discretion to pay it directly to the landlord if the claimant has difficulty managing his financial affairs or it is improbable that the claimant will pay his rent.

Worked examples of HB calculations are given at **9.5**.

9.3.6 Calculating the benefit

There are four steps to be taken when calculating HB.

Step 1: work out the maximum HB to which the claimant is entitled (ie the eligible rent (see **9.3.2.1**) or LHA (see **9.3.2.2**) less any non-dependant deduction(s)). If the claimant is receiving IS, IRESA or IBJSA, or the guarantee credit element of pension credit, no further calculation is necessary.

Step 2: calculate the claimant's applicable amount (ie aggregate the allowances and any premiums to which he is entitled for his benefits household).

Step 3: calculate the claimant's income for the purposes of HB from all relevant sources.

Step 4: determine whether the claimant is entitled to HB and, if so, how much. Do this by comparing the income and the applicable amount. If the income is the same as or less than the applicable amount, the maximum HB calculated at Step 1 is payable. If the income is more than the applicable amount, the maximum HB is tapered downwards (ie 65% of the income that exceeds the applicable amount is deducted from the maximum HB and the resulting figure is the claimant's entitlement).

9.4 Council tax benefit

9.4.1 Who is eligible for council tax benefit?

Council tax is a local tax paid by most residents to their local authority for such local services as rubbish collection, street lighting, leisure facilities, education, social services and policing. Council tax is paid once per household, the amount varying according to the area in which the householder resides and the value of the property in which he lives. Properties were 'banded' on a national basis in 1992 according to their value at that date. It does not matter if house values have increased or decreased since that date, the house remains in the same Band, although there are limited rights of appeal for new owners of property. The Bands range from A to H. Properties in Band A have the lowest value at below £40,000, whilst properties in Band H have the highest in value at over £320,000. Using its annual budget as a basis, the local authority determines the amount of tax to be paid by the householders in each Band.

To be eligible for CTB, the claimant must be liable to pay the tax on a property which is his sole or main residence: see *Parry v Derbyshire Dales District Council* [2006] EWHC 988 (Admin). Unlike HB, it does not have to be a property normally occupied as a home (see **9.3.1**).

9.4.2 Exempt persons

Some occupiers of residential property are not liable to pay council tax. The most important groups are:

(a) full-time students and some trainees, including anyone under 20 in non-advanced education;

(b) people who do not live in their own accommodation: boarders and lodgers, people in residential care.

9.4.3 Special categories

If the householder is a single occupier or a lone parent, he pays only 75% of the normal amount of tax for the valuation Band. If there are two or more non-exempt occupiers (see above), they will pay 100% of the normal tax. A house which has been specially adapted for the needs of a disabled person is placed in the valuation Band below the one into which it would otherwise fall.

9.4.4 The amount of benefit

The administration and payment of the benefit are similar to HB (see **9.3.5**).

Council tax benefit has two forms. The first is calculated in the same way as HB, using allowances and premiums, and the maximum benefit figure subject to any non-dependant deductions, all based on the claimant's personal circumstances. The second form is the 'second adult rebate', which is peculiar in that the claimant's financial circumstances are totally irrelevant to the calculation.

Second adult rebate is an alternative to standard CTB. It may be claimed by a single person who has living in his household a non-dependant on a low income. A non-dependant who is not exempt (ie not a full-time student, in practice) would be expected to contribute to the claimant's liability to pay council tax. The householder is not entitled to the single occupier discount if he has a non-dependant living with him who is not exempt.

The second adult rebate is calculated on the income of the non-dependant. The claimant's capital and income are totally irrelevant. The maximum rebate is 25%, which produces the same tax liability as the single occupier discount. There are smaller rebates for non-dependants with higher incomes.

Some householders who qualify for CTB under the normal rules are better off on second adult rebate. Local authorities must always carry out comparative calculations and award whichever is the more advantageous.

9.4.5 Calculating the benefit

There are five steps to be taken when calculating CTB.

Step 1: calculate the maximum CTB, having regard to the single occupier rate and any non-dependant deduction(s), if appropriate. If the claimant is in receipt of IS, IRESA or IBJSA, or the guarantee credit element of pension credit, he will be entitled to this maximum and no further calculation needs be done.

Step 2: calculate the applicable amount which is made up of the personal allowances and any premiums to which the claimant is entitled for his benefits household.

Step 3: calculate the claimant's income for CTB purposes from all sources.

Step 4: determine whether the claimant is entitled to CTB and, if so, how much. Do this by comparing the income and the applicable amount. If the income is the same or less than the applicable amount, then the maximum CTB calculated at Step 1 is payable. If the income is more than the applicable amount, then the maximum CTB is tapered downward by 20% of the income that exceeds the applicable amount. The resulting figure is the claimant's entitlement.

Step 5: there is, however, a further step to be taken if the claimant is entitled to the second adult rebate. A comparison should be made between the CTB entitlement calculated under the above four Steps and the council tax payable if the second adult rebate is applicable.

9.5 Worked examples

9.5.1 Introduction

We shall now look at two short case studies, which illustrate the calculation of the local authority benefits. These examples are worked using the benefit rates in force for the period 6 April 2008 to 5 April 2009.

Before presenting each calculation, we shall analyse the key facts of each case study.

9.5.2 Tapering

9.5.2.1 Facts

Chen, aged 42, works part time. He earns £150 a week. His wife, Mei, aged 40, also works part time. She earns £100 a week. Mei receives DLA, care component at the lowest rate. Their children are grown up and living away from home. They have savings of £8,135. They are not eligible for IS, IRESA, IBJSA or working tax credit. They rent a one-bedroom, self-contained flat from a private landlord. Their weekly rent is £90.

The LHA for the area in which they reside is as follows:

1 bedroom shared	1 bedroom self contained	2 bedrooms	3 bedrooms	4 bedrooms	5 bedrooms
£54.23	£95.00	£121.15	£132.69	£150	£183.46

What is the couple's entitlement to housing benefit?

9.5.2.2 Analysis

Step 1: calculate maximum HB

As a couple with no children, Chen and Mei are entitled to the LHA at the one-bedroom rate as they are renting property of at least that size.

Their LHA for a one-bedroom, self-contained flat exceeds the amount of their contractual rent by £5 (£95 LHA less £90 rent). That £5 excees is less than the £15 maximum allowed and so in these circumstances they are entitled to the LHA of £95.

There is no non-dependant living with the couple so their maximum HB is £95.

Step 2: calculate applicable amount

Their applicable amount is:

(a) personal allowance for a couple;

(b) disability premium, as Mei receives DLA, care component. As she has a partner, it is paid at the couple rate.

Step 3: calculate income from all sources

Chen and Mei's income is:

(a) their combined earnings less a higher earnings disregard of £20 for being in receipt of the disability premium;

(b) tariff income on £8,135, ie ignore first £6,000 = £2,135 and then calculate at the rate of £1 for every £250 or part = £9;

(c) Mei's DLA care component is ignored.

The calculation

	£	£	£
Step 1: calculate maximum housing benefit			
Local housing allowance			95.00
Step 2: calculate applicable amount			
Allowance for a couple		94.95	
Disability premium (couple rate)		<u>36.85</u>	131.80
Step 3: calculate income from all sources			
Chen's earnings	150.00		
Mei's earnings	<u>100.00</u>	250.00	
LESS disregard (disability premium)		<u>20.00</u>	
		230.00	
Tariff income		9.00	239.00

Step 4: taper as income exceeds applicable amount

Income of £239 exceeds applicable amount of £131.80 by £107.20, so maximum HB is not payable and must be reduced by 65% of the excess.

£107.20 x 65% = £69.68

Maximum HB of £95 less tapered excess of £69.68 means the HB they will receive each week is £25.32.

9.5.3 Non-dependant in house: claimant in receipt of IBJSA

9.5.3.1 Facts

Chris (aged 35) is unemployed and receives IBJSA. He lives in a two-bedroomed flat, which he rents from a private landlord with his wife, Karen (aged 30). Their rent is £160 per week. The flat is in Band D for council tax purposes, which in their area is £658 per year. Karen's younger sister Martina lives with them. Martina is 22 and works as a waitress, earning £180 gross per week.

How much HB and CTB will they receive?

9.5.3.2 Analysis

(a)   Because Chris is in receipt of IBJSA, we know that he will automatically receive the maximum amount of HB and CTB, subject only to the effect of any non-dependants in the household. We do not therefore need to know anything about his resources and do not need to work out his applicable amount.

(b)   Under the room size test, the total number of bedrooms that Chris requires is two, ie one for Karen and himself (an adult couple) and one for Martina (an adult aged 16 or over).

(c)   Assume that the LHA for a two bedroom property in the locality is £150. As their contractual rent exceeds the LHA, they will have to meet the shortfall.

(d)   Martina is a non-dependant, ie a relative sharing the accommodation on an informal basis. She therefore counted when we did the room size test in (b) above, but we must now remember that the LHA will have to be reduced by the amount of the appropriate non-dependant deduction.

(e)   Both Chris and Karen are liable to pay council tax, so there is no single householder discount and no possibility of second adult rebate.

(f)   Martina, as a non-dependant with earnings, will cause the amount of CTB to be reduced.

The calculation

	£	£
Maximum HB		
LHA	150.00	
Less non-dependant deduction (earnings £180 pw)	<u>23.35</u>	
Benefit payable		126.65
Council tax benefit		
Maximum benefit = £658 ÷ 52	12.66	
Less non-dependant (as above)	4.60	
CTB payable		8.06

9.6   The tax credits

9.6.1   What are the tax credits?

As we saw at **9.1.2**, the aim of the child tax credit is to encompass all income-related support for children, and the goal of the working tax credit is to make work pay. So how are these ideals to be achieved? First, child tax credit now contains all the premiums relating to children that used to be claimable with IS or IBJSA (and indeed remain part of a HB or CTB calculation where the benefits household includes at least one qualifying child). Claimants who receive IS, IRESA or IBJSA automatically receive the maximum amount of child tax credit. The only other child-centred benefit is, of course, child benefit (see **6.6**). Secondly, tax credits are subject to an income only test. There is no upper capital limit. Lastly, the category of potential claimants for working tax credit is far wider than any earlier version of this benefit.

Although called credits, these tax credits are 'payable', so that claimants receive them even if they have no income tax or National Insurance contributions to pay.

9.7   Common features of the two tax credits

9.7.1   Age

The claimant must be aged 16 or over or, if under 16, have a partner who least 16.

There is no maximum age.

9.7.2   Immigration requirements

The claimant must not be subject to immigration control and must meet residence requirements (see **Chapter 10**).

9.7.3   Income: an overview

To qualify for either tax credit the claimant and any partner must have a sufficiently low annual income. It is based over a full tax year from 6 April to 5 April. The income of a child or qualifying young person is ignored. If the claimant was part of a couple in the previous tax year but is now single or a lone parent, only the claimant's income counts. So what counts as income? At the start of a claim, it is calculated by reference to income for the previous tax year. For claims for later tax years the award is based initially on income from the previous tax year.

Regulation 3 of the Tax Credits (Definition and Calculation of Income) Regulations 2002 (SI 2002/2006) states that

> the manner in which income of a claimant or, in the case of a joint claim, the aggregate income of the claimants, is to be calculated for a tax year for the purposes of the [2002] Act is as follows.
>
> *Step One:* calculate and then add together—
>
> (a)   the pension income (as defined in regulation 5(1)),
>
> (b)   the investment income (as defined in regulation 10),
>
> (c)   the property income (as defined in regulation 11),
>
> (d)   the foreign income (as defined in regulation 12) and
>
> (e)   the notional income (as defined in regulation 13)
>
> of the claimant, or, in the case of a joint claim, of the claimants.
>
> If the result of this step is £300 or less, it is treated as nil. If the result of this step is more than £300, only the excess is taken into account in the following steps.
>
> *Step Two:* calculate and then add together—
>
> (a)   the employment income (as defined in regulation 4),
>
> (b)   the social security income (as defined in regulation 7),
>
> (c)   the student income (as defined in regulation 8) and
>
> (d)   the miscellaneous income (as defined in regulation 18)
>
> of the claimant, or in the case of a joint claim, of the claimants.
>
> *Step Three*
>
> Add together the results of Steps One and Two.
>
> *Step Four*
>
> Calculate the trading income (as defined in regulation 6) of the claimant, or in the case of a joint claim, of the claimants.
>
> Add the result of this step to that produced by Step Three, unless there has been a trading loss in the year.
>
> If there has been a trading loss in the year, subtract the amount of that loss from the result of Step Three.

Subject to certain qualifications, the result of Step Four is the income of the claimant, or, in the case of a joint claim, of the claimants, for the purposes of the Act.

9.7.4   Income: the detail

We have set out below some examples of the most common type of income that is taken into account.

9.7.4.1   Pension income

This includes State Pension (see **5.2.1**), any adult dependant increase (see **2.4**), any additional State Pension (see **5.2.3**), personal and occupational pensions, and widowed parent's allowance (see **5.4.3**).

9.7.4.2   Investment income

This includes, before tax is deducted, any interest on money invested (eg in a bank or building society), dividends from UK company shares and income from government stocks and bonds.

9.7.4.3   Property income

This basically means rental income after the expenses incurred in running the property (eg repairs). However, if the claimant rents out property as a business that should be included as income from self-employment (see **9.7.4.5**). Note that where the claimant rents out a furnished room in his own home to a boarder or subtenant then up to £4,250 of the annual rent is exempt from tax. Anything above that figure will count.

9.7.4.4   Notional income

The rules are very similar to those relating to notional capital for the four means-tested benefits (see **7.2.1.3**). So if a claimant has deprived himself of income for the purpose of securing entitlement to, or increasing the amount of, a tax credit, he is treated as having that income. Equally, if income would become available to a claimant upon the making of an application for that income he is treated as having that income.

9.7.4.5   Employment income

The gross earnings of an employee count, including any bonuses, overtime etc. However, any contributions made to a personal or occupational pension approved by HMRC can be deducted.

Any SSP (see **4.2**) that is paid is included. Only statutory maternity pay (see **6.3**) exceeding £100 counts.

9.7.4.6   Social security income

The following benefits count:

(a)   bereavement allowance (see **5.4.4**);

(b)   carer's allowance (see **6.7**);

(c)   contribution-based JSA (see **3.4**);

(d)   CESA (see **4.3**); and

(e)   any increase (see **2.4**) paid for an adult dependant.

The following benefits do not count:

(a)   attendance allowance (see **4.9**);

(b)   bereavement payment (see **5.4.5**);

(c)   child benefit (see **6.6**);

(d)   CTB (see **9.4**);

(e)   DLA (see **4.6**);

(f)   HB (see **9.3**);

(g)   IS or IRESA (see **8.2**);

(h)   IBJSA (see **8.2**);

(i)   industrial disablement benefit (see **4.10**);

(j)   maternity allowance (see **6.4**);

(k)   social fund payment (see **9.16**); and

(l)   any adult dependant increase (see **2.4**) that may be payable.

Note that widowed parent's allowance is treated as pension income (see **9.7.4.1**).

9.7.4.7   Trading income

This is the taxable profit made by a self-employed person from a trade, profession or vocation. If the claimant is a partner in a business, it is the taxable profits from his share that count.

9.7.5 Income: an example

9.7.5.1 Facts

Ivan and Lucy claim tax credits in April 2009. HMRC assesses their claim based on their joint income for the previous tax year 6 April 2008 to 5 April 2009. For that tax year, Ivan was employed and earned £25,950 gross (after taking into account contributions to an approved occupational pension deducted by his employer). Lucy received an occupational pension of £750, DLA care component at the lowest rate, industrial disablement benefit (at 30%) and CESA of £4,394. They received gross dividends on their UK company shareholdings of £360.

9.7.5.2 Analysis

Following the five stages outlined at **9.7.3**, their annual income is:

Step One: calculate and then add together:

(a)   the pension income, namely Lucy's occupational pension of £750;

(b)   the investment income, namely the dividends on the shares: £360.

As the result of this step (£1,110) is more than £300, only the excess of £810 is taken into account in the following steps.

Step Two: calculate and then add together—

(a)   the employment income, namely Ivan's earnings of £25,950;

(b)   the social security income, namely Lucy's CESA of £4,394 (her DLA and industrial disablement benefit do not count).

The total for this step is £30,344.

Step Three

Add together the results of Steps One and Two, ie £810 + £30,344 = £31,154.

Step Four

Neither had a trading income.

So £31,154 is the income of Ivan and Lucy for the purposes of the 2002 Act.

9.7.6 Notifying changes in income

Increases in income of £25,000 or less between the current tax year and the previous tax year do not affect an award and there is no need to tell HMRC. Larger increases, or decreases of any size, affect an award and it is best to notify HMRC immediately so the credit(s) can be recalculated and the risk of an overpayment or underpayment minimised.

At the end of the tax year, HMRC finalises the assessment.

9.7.7 Entitlement over a tax year

Tax credits are calculated by reference to a maximum annual amount. So if a claim is made at the beginning of a tax year, the award is made for a whole year. Otherwise, only the appropriate proportion of the annual award is payable. A formula for calculating the latter can be found in the Tax Credits (Income Thresholds and Determination of Rates) Regulations 2002 (SI 2002/2008).

9.8   Conditions of entitlement for child tax credit

To qualify for child tax credit the claimant must:

(a)   be aged 16 or over (or if under 16 have a partner aged at least 16);

(b)   be responsible for at least one dependent child or qualifying young person;

(c)   have a sufficiently low income;

(d)   not be subject to immigration control and meet residence requirements (see **Chapter 10**).

9.8.1   A child or qualifying young person

Section 8(1) of the Tax Credits Act 2002 provides that 'the entitlement of the person or persons by whom a claim for child tax credit has been made is dependent on him, or either or both of them, being responsible for one or more children or qualifying young persons'.

The definitions of a child and qualifying young person are exactly the same as under the Child Benefit (General) Regulations 2006 (see **6.6.2** and **6.6.3**).

9.8.2   Being responsible for the child or qualifying young person

The most common way of establishing responsibility is set out in reg 3 of the Child Tax Credit Reglations 2002 (SI 2002/2007), namely 'a person is treated as responsible for a child or qualifying young person who is normally living with him'. Whilst reg 3 describes this as the 'normally living with test', it does not set out how the test is to be met. Common sense suggests that this is describing a situation where the child lives with the claimant under the same roof. Should a child reside part of the week with one parent (or adult, say grandparent) and the rest with another adult, there are two potential conflicting claims which the parties must resolve, otherwise HMRC will.

9.8.3   The elements making up maximum child tax credit

The maximum rate at which a claimant may be entitled to child tax credit is the aggregate of:

(a)   the family element of child tax credit; and

(b)   an individual element of child tax credit, in respect of each child or qualifying young person.

All the figures that follow are for 2008/09.

The family element of child tax credit is made up as follows:

(a)   in a case where any child is under the age of one year it is £1,090 a year; but

(b)   in any other case it is £545.

Note that only one amount forms the family element. So a family that includes two children aged six months and three years of age gets £1,090, whilst a family that includes three children aged two, four and five years gets £545.

The individual element of child tax credit for any child or qualifying young person may be made up as follows:

(a)   where the child or qualifying young person is disabled it is £4,625; or

(b)   where the child or qualifying young person is severely disabled it is £5,645; or

(c)   in the case of any other child or qualifying young person it is £2,085pa.

The disability element is payable for any child or qualifying young person who receives DLA (either component at any rate of pay: see **4.7** and **4.8**), or is registered blind.

The severe disability element is payable for any child or qualifying young person who receives the highest rate of DLA care component (see **4.7.3.3**).

9.8.4   Examples of maximum child tax credit

(1)   Ann is a single parent. She has two children, Bob aged 6 months and Dan aged 5. She receives DLA care at the lowest rate for Dan. The annual elements used when calculating Ann's maximum child tax credit are:

Family element: £1,090
Child element for Bob: £2,085
Disabled Child element for Dan: £4,625

(2)   Brenda and Mike have three children, Alice aged 13, Clive aged 15 and Derek aged 18. Derek is doing his 'A' levels at the local College (non-advanced education and he is a qualifying young person). The annual elements used when calculating their maximum child tax credit are:

Family element: £545
Child element for Alice: £2,085
Child element for Clive: £2,085
Child element for Derek: £2,085.

9.8.5   Will the maximum child tax credit be paid?

If the claimant is entitled to IS, IRESA or IBJSA, he will receive the maximum child tax credit consisting of the family and child elements as described at **9.8.3** and illustrated at **9.8.4**.

If the claimant is not receiving IS, IRESA or IBJSA, his income (see **9.7.3**) must be compared with a prescribed figure called 'the income threshold' (TCA 2002, s 7(1)(a)). If the claimant is also entitled to working tax credit (see **9.10**), the annual threshold figure is £6,420. If the claimant is not entitled to working tax credit the figure is £15,575.

If the claimant's income is *the same as or less* than the income threshold, the maximum child tax credit is payable.

If the claimant's income is *more* than the income threshold, the maximum child tax credit is not payable. Instead, it will be tapered, that is reduced, by 39% of the excess income (see further **9.11**).

9.9   Calculating child tax credit: a summary of the steps

If the claimant is entitled to IS, IRESA or IBJSA, he will receive the maximum child tax credit. This is made up of the family and child elements as described at **9.8.3** and illustrated at **9.8.4**.

If the claimant is not receiving IS, IRESA or IBJSA, the following steps must be taken:

Step 1: calculate the maximum child tax credit

Step 2: calculate relevant income (see **9.7.3**).

Step 3: compare income with the annual threshold (see **9.8.5**).

Step 4: if the claimant's income is the same or less than the income threshold, the maximum child tax credit is payable.

If the claimant's income is more than the income threshold, the maximum child tax credit is not payable. Instead, it will be tapered, that is reduced, by 39% of the excess income. See the worked examples at **9.13**.

9.10 Conditions of entitlement for working tax credit

To qualify for working tax credit the claimant must:

(a) be aged 16 or over (or if under 16 have a partner aged at least 16);

(b) be in qualifying remunerative work;

(c) have a sufficiently low income;

(d) not be subject to immigration control and meet residence requirements (see **Chapter 10**).

9.10.1 Qualifying remunerative work

By reg 4 of the Working Tax Credit (Entitlement and Maximum Rate) Regulations 2002 (SI 2002/2005), a person must be treated as engaged in qualifying remunerative work if, but only if, he satisfies all of the following conditions.

9.10.1.1 First condition

The person:

(a) is working at the date of the claim; or

(b) has an offer of work which he has accepted at the date of the claim and the work is expected to commence within seven days of the making of the claim.

In relation to a case falling within (b), references in the second, third and fourth conditions (see **9.10.1.2**, **9.10.1.3** and **9.10.1.4**) to work which the person undertakes are to be construed as references to the work which the person will undertake when it commences. In such a case the person is only treated as being in qualifying remunerative work when he actually begins that work.

9.10.1.2 Second condition

The person:

(a) is aged at least 16 and undertakes work for not less than 16 hours per week if:
  (i) there is a child or qualifying young person for whom he or his partner is responsible (see **9.8.1**); or
  (ii) he has a physical or mental disability which puts him at a disadvantage in getting a job (see **9.10.2.1**); or

(b) satisfies the conditions in reg 18 ie is entitled to a 50-plus element (see **9.10.2.7**); or

(c) is aged at least 25 and undertakes not less than 30 hours work per week in any other case.

9.10.1.3 Third condition

The work which the person undertakes is expected to continue for at least four weeks after the making of the claim or, in a case falling within (b) of the first condition (see **9.10.1.1**), after the work starts.

9.10.1.4 Fourth condition

The work is done for payment or in expectation of payment.

The number of hours for which a person undertakes qualifying remunerative work is:

(a)   in the case of an apprentice, employee or office-holder the number of hours of such work which he normally performs:

(i)   under the contract of service or of apprenticeship under which he is employed; or

(ii)   in the office in which he is employed;

(b)   in the case of an agency worker, the number of hours in respect of which remuneration is normally paid to him by an employment agency with whom he has a contract of employment; or

(c)   in the case of a person who is self-employed, the number of hours he normally performs for payment or in expectation of payment.

This is subject to the following qualification. In reckoning the number of hours of qualifying remunerative work which a person normally undertakes the following are disregarded:

(a)   any period of customary or paid holiday; and

(b)   any time allowed for meals or refreshment, unless the person is, or expects to be, paid earnings in respect of that time.

What about a claimant on maternity leave? For the purposes of the second and fourth conditions (see **9.10.1.2** and **9.10.1.4**) in reg 4(1) a woman is treated as engaged in qualifying remunerative work for the requisite number of hours during any period for which maternity allowance or statutory maternity pay is paid to her; if she was so engaged (under a contract of service or a contract for services) immediately before the time when that payment began.

What about a claimant on SSP? For the purposes of the second and third conditions (see **9.10.1.2** and **9.10.1.3**) in reg 4(1), a person is treated as engaged in qualifying remunerative work for the requisite number of hours during any period for which statutory sick pay is paid to him, if he was so engaged immediately before that payment began.

Note that a person who is self-employed is treated as engaged in qualifying remunerative work for the requisite number of hours during any period for which he would have been entitled to statutory sick pay but for the fact that the work he performed in the week immediately before the period began, although done for payment or in expectation of payment, was not performed under a contract of service.

9.10.2   The elements making up maximum working tax credit

If the claimant satisfies the conditions of entitlement (see **9.10**), he will be entitled to the basic element. It was £1,800 in 2008/09.

In addition, the following elements may be included if the qualifying conditions are met.

9.10.2.1   Disability element

By reg 9, the determination of the maximum rate must include the disability element, if any person in respect of whom the claim is made:

(a)   undertakes qualifying remunerative work for at least 16 hours per week; and

(b)   satisfies para (2); and

(c)   has any of the disabilities listed in Pt 1 of Sch 1 (see **Appendix 5**).

A person satisfies para (2) in any of the Cases listed in reg 9. These include:

Case A

For at least one day in the 182 days immediately preceding the making of the claim, the claimant, or, in the case of a joint claim, at least one of the claimants, must have been in receipt of CESA.

Case B

For at least one day in the 182 days immediately preceding the making of the claim, the applicable amount for the claimant, or, in the case of a joint claim, at least one of the claimants, must have included as part of IS, IRESA, IBJSA, HB or CTB a higher pensioner or disability premium (see **7.7**).

Case C

At the date of the claim there is payable to the claimant, or in the case of a joint claim, to at least one of the claimants, DLA (either component at any rate of pay) or attendance allowance (at any rate of pay).

Evidence of how the disability affects the claimant or co-claimant may be provided by his doctor, occupational therapist, community nurse or the like.

A claimant or co-claimant must meet conditions (a), (b) and (c) in his own right for a disability element to be payable. So, if both members of a couple satisfy conditions (a), (b) and (c) then two disability elements are payable. See *Commissioner's Decision CSTC/76/2006*.

Example 1

Alan works 20 hours a week (condition (a) met). He receives DLA care component at the lowest rate (condition (b) met). People who know him well have difficulty in understanding what he says (condition (c) met – see disability 13).

Example 2

Bryan works 16 hours a week and his civil partner, Clive, works 20 hours a week (each meet condition (a)). Bryan receives DLA care component at the middle rate and Clive receives DLA mobility component at the higer rate (each meets condition (b)). Bryan cannot, due to lack of manual dexterity, pick up with his left hand a coin of less than 2.5 cm, and Clive will lose his balance when standing unless he continually holds onto something (each meets condition (c) – see disabilities 6 and 1 respectively).

9.10.2.2   30-hour element

By reg 10, the determination of the maximum rate must include a 30-hour element if the claimant, or in the case of a joint claim, at least one of the claimants, is engaged in qualifying remunerative work for at least 30 hours per week.

The determination of the maximum rate must also include the 30-hour element if:

(a)   the claim is a joint claim;
(b)   at least one of the claimants is responsible for one or more children or qualifying young people (see **9.8.1**);
(c)   the aggregate number of hours for which the couple engage in qualifying remunerative work is at least 30 hours per week; and
(d)   at least one member of the couple engages in qualifying remunerative work for at least 16 hours per week.

Examples

(1)   Bob, a single claimant, works full time 30 hours a week (qualifying remunerative work).

(2)   Carol and Mike are joint claimants. Carol works 35 hours a week (qualifying remunerative work). Mike works part time for 10 hours (so on his own Mike would not qualify for this element).

(3)   Debra and John are joint claimants. Their two children aged six and eight live with them (and so they are responsible for two children). Debra works 16 hours each week (qualifying remunerative work) and John works part time for 14 hours. Between them they work 30 hours a week and so qualify for the 30-hour element.

Note that in example (3), even if both Debra and John had each worked 30 hours or more a week they would still only receive one 30-hour element.

9.10.2.3   A second adult element

By reg 11, the determination of the maximum rate must include the second adult element if the claim is a joint claim unless:

(a)   one of the claimants is aged 50 or over; and

(b)   the 50-plus element is payable (see **9.10.2.7**); and

(c)   neither of the claimants is engaged in qualifying remunerative work for at least 30 hours per week. However, this condition does not apply if at least one of the claimants is responsible for a child or a qualifying young person; or is entitled to the disability element (see **9.10.2.1**).

Examples

(1)   Alice, aged 40 and her civil partner, Lucy aged 45, apply jointly.

(2)   Claire, aged 51 and her partner, Dan aged 47, apply jointly. Claire is not entitled to the 50-plus element.

(3)   Eileen, aged 46 and her partner, Fred, aged 50, apply jointly. Fred is entitled to the 50-plus element but the couple are responsible for their 13-year-old grandson who is living with them. Or, alternatively, assume Eileen was entitled to the disability element.

9.10.2.4   A lone parent element

By reg 12, the determination of the maximum rate must include the lone parent element if:

(a)   the claim is a single claim; and

(b)   the claimant is responsible for one or more children or qualifying young people (see **9.8.1**).

9.10.2.5   A child care element

By reg 13, the determination of the maximum rate must include a child care element where that person, or in the case of a joint claim at least one of those persons, is incurring relevant child care charges and:

(a)   is a person, not being a member of a married or unmarried couple or civil partnership, engaged in remunerative work; or

(b)   is a member or are members of a married or unmarried couple or civil partnership where:

(i)   both are engaged in remunerative work; or

(ii)   one member is engaged in remunerative work and the other is incapacitated.

Note that for the purposes of this regulation a person is a child until the last day of the week in which falls the first day of September following that child's fifteenth birthday or sixteenth birthday if the child is disabled. A child is disabled for these purposes if he receives disability living allowance (either component at any rate of pay) or is registered blind.

So what are relevant child care charges? By reg 14, 'child care' means care provided for a child in England and Wales (there are different rules for other parts of the UK):

(a)   by an Ofsted-registered child minder or child care provider (such as an approved nanny or au pair), nursery or child care scheme;

(b)   in schools or establishments which are exempted from registration;

(c)   in respect of any period on or before the day preceding the first Tuesday in September following his twelfth birthday, where the care is provided out of school hours, by a school on school premises or by a local authority; or

(d)   in respect of a child aged seven or over, that provided by a child care provider approved by Ofsted or exempt organisations such as school breakfast clubs, after-school clubs and school holiday clubs.

Relevant child care charges are calculated on an average weekly charge basis in accordance with reg 15. The annual amount of the element therefore depends on whether the charges are paid weekly or monthly and whether the amount fluctuates over a year. So if charges are incurred every week for the same amount, simply multiply by 52. If charges are incurred weekly but vary over time, add together the charges in the 52 weeks before the claim and divide by 52. If charges are not incurred every week, simply add those together that are incurred in the year and divide by 52. For example, where a child attends an after-school club, he will do so during term time only (in the region of 40 weeks). If charges are paid monthly for a fixed monthly amount, multiply that amount by 12 and divide the result by 52. If charges are for variable monthly amounts, aggregate the charges for the previous 12 months and divide the total by 52.

Examples

(1)   Amanda pays £50 a week for relevant child care during the school terms (40 weeks). She incurs no relevant charges during school holidays. Her average weekly child care costs are £50 multiplied by 40 divided by 52 = £38.46.

(2)   Brian pays £40 a week relevant child care costs during school terms (40 weeks) and during school holidays (12 weeks) he pays £140 a week. His average weekly child care costs are £40 multiplied by 40 (£1,600) plus £140 multiplied by 12 (£1,680) = £3,280 divided by 52 = £63.08.

(3)   Claire has paid relevant child care costs over the last 12 months as follows: April, £190; May, October and December, £210; July and August, £290; the other six months at £170. Her average weekly costs are £190 plus £210 multiplied by 3 (£630) plus £290 multiplied by 2 (£580) plus £170 multiplied by 6 (£1,020) = £2,420 divided by 52 = £46.54.

If the claimant's average relevant weekly child care costs fall or rise by £10 or more a week, he should inform HMRC.

If the claimant is entitled to the child care element, it will be paid at the rate of 80% (ie 80 pence for every £1 actually paid) but limited to a maximum, namely:

(a)   £175 per week, where the claimant's family includes only one child in respect of whom relevant child care charges are paid; and

(b)   £300 per week where the claimant's family includes more than one child in respect of whom relevant child care charges are paid.

This means that the most a claimant can receive for this element is £140 for one child or £240 for two or more children for any week that relevant child care costs are actually incurred.

To summarise, the key questions to answer are as follows:

(a)   Are relevant child care costs being incurred? If so, go to question (b).

(b)   What is the average weekly charge? Work out the annual charge if the costs are not incurred for all 52 weeks in the year. Ascertain these figures and go to question (c).

(c)   Does the average weekly charge incurred exceed the maximum? If not, go to question (d). If so, go to question (e).

(d)   What is the annual allowable child care element (ascertain it by multiplying the annual charges incurred by 80%).

(e)   What is the annual allowable child care element (ascertain it by multiplying the maximum annual charges incurred by 80%).

See the worked example at **9.13.3**.

In what circumstances is the member of a joint claim said to be 'incapacitated'? This is where:

(a)   HB or CTB is payable to the claimant or partner and the applicable amount includes a disability premium or a higher pensioner premium by virtue of incapacity; or

(b)   CESA is payable to that person; or

(c)   attendance allowance (at any rate of pay) or DLA (either component at any rate of pay) is payable to that person; or

(d)   industrial disablement benefit with constant attendance allowance (at any rate of pay) is payable to that person.

9.10.2.6   A severe disability element

By reg 17, the determination of the maximum rate must include the severe disability element if the claimant, or, in the case of a joint claim, one of the claimants receives disability living allowance care component payable at the highest rate, or attendance allowance payable at the higher rate.

Note that if both members of a couple satisfy a condition then two severe disability elements are payable.

9.10.2.7   A 50-plus element

By reg 18, the determination of the maximum rate must include the 50-plus element if:

(a)   in the case of a single claim, the claimant satisfies para (3); or

(b)   in the case of a joint claim, at least one of the claimants satisfies that paragraph.

A claimant satisfies para (3) if:

(a)   he is aged at least 50;

(b)   he started work within the preceding three months; and

(c)   he undertakes qualifying remunerative work for at least 16 hours per week; and

(d)   he satisfies any of the conditions set out in paras (4) or (6) or (7) or (8).

The condition in para (4) is that for a period of at least six months immediately before his starting work for consecutive periods, amounting in the aggregate to at least six months, the last of which ends immediately before his starting work, para (5) is satisfied.

Paragraph (5) is satisfied while the claimant is receiving:

(a)   IS; or

(b)   a JSA; or

(c)   CESA.

Examples
(1)   Ethel is 52 years of age. For the last year she has received income support. Today she takes up a full-time job of 25 hours a week.

(2)   Sam is 53 years of age. Over the last twelve months he has received three months' worth of CESA and six months' worth of CBJSA. For the last two months he has received IBJSA. He is about to take up full-time work of 30 hours a week.

The condition under para (6) is that for at least six months immediately prior to his starting work, another person was receiving an increase in IS, IRESA or JSA in respect of the claimant, as a dependant of the other person.

The condition under para (7) is that for at least six months immediately prior to his starting work he satisfied the conditions entitling him to be credited with National Insurance contributions or earnings (see **2.2.5**).

The condition under para (8) is that:

(a)   for a period immediately prior to his starting work another person was receiving an increase in their IS, IRESA or JSA in respect of the claimant, as a dependant of the other person; and

(b)   for a period immediately before this, the claimant or any partner was receiving carer's allowance, bereavement allowance, or widowed parent's allowance; and

(c)   these two periods add up to at least six months.

Note that this element is only payable for a 12-month period starting from when the claimant returns to work. It can be paid for one continuous period of 12 months; or for periods amounting in aggregate to 12 months if the gap between any consecutive pair of those periods is not more than 26 weeks.

The rate of pay of this element depends on the amount of qualifying remunerative work undertaken. It is paid at a lower rate if the work is for 16 to 29 hours a week but at a higher rate where the work is for 30 hours or more a week. As to the latter, a 30-hour element (see **9.10.2.2**) will also be payable.

If joint claimants each meet the qualifying criteria, then two 50-plus elements are payable at the appropriate rate.

9.10.3   The annual amount of each element

For 2008/09 the rate of each element was as follows:

Basic element: £1,800

Disability element: £2,405

30-hour element: £735

Second adult element: £1,770

Lone parent element: £1,770

Severe disability element: £1,020

50-plus element: £1,235 if any claimant normally undertakes qualifying remunerative work of at least 16 hours but less than 30 hours per week but £1,840 if any claimant normally undertakes qualifying remunerative work of at least 30 hours per week.

9.10.4   Examples of maximum working tax credit

(1)   Arthur, aged 52 and his partner, Belinda, aged 47, both work 35 hours a week. Arthur started his job one month ago. Immediately before that he received contribution-based JSA for six months. Their maximum working tax credit will include the following annual elements:

(a)   basic element;

(b)   second adult element (although Arthur is over 50 and eligible for the 50-plus element he and indeed Belinda are working for at least 30 hours a week);

(c)   30-hour element (only one such element is payable even though both are working at least 30 hours a week);

(d)   50-plus element at the higher rate (Arthur is over 50, started full-time work of at least 16 hours a week work in the last three months and immediately before that received jobseeker's allowance for at least six months. It is paid at the higher rate as he is working for at least 30 hours a week).

(2)   Viv is aged 26. She is a single parent. Her daughter is aged eight. She pays £10 a week for her daughter to attend the school's breakfast club on the mornings that she works. Viv works 25 hours a week. Viv receives disability living allowance mobility component at the lower rate. When standing she cannot keep her balance and continually holds onto something. Her maximum working tax credit will include the following annual elements:

(a)   basic element;

(b)   disability element (she is working at least 16 hours a week, she has a disability that puts her at a disadvantage in getting a job and she receives disability living allowance);

(c)   lone parent element (she is a single parent);

(d)   child care charges (more details are needed to work out the annual element).

Note that since Viv is responsible for a child, she may also qualify for child tax credit (see **9.8**).

9.10.5   Will the maximum working tax credit be paid?

The maximum credit will be paid only if the claimant's income (see **9.7.3**) does not exceed the annual threshold. For 2008/09 that was £6,420.

If the claimant's income is *the same as or less* than the income threshold, the maximum working tax credit is payable.

If the claimant's income is more than the income threshold, the maximum working tax credit is not payable. Instead, it will be tapered, that is reduced, by 39% of the excess income (see further **9.11**).

Note that the different elements are tapered away in a set order. First, reduce all the elements apart from any child care element. Only if that reduces those elements to nil must you then reduce the child care element. See the examples at **9.13**.

9.11 Tapering when entitled to both credits

As we saw at **9.8.5** and **9.10.5**, when calculating entitlement to either tax credit, you apply the appropriate annual income threshold.

If the annual income exceeds the threshold, the maximum credit must be reduced by 39% of the excess.

Where a claimant is entitled to both credits, the different elements are tapered away in the following set order:

(a)   first, reduce all the elements of working tax credit, apart from any child care element;

(b)   secondly, reduce any child care element of working tax credit;

(c)   thirdly, reduce the child elements of child tax credit;

(d)   finally, note that the family element of child tax credit is not reduced unless the claimant has an annual income in excess of £50,000. If so, the family element is reduced by 6.67% of the excess (namely at the rate of £1 for every £15 of income exceeding £50,000).

Example:

Assume a claimant qualifies for both tax credits but as he has a high income all elements, apart from the family element, have been reduced to nil. If his income were say £55,000pa then his family element would have to be reduced by £333.50 (ie £5,000 × 6.67%).

See further the worked examples at **9.13**.

9.12 Calculating working tax credit: a summary of the steps

Step 1: calculate the maximum working tax credit.

Step 2: calculate relevant income (see **9.7.3**).

Step 3: compare income with the annual threshold (see **9.10.5**).

Step 4: if the claimant's income is the same or less than the income threshold, the maximum working tax credit is payable.

If the claimant's income is more than the income threshold, the maximum working tax credit is not payable. Instead, it will be tapered, that is reduced, by 39% of the excess income (see the worked examples at **9.13**).

9.13 Tax credits: worked examples

9.13.1 Claimant entitled to child tax credit only

Jan, aged 20, is a single parent. She has two children, Amanda, aged 9 months and Keith aged 3 years. She receives DLA care component at the middle rate for Keith. Jan is receiving IS and as a result she is entitled to maximum child tax credit. This will consist of the following annual elements.

Family: £1,090 (as she is responsible for a child under 1 year of age).
Child element for Amanda: £2,085.
Disabled child element for Keith: £4,625 (as he is in receipt of DLA).
Total: £7,800pa or £150 per week.

9.13.2 Claimant entitled to working tax credit only

Elizabeth, aged 25, works 35 hours a week. She earned £8,000 gross in the last tax year. Her partner, Lionel, aged 35 has been permanently disabled for the last year. He receives CESA (of which he is in the work-related activity group) of £4,394 per annum. He also receives DLA care component at the middle rate and DLA mobility component at the lower rate. The couple received interest on their building society account for the last tax year of £37.

Step 1: maximum working tax credit

This will consist of the following annual elements:

> Basic element: £1,800.
> 30-hour element: £735.
> Second adult element: £1,770.
> Total: £4,305.

Step 2: income from all relevant sources

As the investment income (£37 interest on savings) does not exceed £300, it is ignored.

Elizabeth's employment income is £8,000.

Lionel's CESA is social security income of £4,394.

Total: £12,394.

Lionel's DLA does not count.

Step 3: compare income with annual threshold

> Income: £12,394
> Threshold: £6,420
> Excess: £5,974.

As income exceeds annual threshold, proceed to Step 4.

Step 4: reduce maximum by excess

Maximum credit must be reduced by 39% of the excess, namely:

> £5,974 × 39% = £2,329.86

> Maximum credit: £4,305
> Less tapered excess: £2,329.86
> Credit payable is: £1,975.14 or £37.98 per week.

9.13.3 Claimant entitled to child tax credit and working tax credit

Gareth is aged 35. He is a single parent. His wife died two years ago. For the last tax year he received weekly widowed parent's allowance of £90.70 or £4,716.40 a year and child benefit. His son, Jack, is aged 9. Ever since his wife died, Gareth pays £60 a week for Jack to attend the after-school club. He attends each school week, totalling 40 weeks a year. Gareth is self-employed. His taxable profit for last year was £17,000. He has no savings and no other sources of income.

Step 1: maximum tax credits entitlement

Child tax credit:

His maximum child tax credit will include the following annual elements:

Family element: £545

Child element for Jack: £2,085.

Working tax credit:

As to the child care costs, let us answer the questions at **9.10.2.5**:

(a)　Are relevant child care costs being incurred by Gareth for his 9-year-old child, Jack? Yes, as Jack is over 7 and the care is at his after-school club.

(b)　What is the average weekly charge? He spends £60 for 40 weeks, ie £2,400 pa or £46.15 (£2,400 ÷ 52).

(c)　Does the average weekly charge exceed the maximum? The weekly amount of £46.15 does not exceed the maximum for one child of £175.

(d)　So we ascertain the annual allowable child care element by multiplying the allowable annual charge by 80%, ie £2,400 × 80% = £1,920.

His maximum working tax credit will include the following annual elements:

Basic element: £1,800

Lone parent element: £1,770

Child care charges: £1,920 (ie £60 × 40 × 80%)

Total maximum credits: £8,120

Step 2: income from all relevant sources

Pension income, ie widowed parent's allowance of £4,716.40 exceeds £300 and so the balance of £4,416.40 counts.

Employment income is £17,000.

Total: £21,416.40

Child benefit is ignored.

Step 3: compare income with annual threshold

Income: £21,416.40

Threshold: £6,420.00

Excess: £14,996.40.

As income exceeds annual threshold, proceed to Step 4.

Step 4: reduce maximum by excess

Maximum credit must be tapered by 39% of the excess, namely:

£14,996.40 × 39% = £5,848.60.

First, the elements of working tax credit apart from his child care costs must be reduced, ie £3,570 (basic element: £1,800 and lone parent element: £1,770) is reduced by the excess to nil. That leaves a tapered excess of £2,278.60 still to be made.

Secondly, the child care costs of £1,920 are reduced by the excess to nil. That leaves a tapered excess of £358.60 still to be made.

Thirdly, the child element of child tax credit of £2,085 is reduced by the remaining tapered excess of £358.60 to £1,726.40.

He will receive the family element in full.

So he will receive an annual child tax credit totalling £2,271.40 (or £43.68 per week). This is made up of £1,726.40 child element and £545 family element. His income is too large to receive any working tax credit.

9.14 The tax credits and other benefits

Child tax credit does not count as income when calculating IS, IRESA or IBJSA (see **7.3**) or pension credit (see **5.3**).

Child tax credit does count as income when calculating HB or CTB (see **9.2**).

Working tax credit counts as income when calculating IS, IRESA and IBJSA.

Whilst working tax credit counts as income when calculating HB and CTB there are two points to note. First, if any 30-hour element (see **9.10.2.2**) is payable, that is ignored. Secondly, if any child care costs (see **9.10.2.5**) are payable, these are ignored subject to a weekly maximum of £140 for one child or £240 for two or more children.

Working tax credit is taken into account when assessing eligibility for the pension credit, but it is ignored when calculating any savings credit.

Some non means-tested benefits are treated as income when calculating entitlement to a tax credit whilst others are not (see **9.7.4**).

9.15 Payment of tax credits

Payments of child tax credit are usually made each week or month, whichever is more convenient for the claimant. They are usually paid directly to the bank, building society or post office account of the child's main carer.

Payments of working tax credit are usually made each week or month, whichever is more convenient for the claimant, directly to his bank, building society or post office account. However, if the award includes a child care element, that part is paid directly to the main carer of the child.

9.16 The social fund

9.16.1 What is the social fund?

The social fund makes grants and loans to assist with expenses that are not covered by other means-tested benefits. It has two elements, the regulated social fund and the discretionary social fund.

9.16.2 The regulated social fund

The regulated social fund makes outright payments, as of right, to any claimant who satisfies the criteria. There is a right of appeal to an appeal tribunal against an adverse decision. The regulated social fund includes the sure start maternity grant (see **6.5**), funeral costs and cold weather payments.

9.16.3 Funeral payments

9.16.3.1 Who may claim?

A claimant may receive a funeral payment if:

(a) he is responsible for arranging a funeral to be held in the UK (or in certain cases an EEA State); and

(b)   he is in receipt of a 'qualifying benefit' (IS, IRESA, IBJSA, HB, CTB, child tax credit at the maximum rate or any rate greater than the appropriate family element, working tax credit that includes a disability or severe disability element); and

(c)   it is reasonable for him to take responsibility for arranging the funeral because there is no closer relative of the deceased who could have taken responsibility and would not qualify for a social fund payment; and

(d)   he makes a claim within three months of the funeral taking place.

The resources of the person who has died are largely irrelevant.

Is the requirement that the funeral must be held in the UK (or in certain cases an EEA State) compatible with the ECHR? Yes, held the Court of Appeal in *Esfandiari v Secretary of State for Work and Pensions* [2006] EWCA Civ 282.

9.16.3.2   Amount of the payment

The maximum payment is made up of:

(a)   the necessary cost of a burial (including a burial plot) or cremation;

(b)   the cost of transporting the body to a funeral director's premises, if this is over 50 miles;

(c)   the cost of a hearse and one car for mourners on the day of the funeral;

(d)   the cost of one return journey for the responsible person to arrange or attend the funeral; and

(e)   a maximum of £600 for all other expenses.

This low limit is well below the typical cost of a funeral. It creates problems if the claimant does not know about it before contracting with the funeral director. Most appeals to tribunals about the social fund are trying to get more money to meet a funeral bill, but they are usually doomed to failure.

9.16.3.3   Resources taken into account

The payment is reduced by:

(a)   any assets of the deceased which are readily accessible without probate;

(b)   payments from pre-paid funeral plans.

The costs of a funeral are the first charge on the estate of anyone who has died. The social fund has first charge on any assets that only become available after probate, to recoup the payment.

9.16.4   Cold weather payments

Cold weather payments are paid as an automatic addition to IS, IRESA or IBJSA if:

(a)   the claimant has a child under the age of five; or

(b)   the claimant's applicable amount includes any of the disability or pensioner premiums, including the disabled child premium; and, in either case

(c)   a 'period of cold weather' has been forecast or recorded in his home area.

9.16.4.1   Period of cold weather

A period of cold weather is a period of seven or more consecutive days when the average daily temperature is recorded as freezing (0° Celsius) or below. Weather records are collated at 72 centres across the country to allow for local variations in temperature. It is unusual for cold weather payments to cause problems.

9.16.4.2   Winter fuel payments

In recent winters, the Government has announced one-off additional payments to help with winter heating bills for all people on income support, and pensioners. This scheme is not part of the social fund and is dealt with on a year-by-year basis.

9.16.5   The discretionary social fund

Payments from the discretionary social fund are indeed discretionary, which means that there is no right of appeal against refusal. Claimants may always ask for a review, especially if it appears that there is evidence to support the application which has been overlooked. The details of the administration of this fund are not in legislation but Social Fund Directions (SFD). These directions define the circumstances in which social fund payments may be made, but leave it to the discretion of the Department whether to make a payment in any case.

There are two forms of social fund payments, grants and loans. Grants are outright payments which are not repayable. Loans are repayable, by weekly deduction from other benefits. A loan may be refused if it is unlikely that the claimant will be able to repay it. This could be because of the amount borrowed, or because of other deductions from benefit (see **7.13**).

9.16.5.1   Community care grants (SFD 25–29)

To be eligible for a community care grant, the claimant must be in receipt of IS, IRESA or IBJSA and need the grant for one of the following reasons:

(a)   to re-establish himself in the community after a long spell in institutional or residential care. This includes prisons, youth custody, hospitals, residential care homes and special schools. These grants would include help with the costs of removals, essential furniture and clothing;

(b)   to enable him to live in the community without having to go into residential care. The commonest use for these grants is to make alterations to a disabled claimant's home, or buy him aids to make life easier;

(c)   to ease 'exceptional pressure on families'. This includes helping people to move away from or otherwise cope with the breakdown of a non-marital relationship (especially if there is domestic violence), or the stresses of caring for a very seriously disabled or disturbed family member;

(d)   to pay some travelling costs, for example to visit relatives in hospital or attend a family funeral.

The claim must be for at least £30, except for the travelling costs which have no lower limit. Capital of £500 or more reduces the payment pound for pound.

9.16.5.2   Budgeting loans (SFD 1 and 8–12)

A claimant receiving IS, IRESA or IBJSA is supposed to be able to put aside small sums regularly for predictable future bills. But a claimant may face the need to make a large payment for which it would not be reasonable to expect him to budget in this way. This could include essential items of furniture, essential household repairs and maintenance, and purchase of fuel such as oil or coal, which has to be bought in bulk. A budgeting loan is one way of meeting such payments.

To qualify for a loan, the claimant must have been in receipt of IS, IRESA or IBJSA for at least 26 weeks. The maximum loan is £1,000, but the DfWP may be unwilling to lend so much because claimants may have difficulty in repaying it.

9.16.5.3   Crisis loans (SFD 14–23)

Crisis loans may be paid to someone who has suffered a crisis or disaster, has no resources to meet his immediate needs and is facing the serious risk of damage to his health or safety. A domestic flood or fire will always qualify, as will being penniless while waiting for first wages from a new job, or being stranded away from home with no money and no transport.

A second form of crisis loan may be made to a person who is receiving a community care grant, to help him pay rent in advance to a private landlord (advance rent is not covered by HB).

9.17   Passport benefits

9.17.1   What are passport benefits?

The term 'passport benefits' is used to describe a collection of more or less means-tested benefits which are outside the social security system. Most of them are connected with the National Health Service and are collectively called 'NHS benefits'. The word 'passport' is used because a person who is receiving some of the main means-tested benefits is often automatically entitled to the NHS benefits. In other words, the social security benefit is a passport to them, just as it may be to CTB or HB (see **9.17.2**).

9.17.2   Who is entitled to NHS benefits?

Although the rules of entitlement vary with the benefits, there are four main qualifying groups of people who will be entitled to most of them.

(a) Anyone who is receiving IS, IRESA or IBJSA or if the claimant's gross annual income is no more than £14,200 and he receives child tax credit only or both tax credits or working tax credit only but with a disability element, and any member of their families.

(b) Other people on low incomes, subject to undergoing a means test.

(c) Children under 16, and anyone under 19 who is in full-time education.

(d) War pensioners disabled as a result of military service (including peace-time service), if they need the benefit because of their disability.

For the rest of this section, these four groups will be described as 'the qualifying groups'.

9.17.3   The benefits and those entitled to them

9.17.3.1   Free prescriptions

All the qualifying groups are exempt from paying prescription charges, as are the following:

(a) hospital in-patients;

(b) women who are pregnant or have had a baby within the last 12 months;

(c) some people with chronic illnesses, or who are so disabled that they cannot leave the house alone; and

(d) any person of State Pension age.

A person who wishes to claim free prescriptions from a chemist will have to produce evidence of his entitlement.

9.17.3.2   Free dental treatment

Members of all the qualifying groups are entitled to free dental treatment and dentures, as are women who are pregnant or have had a baby in the last 12 months. In addition, anyone under 18 is entitled to free treatment only. People whose income is low, but not low enough to have free treatment, may be entitled to reduced charges.

These rights may be difficult to enforce. They apply only to dentists who work for the National Health Service, who can be hard to find.

9.17.3.3   Sight tests and glasses

Members of the qualifying groups are entitled to free sight tests, as are the following:

(a)   anyone registered blind or partially sighted;

(b)   anyone aged 60 or over;

(c)   anyone suffering from diabetes or glaucoma, and anyone aged at least 40 who has a close relative with glaucoma; and

(d)   anyone who has in the past needed exceptionally complex lenses (this does not mean bifocals or varifocals).

The prescribing oculist who carries out the examination will issue a voucher to cover some or all of the cost of glasses or contact lenses if the patient:

(a)   is in one of the qualifying groups; or

(b)   needs frequent changes of prescription; or

(c)   needs particularly complex lenses; and, in any case

(d)   there is a reason why new glasses are needed, for example because the prescription has changed, the patient has not needed glasses before, the glasses have worn out, or (exceptionally) the glasses have been lost or damaged.

9.17.3.4   Fares to hospital

Members of all the qualifying groups except the fourth may be entitled to help from the hospital with the cost of transport to and from hospital. This usually means public transport or private car, and covers only the patient's costs, although taxi fares and the cost of a companion may be allowed, where appropriate.

War pensioners do not need this benefit, as there is a parallel provision within the war pensions system.

9.17.4   Free milk and school meals

9.17.4.1   Free milk and vitamins

Free tokens to buy one pint of milk per day, for each qualifying person, are given to:

(a)   children who are too disabled to go to school; and

(b)   pregnant women and children under five in families receiving IS, IRESA or IBJSA.

Pregnant and nursing women and children under five in families receiving IS, IRESA or IBJSA are also entitled to free vitamin tablets or drops.

Free milk and vitamins are also available to children under five who are members of a family of someone who receives child tax credit and has an annual taxable income of no more than £14,495.

Any person who is attending a maternity or childcare clinic is entitled to buy dried milk and vitamins at reduced prices.

9.17.4.2 Free school meals

All State schools must provide children with a midday meal, though it need not be suitable as the main meal of the day. They must generally charge for the meals, but must provide them free to children from families in receipt of IS, IRESA or IBJSA only. This can be a valuable right to a family with several children of school age.

9.18 Claimant profiles

9.18.1 Housing benefit

This is payable to a claimant liable to pay rent for his home and who is on a low income with a limited amount of capital.

9.18.2 Council tax benefit

This is payable to a claimant liable to pay council tax and who is on a low income with a limited amount of capital.

9.18.3 Child tax credit

This is payable to a claimant responsible for a child or qualifying young person and who is on a low income.

9.18.4 Working tax credit

This is payable to a claimant who is in qualifying remunerative work but on a low income. Only four types of claimants may be in qualifying remunerative work, namely:

(a)   working at least 16 hours a week and responsible for a child or qualifying young person; or

(b)   working at least 16 hours a week, entitled to the disability element and with a prescribed job market disadvantage; or

(c)   aged at least 50, working at least 16 hours a week and entitled to the 50-plus element; or

(d)   aged at least 25 and working at least 30 hours a week.

Chapter 10
Immigration Tests for Welfare Benefits

10.1 The scope of this chapter

So far, we have been considering the basic rules of entitlement to benefit only as they apply to people who have been living and working in Great Britain for several years. We have not considered the rules relating to residence and presence in Great Britain, and their effect on people who have only recently come into the country. Neither have we considered what benefit rights can be taken or acquired abroad. This chapter is concerned with those rules, which form an area of overlap between the law of welfare benefits and immigration law. As to the latter, see *Immigration Law*.

For most benefits, entitlement is directly linked to the claimant's nationality and immigration status within the UK generally, and Great Britain specifically (ie England, Scotland and Wales). The reason for this focus on Great Britain is that, as we saw at **1.3**, welfare law is the law of Great Britain. This contrasts with immigration law, which is the law of the UK as a whole (ie including Northern Ireland).

In order to decide on a claimant's entitlement to benefits, it is necessary to have a good understanding of immigration law. All potential sources of entitlement need to be considered. Two key questions should be asked: first, does the claimant's immigration status disqualify him from a benefit; and secondly, are any residence requirements met? The claimant's nationality and current immigration status are always good starting points from which to analyse his rights in welfare law.

10.2 Potential sources of entitlement to benefits in Great Britain

10.2.1 Introduction

A person who has recently arrived in the UK may have rights to welfare benefits arising from several different sources. Some of these rights run in parallel, while others may confer rights completely independent of any other source of rights.

The sources of rights are:

(a)   domestic legislation, covering Great Britain alone or including the rest of the UK;

(b)   EC legislation and international conventions to which the UK is a signatory;

(c)   reciprocal agreements between the British Government and governments of other countries (see **10.2.2**);

(d)   the law of the country from which the claimant has arrived.

Of these, the last is outside the scope of this book.

10.2.2   Reciprocal agreements

The governments of several countries have entered into reciprocal agreements with the UK Government, for the payment of social security benefits. By these agreements the nationals of the other countries may be able to claim a benefit, whilst living in the reciprocal agreement country, from that country's government. In some circumstances an agreement may help a UK national continue to receive a benefit whilst living in the reciprocal agreement country. In limited circumstances an agreement may provide that presence and residence in a reciprocal agreement country constitutes such in Great Britain for the purposes of claiming the benefit here.

The countries with which the UK Government has reciprocal agreements are Barbados, Bermuda, Bosnia-Herzegovina, Canada, Croatia, Guernsey, Isle of Man, Israel, Jamaica, Jersey, Macedonia, Mauritius, New Zealand, The Philippines, Serbia and Montenegro, Turkey and the USA.

The scope of the agreements varies widely and should always be checked carefully. Benefit coverage is outlined in a chart at **Appendix 6** to this book. However, the following features are common:

(a)   means-tested benefits are always excluded;

(b)   benefits for the unemployed can never be claimed outside the country where contributions were paid;

(c)   retirement and bereavement benefits are always covered in some way.

Rights to benefits for sickness, disability and children are variable. The DfWP has a range of leaflets which explain the agreements.

Example

(1)   Bob is entitled to State Pension. He decides to go and live permanently in Barbados. Under UK law his pension would be frozen at the rate paid when he left the UK. However, under the provisions of the UK–Barbados agreement, it will not be frozen.

(2)   Claire is entitled to CBJSA. If she is absent from the UK in the Isle of Man, it can still be paid to her under that agreement. In respect of the other agreements that cover CBJSA, periods of residence in the reciprocal agreement country by a UK national only count as periods for which National Insurance contributions are deemed to be paid.

There are also reciprocal agreements with most EEA countries (and Switzerland). However, a member of an EEA Member State will be able to rely on a reciprocal agreement only if he has no rights to benefit in EC law. Whether he has will depend in part upon his reasons for going to another Member State and the date upon which his rights arose.

10.2.3 Contributory benefits and the EC

Contributory benefits are not affected by a claimant's immigration status.

The right of free movement of labour, under Article 39 EC, would be of reduced value if citizens of Member States had to start afresh to build up contribution records every time they exercised this right. EC law requires the mutual recognition of NICs, so that a claimant can use contributions paid in one Member State to help satisfy the contribution conditions for a benefit claimed in another.

The basic principle is that the claimant must claim the benefit of the Member State in which he last worked and paid NICs, and comply with the laws of that State. There is an exception if the claimant remained 'resident' in one State while working in another. This will only happen if his work was of a temporary nature, whether as an employee or self-employed.

> #### Example 1
> Dieter has just arrived in Great Britain for the first time from Germany, where he has paid contributions for six years. He has no work. Can he claim CBJSA?
>
> No. He last paid contributions in Germany, so can only claim German unemployment benefits. But they can be paid to him in Great Britain.
>
> #### Example 2
> Marie-Claire has been working in London for six months, paying Class 1 contributions. Before that she lived and worked for many years in Brussels. She has just been made redundant. Can she claim contribution-based JSA?
>
> Yes. She last paid contributions in Great Britain. She can use contributions paid in Belgium to help her qualify for CBJSA.
>
> #### Example 3
> Sai-ling has just returned home to Edinburgh after spending three months in Seville learning Spanish and doing various temporary jobs for which she paid contributions. She broke her arm the day after she got back. Can she claim CESA?
>
> Provided she has the necessary contribution record, yes. She last paid contributions in Spain, but the nature of her work was not such as to prevent her from remaining resident in Great Britain during her absence.

10.3 Immigration status and entitlement to certain non-contributory benefits in Great Britain

10.3.1 The general s 115 exclusionary rule

A person to whom s 115(1) of the Immigration and Asylum Act 1999 (IAA 1999) applies is not entitled to:

(a)   income-based jobseeker's allowance;

(b)   attendance allowance;

(c)   carer's allowance;

(d)   disability living allowance;

(e)   income support or IRESA;

(f)   working tax credit;

(g)   child tax credit;

(h)   a social fund payment;

(i)   child benefit;

(j)   housing benefit;

(k)   council tax benefit;

(l)   State pension credit,

while he is a person to whom this section applies.

Subsection (3) of s 115 provides that:

> This section applies to a *person subject to immigration control* unless he falls within such category or description, or satisfies such conditions, as may be prescribed. (emphasis added)

Regulations under s 115(3) may provide for a person to be treated for prescribed purposes only as not being a person to whom s 115 applies (see **10.3.2**).

Subsection (9) of s 115 defines 'a person subject to immigration control' as meaning:

> a person who is not a national of an EEA State and who—
>
> (a)   requires leave to enter or remain in the United Kingdom but does not have it [eg an illegal entrant or overstayer];
>
> (b)   has leave to enter or remain in the United Kingdom which is subject to a condition that he does not have recourse to public funds [see **10.8**];
>
> (c)   has leave to enter or remain in the United Kingdom given as a result of a maintenance undertaking [defined by subsection 10 as 'a written undertaking given by another person in pursuance of the immigration rules to be responsible for that person's maintenance and accommodation']; or
>
> (d)   has leave to enter or remain in the United Kingdom only because he has appealed a decision to vary or refuse to vary that leave [see **Chapter 16**].

10.3.2   Exceptions to the general s 115 exclusionary rule

The Social Security (Immigration and Asylum) Consequential Amendments Regulations 2000 (SS(I&A)CA Regs 2000) (SI 2000/636) provide that certain categories of persons are not treated as being subject to s 115. In respect of IBJSA, IS, IRESA, a social fund payment, HB and CTB, reg 2(1) provides that the following people are entitled to claim the benefit:

(a)   persons with limited leave whose funds from abroad have been temporarily interrupted provided there is a reasonable expectation that the supply of those funds will be resumed;

(b)   sponsored immigrants whose sponsor has died before completing five years residence;

(c)   sponsored immigrants who have been in the UK for at least five years, beginning on the date of entry or the date on which the undertaking was given, if later;

(d)   nationals of Turkey who are lawfully present in the UK.

By reg 2(2), the categories of persons entitled to claim AA, CA, DLA, a social fund payment and child benefit are:

(a)   a member of the family of a national of an EEA country (it is unclear who is covered by this provision given that family members of qualifying EEA nationals do not need leave to enter the UK and so cannot be excluded by s 115);

(b)   a person who is legally working and living in Great Britain and is a national of a State with which the EU has made an agreement relating to equal treatment (namely Turkey, Morocco, Algeria and Tunisia) and any members of their family living with them;

(c)   a sponsored immigrant regardless of the length of stay in the UK.

By reg 2(3), the categories of persons entitled to claim AA, DLA and child benefit are nationals of a country where there is a reciprocal agreement (see **10.2.2**) in force in respect of the benefit.

The Tax Credits (Immigration) Regulations 2003 (SI 2003/653) provide that no person is entitled to child tax credit or working tax credit while he is a person subject to immigration control, except in five prescribed cases. In summary these are:

> *Case 1:* (a) The claimant has been given leave to enter, or remain in, the UK upon the written undertaking of another person to be responsible for his maintenance and accommodation; and (b) he has been resident in the UK for a period of at least five years commencing on or after the date of his entry into the UK, or the date on which the undertaking was given in respect of him, whichever is the later.
>
> *Case 2:* The claimant is a person who falls within Case 1(a) and he has been resident in the UK for less than the five years mentioned in Case 1(b) but the person giving the undertaking has died.
>
> *Case 3:* The claimant has limited leave to enter or remain in the UK; his funds from abroad have been temporarily interrupted but there is a reasonable expectation that his supply of funds will be resumed. Note that the period (or aggregate of periods) for which this Case applies must not exceed 42 days during any single period of limited leave (including any extension to that period).
>
> *Case 4:* Where the claim is for working tax credit, that the claimant is a national of Turkey (see above) and he is lawfully present in the UK.
>
> *Case 5:* Where the claim is for child tax credit, that the claimant is a person who is lawfully working in the UK and a national of a State with which the EU has made an agreement relating to equal treatment and their family members (see above).

10.4 Residence requirements and entitlement to benefits in Great Britain and 'exporting' benefits

It is obvious from **10.3** that you must first check that a person is not excluded from a benefit due to his immigration status. However, even if a claim can be made it is then important to check that any residence requirements are met.

10.4.1 Attendance allowance, disability living allowance and carer's allowance

To qualify for any such benefit, the claimant must:

(a) be ordinarily resident (see **10.6**) in Great Britain; and

(b) be present in Great Britain; and

(c) have been present in Great Britain for a total of 26 weeks, in the last 12 months (unless claiming DLA or AA on the basis that he is terminally ill).

For AA and DLA, claimants who are absent from Great Britain on any day during the claim are treated as being present if the absence is for a temporary purpose and lasts no longer than 26 weeks; or the absence is for the specific purpose of being treated for a pre-existing incapacity or a disabling condition as certified by the Secretary of State.

For CA, claimants who are absent from Great Britain on any day during the claim are treated as being present if the absence is for a temporary purpose and lasts no longer than four weeks, or for an indefinite period if the temporary absence is for the specific purpose of caring for a severely disabled person who himself is absent from Great Britain.

UK law does not generally allow claimants to go abroad permanently to live and still receive such a benefit. The reciprocal agreements that cover the benefit do not help claimants to export it. However, in some circumstances a person being paid AA, DLA care component or CA may be able to continue to receive it on taking up residence in another EEA country: see *Commission of the European Communities v The European Parliament and the Council of the European Union* [2007] LTLEU, 18 October.

10.4.2 Child benefit

As a general rule, to qualify for this benefit:

(a)   the qualifying child or young person and claimant must be in Great Britain; and

(b)   the qualifying child or young person and claimant must be ordinarily resident (see **10.6**) in Great Britain; and

(c)   the qualifying child or young person and claimant must have a legal right to reside in the UK under either domestic or EC law.

As a general rule, a child or young person is treated as present if the absence is for a temporary purpose and lasts no longer than for 12 weeks; or, if longer, the child or young person is abroad receiving full-time education in an EEA State or Switzerland at a recognised educational establishment or for the purpose of treatment for a pre-existing illness or disability.

Claimants who are absent from Great Britain are treated as being present if the absence is for a temporary purpose and lasts no longer than for eight weeks.

Under EEA law, this benefit constitutes a 'family benefit or allowance'. The payment of such is generally the responsibility of the EEA country in which an employed or self-employed person is insured (or an unemployed person is drawing an unemployment benefit) even though the person's family may be living in another EEA country.

There are various reciprocal agreements which enable residence and/or presence in other countries to be treated for child benefit purposes as constituting such in Great Britain. The extent to which reciprocity exists varies, according to the particular agreement.

10.4.3 Working tax credit and child tax credit

By the Tax Credits (Residence) Regulations 2003 (SI 2003/654) (as amended), a claimant must be ordinarily resident (see **10.6**) in the UK and have a legal right to reside in the UK under either domestic or EC law.

Each tax credit can be paid during a period of absence from the UK of the claimant:

(a)   for up to eight weeks of any period of absence; or

(b)   for up to 12 weeks of any period of absence, provided that period of absence is in connection with:

(i)   the treatment of the claimant's illness or physical or mental disability;

(ii)   the treatment of his partner's illness or physical or mental disability;

(iii)   the death of a person who, immediately prior to the date of death, was his partner;

(iv)   the death, or the treatment of the illness or physical or mental disability, of a child or qualifying young person for whom either he or his partner is, or both of them are, responsible; or

(v)   the death, or the treatment of the illness or physical or mental disability, of his or his partner's brother, sister, ancestor or lineal descendant.

Note that a person is treated as temporarily absent from the UK only if at the beginning of the period of absence his absence was unlikely to exceed 52 weeks.

What if the claimant is eligible for tax credits but his partner is excluded by s 115? See **10.8.4**.

10.4.4   Income support, income-based jobseeker's allowance, housing benefit and council tax benefit

To qualify for any such benefit, the person must be, or must be treated as being, habitually resident (see **10.7**) in the Common Travel Area (see **10.5**). To be treated as habitually resident the claimant must have a legal right to reside in the UK under either domestic or EC law (see **10.7**).

For IS purposes, the benefit can usually be paid for the first four weeks of temporary absence. This is extended to eight weeks if the claimant is accompanying a qualifying child abroad for the purposes of medical treatment.

For JSA purposes, it is a fundamental condition of entitlement that the person is in Great Britain so as to be available for work. However, it can be paid during an absence from Great Britain:

(a)   for up to four weeks if the claimant has a partner who is either disabled, or aged 60 or over, and a premium (see **7.7**) is payable as a result;

(b)   for up to eight weeks (as for IS, above);

(c)   for up to seven days if the claimant is attending a job interview;

(d)   for up to three months if the claimant is looking for work in another EEA country.

For HB and CTB purposes, the benefit can be paid during a temporary absence of no longer than 13 weeks (or 52 weeks if the claimant is abroad for the purposes of medical treatment).

None of these benefits is within the scope of either EC law or any of the reciprocal agreements.

What if the claimant is eligible for IS or IBJSA but his partner is excluded by s 115? See **10.8.3**. As to HB or CTB for partners where one is excluded, see **10.8.4**.

10.4.5   Industrial disablement benefit

A claimant does not have to satisfy any residence conditions to claim the benefit. However, it may not be payable if the accident occurred or the prescribed disease was contracted outside Great Britain or the EEA.

If a person sustains an industrial accident or contracts a prescribed disease outside Great Britain or the EEA but, during his absence, he has paid Class 1 contributions (or Class 2 as a volunteer development worker), the benefit can be claimed on returning to Great Britain.

A claimant who sustains an industrial accident or contracts a prescribed disease in a country with a reciprocal agreement may qualify under the terms of that agreement.

A person is not disqualified from receiving the benefit whilst absent from Great Britain. It can usually be permanently exported to another EEA country or one with a reciprocal agreement.

10.4.6 Statutory sick pay and statutory maternity pay

There are no presence or residence requirements for these benefits, which can be continued to be paid whilst the claimant is abroad so long as the normal conditions of entitlement are met.

10.4.7 Employment and support allowance

Regulations 152 to 154 of the Employment and Support Allowance Regulations 2008 (SI 2008/794) provide that a claimant's entitlement to either or both types of ESA continues during a period of absence from Great Britain if:

(a)   it is unlikely to exceed 52 weeks; and

(b)   whilst absent the claimant continues to satisfy the other conditions of entitlement; and

(c)   it is for no longer than four weeks; or

(d)   it is for no longer than 26 weeks and solely–

    (i)   in connection with arrangements made for the treatment of the claimant for a disease or bodily or mental disablement directly related to the claimant's limited capability for work which commenced before leaving Great Britain, or

    (ii)   because the claimant is accompanying a dependent child in connection with arrangements made for the treatment of that child for a disease or bodily or mental disablement, and before leaving the claimant obtained the permission of the Secretary of State to do so.

There are similar provisions, but for an unlimited period of absence, to have NHS treatment outside Great Britain.

Note that, to satisfy the National Insurance conditions (see **Chapter 2**) for the contributory version of the benefit, the claimant may be able to rely on EC provisions (see **10.2**) or a reciprocal agreement with another country (see **10.2.2**).

What if the cliamant is eligible for IRESA but his partner is excluded by s 115? See **10.8.3**.

10.4.8 Non-contributory ESA for youths

Regulation 11 of the Employment and Support Allowance Regulations 2008 imposes residence and presence requirements for this version of ESA (see generally **3.3**), namely that the claimant:

(a)   is ordinarily resident in Great Britain; and

(b)   is present in Great Britain; and

(c)   has been present in Great Britain for a period of, or for periods amounting in aggregate to, not less than 26 weeks in the 52 weeks immediately preceding the claim; and

(d)   is not a person subject to immigration control within the meaning of s 115(9) of the IAA 1999. However, note that claimants who fall within the exception to s 115 by SS(I&A)CA Regs 2000, reg 2(2) (see **10.3.2**) can claim.

As to periods of absence from Great Britain, see **10.4.7**.

10.4.9 Contribution-based jobseeker's allowance

For JSA purposes, it is a fundamental condition of entitlement that the person is in Great Britain so as to be available for work. However, it can be paid during an absence from Great Britain:

(a)   for up to four weeks if the claimant has a partner who is either disabled, or aged 60 or over, and a premium (see **7.7**) is payable as a result;

(b)   for up to eight weeks if the claimant is accompanying a qualifying child abroad for the purposes of medical treatment;

(c)   for up to seven days if the claimant is attending a job interview;

(d)   for up to three months if the claimant is looking for work in another EEA country.

In addition, as a general rule, a person remains entitled to the benefit whilst absent from Great Britain in another EEA country for up to three months, provided he has registered with the employment services of that country within seven days.

Note that, to satisfy the National Insurance conditions for CBJSA (see **Chapter 2**), the claimant may be able to rely on EC provisions (see **10.2.3**). However, any reciprocal agreement with another country cannot affect the entitlement to British CBJSA as it is a benefit for the unemployed (see **10.2.2**).

10.5 Northern Ireland and the Common Travel Area

We have already noted that the law of social security is the law of Great Britain. What is the position of a person who arrives in Great Britain from Northern Ireland or the Common Travel Area (this consists of the UK, the Republic of Ireland, the Channel Islands and the Isle of Man)? The answer depends more on the type of benefit being claimed than the place of origin of the claimant.

10.5.1 Means-tested benefits

If the claimant has been habitually resident within any part of the UK or the Common Travel Area, and is not a person subject to immigration control under s 115 of the IAA 1999, he can claim means-tested benefits on the same basis as any British resident who has no restrictions on his leave to be in the UK.

10.5.2 Contributory benefits

(a)   Contributions paid by a person from Northern Ireland can be used to claim any contributory benefit in Great Britain, including CBJSA.

(b)   People from the Channel Islands and the Isle of Man depend on reciprocal agreements which effectively give them full rights to claim all British benefits except CBJSA, relying on their contribution records at home.

(c)   Citizens of the Republic of Ireland can rely on EC law rights (see **10.2.3**).

Note that the Channel Islands and the Isle of Man have an anomalous status within the UK; their citizens are British citizens but not EU nationals, as these islands do not belong to the EU. People from the islands therefore do not have special rights in EC law.

10.5.3 Non-contributory, non means-tested benefits

A combination of EC law, domestic British law and the reciprocal agreements between them gives people from Northern Ireland and the Common Travel Area the same right to non-contributory, non means-tested benefits as British residents.

10.6   Ordinarily resident

The words 'ordinary residence' were considered by the House of Lords in two tax cases reported in 1928. In each, the House sought the natural and ordinary meaning of the words. In *Levene v Inland Revenue Commissioners* [1928] AC 217 at 225, Viscount Cave LC said, 'I think that [ordinary residence] connotes residence in a place with some degree of continuity and apart from accidental or temporary absences'. In *Inland Revenue Commissioners v Lysaght* [1928] AC 234 at 243, Viscount Sumner said, 'I think the converse to "ordinarily" is "extraordinarily" and that part of the regular order of a man's life, adopted voluntarily and for settled purposes, is not "extraordinary"'.

In *R v Barnet London Borough Council, ex p Shah* [1983] 2 WLR 16, Lord Scarman said (at 28):

> There are two, and no more than two, respects in which the mind of the [claimant] is important in determining ordinary residence. The residence must be voluntarily adopted. Enforced presence by reason of kidnapping or imprisonment, or a Robinson Crusoe existence on a desert island with no opportunity of escape, may be so overwhelming a factor as to negative the will to be where one is. And there must be a degree of settled purpose. The purpose may be one; or there may be several. It may be specific or general. All the law requires is that there is a settled purpose. This is not to say that the [claimant] intends to stay where he is indefinitely; indeed his purpose, while settled, may be for a limited period. Education, business or profession, employment, health, family, or merely love of the place spring to mind as common reasons for a choice of regular abode. And there may well be many others. All that is necessary is that the purpose of living where one does has a sufficient degree of continuity to be properly described as settled.

10.7   Habitual residence

10.7.1   The test

For IS, IRESA, IBJSA, HB and CTB, the test is 'habitual residence'. The question is whether the claimant is habitually resident within the Common Travel Area, not just Great Britain or even the UK. This extension to the rest of the Common Travel Area means that residents of the Republic of Ireland, the Channel Islands and the Isle of Man can claim these benefits on the same basis as British residents.

The habitual residence test is itself made up of three tests, namely:

(a)   that the UK is the claimant's so-called 'centre of interest';

(b)   that residence has been for an appreciable period of time with a settled intent; and

(c)   that the claimant has a right to reside in the UK under domestic or EC law.

10.7.1.1   Centre of interest

'Habitual residence' is more than just 'residence'; it is a complex question of fact. It is often paraphrased as indicating the claimant's 'centre of interest'. The DfWP's standard questionnaire for recent arrivals includes the following:

(a)   Does the claimant have another home elsewhere?

(b)   Where are the members of his immediate family living?

(c)   Where are his personal possessions?

(d)   Does he have a bank account, utility accounts and so on within Great Britain?

(e)   Community ties: is he registered with a local doctor? Where do his children go to school? Does he belong to a local church/mosque/temple?

(f)   How is he proposing to support himself?

The DfWP *Decision Maker's Guide* says:

> People who maintain their centre of interest in the United Kingdom, for example a home, a job, friends, membership of clubs, are likely to be habitually resident in the United Kingdom. People who have retained their centre of interest in another country and have no particular ties here are unlikely to be habitually resident in the United Kingdom.

In *Commissioner's Decision CIS 12703/96*, the claimant arrived from Bangladesh. She had never been in the UK before and was living with relatives. One factor taken into account was, as Commissioner Henty stated, 'her husband and children, to be presumed to be her centre of interest, remained resident in Bangladesh'.

10.7.1.2   Appreciable period and settled intent

Lord Brandon in *Re J (A Minor) (Abduction: Custody Rights)* [1990] 2 AC 562 at 578–9 said:

> It follows, I think, that the expression [habitually resident] is not to be treated as a term of art with some special meaning, but as rather to be understood according to the ordinary natural meaning of the two words which it contained. The second point is that the question whether a person is or is not habitually resident in a specified country is a question of fact to be decided by reference to all the circumstances of any particular case. The third point is that there is a significant difference between a person ceasing to be habitually resident in country A, and his subsequently becoming habitually resident in country B. A person may cease to be habitually resident in country A in a single day if he or she leaves it with a settled intention not to return to it but to take up long-term residence in country B instead. Such a person cannot, however, become habitually resident in country B in a single day. An appreciable period of time and a settled intention will be necessary to enable him or her to become so. During that appreciable period of time the person will have ceased to be habitually resident in country A but not yet have become habitually resident in country B.

10.7.1.3   The right to reside test

The Social Security (Persons from Abroad) Amendment Regulations 2006 (SI 2006/1026) provide that no person is treated as habitually resident in the Common Travel Area unless he has a right to reside in the UK under domestic or EC law. As to the latter, see **10.7.2**.

10.7.2   EEA nationals and their family members

An EEA national and his family members are entitled to reside in the UK for a period not exceeding three months, where the only condition is that the EEA national and any family member must not become an unreasonable burden on the social assistance system of the UK. This includes economically inactive people, who are not required to be self-sufficient during this period, but the United Kingdom Border Agency ('UKBA') guidance is that claimants who have a right to reside solely on this basis will not satisfy the right to reside aspect of the habitual residence test (see **10.7.1.3**).

After three months, an EEA national and his family members may reside in the UK if the EEA national is a qualified person. EEA workers and self-employed persons satisfy the right to reside test. What about the other categories?

Guidance from UKBA is that those EEA jobseekers who have registered with Jobcentre Plus and have claimed JSA will have a right to reside for an initial period of six months, and for longer if they are genuinely seeking work and have a reasonable chance of securing employment.

The UKBA also state that an EEA national who has the right to reside as a jobseeker will not satisfy the right to reside aspect of the habitual residence test for IS. Such a right to reside will satisfy the test for IBJSA.

It is therefore vital to be able to identify whether an EEA national is a worker or a jobseeker. Regulation 6(2) of the Immigration (EEA) Regulations 2006 (SI 2006/1003) (see *Immigration Law*) provides that an EEA national who has worked in the UK but has ceased working, may in certain limited circumstances still be treated as a worker, for example if he is temporarily unable to work due to illness or accident.

Those EEA nationals who are in the UK as students or self-sufficient persons have a right to reside. However, they risk losing their right of residence if they become an unreasonable burden on the social assistance system of the UK.

The above was confirmed by the Court of Appeal in *Abdirahman and Ullusow v Secretary of State for Work and Pensions* [2007] EWCA Civ 657. As neither EEA national claimant was a worker or otherwise economically self-sufficient, their claims for any one of these benefits were rejected on the basis that they did not have a right to reside in the UK under EC law.

Family members of an EEA worker, a self-employed person, student or self-sufficient person satisfy the right to reside test. More distant relatives, known as extended family members, satisfy the right to reside test if they have been issued with a family permit, registration certificate or residence card.

Family members of an EEA national who has the right to reside as a jobseeker will not satisfy the right to reside aspect of the habitual residence test for IS. Such a right to reside will satisfy the test for IBJSA.

10.7.3   Other exempt categories

People granted refugee status or humanitarian protection are treated as being habitually resident.

10.7.4   First-time entrants

If a British citizen, a Commonwealth citizen with the right of abode or a person granted entry clearance for the purposes of settlement has never lived in the Common Travel Area before, he will need to establish habitual residence before being entitled to the benefit.

In the case of *Nessa v Chief Adjudication Officer* [1999] 1 WLR 1937, Mrs Nessa arrived at Heathrow on 22 August 1994. She was then aged 55 and she had lived all her life in Bangladesh. She had a right of abode in the UK. In Bangladesh, she had lived in the house of her husband's father with her husband's other wife and the children of both wives. On arrival, she planned to live at the home of her husband's brother in England. Her three children, all adults, wanted to come to join her. She applied for income support. Her application was dated 2 September 1994. It was refused as the decision-maker found she was 'not habitually resident in the United Kingdom' as 'Customer has never lived in the UK. Husband died in UK 1.5.75. All other family ties and home in Bangladesh'.

Lord Slynn of Hadley said:

> If Parliament had intended that a person seeking to enter the United Kingdom or such a person declaring his intention to settle here is to have Income Support on arrival, it could have said so. It seems to me impossible to accept the argument at one time advanced that a person who has never been here before who says on landing, 'I intend to settle in the United Kingdom' and who is fully believed is automatically a person who is habitually resident here. Nor is it enough to say I am going to live at X or with Y. He must show residence in fact for a period which shows that the residence has become 'habitual' and, as I see it, will or is likely to continue to be habitual.

> I do not consider that when he spoke of residence for an appreciable period, Lord Brandon [see **10.7.1.2**] meant more than this. It is a question of fact to be decided on the date where the determination has to be made on the circumstances of each case whether and when that habitual residence had been established. Bringing possessions, doing everything necessary to establish residence before coming, having a right of abode, seeking to bring family, 'durable ties' with the country of residence or intended residence, and many other factors have to be taken into account.

> The requisite period is not a fixed period. It may be longer where there are doubts. It may be short (as the House accepted in *In re S (A Minor) (Custody: Habitual Residence)* [1998] AC 750, my speech at p 763A; and *Re F (A Minor) (Child Abduction)* [1994] 1 FLR 548, 555 where Butler-Sloss, LJ said 'A month can be ... an appreciable period of time.')

10.7.5   Returning 'residents'

What if a British citizen, a Commonwealth citizen with the right of abode or a person with settled status has lived in the Common Travel Area before and is now returning? In Case C–90/97 *Swaddling v Adjudication Officer* [1999] All ER (EC) 217, the ECJ had to consider the position of a British citizen who had spent much of his adult life working in France. Between 1980 and 1994, Mr Swaddling had worked for various employers mainly in France but occasionally in the UK. In 1994, his French employer's business collapsed and in January 1995, after an unsuccessful attempt to find work in France, Mr Swaddling returned to the UK to live with his brother. Mr Swaddling declared that he no longer wished to take a job which entailed spending long periods of time abroad and on 9 January he applied for income support. The application was refused on the grounds that Mr Swaddling did not meet the habitual residence requirement prescribed by reg 21 of the IS Regs 1987. However, the Social Security Appeal Tribunal allowed Mr Swaddling's appeal on the ground that he had shown the necessary intention to establish habitual residence in the UK as of 9 January. On a further appeal, the Social Security Commissioner considered that, for the purposes of the national legislation, 'habitual residence' presupposed an appreciable period of residence (such as eight weeks) in the UK in addition to the settled intention of residing there. However, the Commissioner stayed the proceedings and referred to the European Court of Justice (ECJ) for a preliminary ruling the question whether, in the circumstances, the imposition of a condition of habitual residence, involving the existence of an appreciable period of residence, was compatible with Community law.

The ECJ held that under Articles 1(h) and 10a of Council Regulation 1408/71 on the application of social security schemes to employed persons, to self-employed persons and to members of their families moving within the Community, payment of income support was conditional on the claimant being resident in the territory of the Member State under whose legislation he was claiming and having the habitual centre of his interests there. In determining whether that was the case, account had to be taken of the person's family situation, the reasons which had led him to move, the length and continuity of his residence, and his intention as it appeared in all the circumstances. However, the length of residence in the Member State in which payment of the benefit was sought could not be regarded as an intrinsic element of the concept of residence within the meaning of art 10a. In particular, when, as in the instant case, an employed person, on returning to his State of origin after exercising his right to freedom of movement, had made it clear at the time of applying for income support that he intended to remain in his State of origin where his close relatives lived, he did not fail to satisfy the Article 10a residence condition merely because the period of residence completed there was too short. It followed that in such circumstances, the application of the rule at issue was precluded by Regulation 1408/71.

Whilst the *Swaddling* case concerned EC law, the Government issued a press release on 14 June 1999 saying:

> People returning to the UK from living abroad are to get fairer access to benefits – but tough action to prevent 'benefit tourism' will continue.

Social Security Minister Angela Eagle said:

> We have accepted a recent judgment of the European Court of Justice which has made it clear that people returning to the UK from an EU member state and re-establishing their ties here should be treated as habitually resident immediately upon their return.

The DfWP has issued guidance (Memo DMG Vol 2 01/02) as to the application of EC law in this area. It stresses that a claimant who was previously habitually resident in the Common Travel Area and moved to live and work in another EU State and returns to resume the previous habitual residence is habitually resident immediately on arrival in the Common Travel Area. In deciding whether the claimant is resuming previous residence a decision-maker should take into account the length and continuity of the previous residence in the Common Travel Area, his employment history in the EU State and whether the claimant has maintained sufficient links with the previous residence to be said to be resuming it rather than commencing a new period of residence. The guidance also gives the following example. The claimant, a UK national, lived and worked in the UK before moving to Germany where he worked for several years. He was made redundant and having failed to find work in Germany for three months returned to the UK where he had his family and friends. On claiming IBJSA, he stated that his intention was to find work and remain permanently in the UK. JSA was awarded because he was resuming a previous habitual residence.

Is the habitual residence test compatible with EC law? In Case C-138/02 *Collins v Secretary of State for Work and Pensions* (2004) *The Times*, 30 March, the ECJ held that the right to equal treatment laid down in Article 39(2) EC, read in conjunction with Articles 12 EC and 17 EC, does not preclude national legislation which makes entitlement to a jobseeker's allowance conditional on a residence requirement, in so far as that requirement may be justified on the basis of objective considerations that are independent of the nationality of the persons concerned and proportionate to the legitimate aim of the national provisions. When the case returned to the domestic courts, the Court of Appeal held that the habitual residence test is compatible with EC law: see *Collins v Secretary of State for Work and Pensions* [2006] EWCA Civ 376.

What if EC law does not apply? The DfWP also issued its own guidance (AM(AOG) 109), which includes the following:

> A JSA (IB) or IS claimant of any nationality who was previously habitually resident in the UK, Republic of Ireland, Channel Islands or Isle of Man and moved and lived in another country and returns to resume the previous residence is habitually resident immediately on arrival in the UK, Republic of Ireland, Channel Islands or Isle of Man. In deciding habitual residence questions [decision-makers] should take account of the length and continuity of the previous residence in the UK, Republic of Ireland, Channel Islands or Isle of Man and whether the claimant has sufficient links with that previous residence to be regarded as picking up the pieces of their old life ... a claimant who is temporarily absent from the UK may in any case retain habitual residence in the UK.

The DfWP guidance (Memo DMG Vol 2 01/02) accepts that there may be special cases where a person is resuming a previous habitual residence following a period living abroad. It states that if a person abandons their life in the other country in circumstances which make the decision irrevocable and returns to take up residence previously held in the UK they may be habitually resident immediately on their return. The following example is given. A woman who lived with her partner, an Australian national, in Canada for several years returned to the UK where she had previously lived and worked until she was 27 years old. She stated that following her partner's imprisonment, it was necessary for her to remove the two children of the family from any influence he might try to exert. Before embarking on the journey to rejoin her parents in Wales she had arranged for the future schooling of her children and had obtained a firm offer of employment. She had left nothing behind in Canada and intended to bring up the children in her parents' household.

10.8 Immigration law and public funds

10.8.1 Immigration rules

A person who has limited leave to enter the UK will be placed under a prohibition on 'resorting to public funds' as part of the conditions attached to his leave to enter. The various categories of entrants subject to this condition include visitors, students, fiancé(e)s, spouses in their two-year probationary period, business persons, workers and sponsored immigrants under a written undertaking. See *Immigration Law*.

10.8.2 Public funds

As we have seen at **10.3**, a person with limited leave is not entitled to certain benefits and, perhaps not surprisingly, these constitute 'public funds'.

Note that by Immigration Rules, para 6B, a person is not regarded as having recourse to public funds if he is entitled to such as a member of an exempt group: see **10.3.2**.

10.8.3 Claims by a couple for IS, IRESA or IBJSA

Where one partner is eligible to claim but the other is excluded by s 115, the qualifying partner should apply but the excluded partner will be deemed to have a *nil* applicable amount. This means that the claimant is therefore awarded a single person's allowance according to his or her age. Any premiums appropriate to the claimant (but not the excluded partner) are payable. Any allowable housing costs will form part of the applicable amount in the usual way. Moreover, the capital and income of both partners is also aggregated in the usual way.

10.8.4   Claims by a couple for HB or CTB

If the couple are already receiving IS, IRESA or IBJSA (see **10.8.3**), they will be awarded maximum HB or CTB, and so no additional benefit is payable for the partner who is subject to immigration controls. But if the couple do not receive any of those benefits, their HB and CTB are calculated in the usual way, that is, the partner subject to immigration controls counts when working out allowances and premiums. This may therefore result in the claimant being awarded additional public funds. The danger for the partner subject to immigration controls is that his exisiting leave might be curtailed, or any application in the future for settlement refused.

10.8.5   Claims by a couple for tax credits

Regulation 3(2) of the Tax Credits (Immigration) Regulations 2003 (SI 2003/653) provides that where one member of a couple is a person subject to immigration control, but the other member is not, or that person is within any one of the five prescribed cases (see **10.3.2**), then:

(a)   the calculation of the amount of tax credit (including any second adult element or other element in respect of, or determined by reference to, that person);

(b)   the method of making (or proceeding with) a joint claim by the couple; and

(c)   the method of payment of the tax credit;

is to be determined in the same way as if that person were not subject to immigration control.

Note that where the other member is within prescribed case 4 or 5 (see **10.3.2**), the above applies only to the appropriate tax credit to which he is entitled.

Also note that by Immigration Rules, para 6B, the member of the couple who is subject to immigration controls will not be regarded as resorting to public funds.

10.8.6   Not 'public funds'

The benefits which do not count as 'public funds', and which can theoretically be claimed by a person with limited leave, are:

(a)   statutory sick pay and statutory maternity pay;

(b)   all the contributory benefits; and

(c)   industrial disablement benefit.

10.8.7   Practical problems of claiming benefits which are not public funds

Even if a benefit is not public funds, few new arrivals are likely to be eligible. There are a number of reasons for this, as outlined below.

10.8.7.1   Contributory benefits

Few people who have recently arrived in Great Britain will have the appropriate National Insurance contribution record to claim any contributory benefit (see **Chapter 2**).

10.8.7.2   Contribution-based jobseeker's allowance

A foreign natiional worker could easily satisfy the contribution conditions for CBJSA if he has worked in Great Britain for three years or more. But his employment may be dependent on his employer obtaining Home Office permission for him to work. Can he be said to be 'available for work' (see **3.2.6** and **3.2.7**) in these circumstances? According to the DfWP *Decision Maker's Guide*, the answer is no.

10.8.7.3 Statutory sick pay, statutory maternity pay and industrial disablement benefit

The right to SSP, SMP or disablement benefit depends upon status as an employee. If the claimant is prohibited from working by the terms of his leave to enter, there is a risk that a claim for any of these benefits will lead to the Home Office becoming aware that the claimant is working unlawfully.

If a person has entered the UK in a category which allows him to work, there is no reason whatever why he should not claim any of the benefits in this group, provided that he satisfies the other qualifying conditions.

10.9 Asylum seekers

Section 115 of the IAA 1999 excludes asylum seekers from the main benefits. Part 3 of the Nationality, Immigration and Asylum Act 2002 laid down a blueprint for giving financial support to asylum seekers. The detail is outside the scope of this book.

10.10 Urgent cases payments

As we saw at **10.3**, persons with limited leave whose funds from abroad have been temporarily interrupted can claim IS provided there is a reasonable expectation that the supply of those funds will be resumed. In fact, the claim is for an urgent case payment(s) in the short term. See further **8.12**.

10.11 Social fund payment

As we saw at **10.3**, a social fund payment can be sought by the following: a person with limited leave whose funds from abroad have been temporarily interrupted provided there is a reasonable expectation that the supply of those funds will be resumed; nationals of Turkey who are lawfully present in the UK; a member of the family of a national of an EEA country; a person who is legally working and living in Great Britain and is a national of a State with which the EU has made an agreement relating to equal treatment (namely Turkey, Morocco, Algeria and Tunisia) and any members of their family living with them; and a sponsored immigrant regardless of the length of stay in the UK.

See further **9.15**.

10.12 EEA nationals claiming benefits

As we have seen, EEA nationals are not excluded from benefits. But can claiming benefits affect their right of residence in the UK? That right derives after three months from having a qualifying status, ie a jobseeker, a worker, a self-employed person, a self-sufficient person or a student.

An EEA jobseeker who has registered with Jobcentre Plus and has claimed JSA will have a right to reside for an initial period of six months, and for longer if he is genuinely seeking work and has a reasonable chance of securing employment. If the Home Office considers that he no longer satisfies those requirements, it may seek to remove him. EEA nationals who are in the UK as students or self-sufficient persons have a right to reside. However, they risk losing their right of residence if they become an unreasonable burden on the social assistance system of the UK.

Workers and self-employed EEA nationals retain their qualifying status if they temporarily cease economic activity due to involuntary redundancy or illness. In those circumstances, resorting to public funds would be acceptable.

APPENDICES

Appendix 1

Specimen Jobseeker's Agreement

Jobseeker's
Allowance   *Jobseeker's*   Agreement

Jobseeker's Agreement
This Jobseeker's Agreement sets out

- when I can work
- the types of work I am willing to do
- what I am going to do to find work and increase my chances of finding work.

I, or an Employment Services adviser, can ask for it to be changed at any time. If we cannot agree about changing the Agreement, an independent adjudication officer will be asked to look at it. If I am not satisfied with their decision, I can have it looked at by another adjudication officer. If I am still not satisfied, I can appeal to an independent tribunal.

Availability of work
I understand I must

- be available for work
- (unless the limitation is for health reasons) have a reasonable chance of getting work if I limit
    - the kind of work I am willing to do
    - the rate of pay I will accept
    - where I am willing to work
    - the hours I am willing to work
- be capable of work.

Permitted period
*I know I can limit myself to accepting work in my usual job and at my usual wages from / / to / / After this I will be interviewed about broadening my availability and job search.

Actively seeking work
I understand that I must actively seek work. I will be asked regularly to show what I have done to find work. I have been advised to keep a record of what I do to find work.

Jobseeker's Allowance
I understand my allowance may be affected if I

- do not do enough to find work
- am not available for work
- reduce my chances of getting work, or
- become incapable of work.

If this happens, I will be told and my case may be sent to an independent adjudication officer for a decision. If I am not satisfied with the decision, I can appeal to an independent tribunal. I understand that this is general information and not a full statement of the law.

* The adviser had read this Agreement to me.

Jobseeker's signature	
Date	/ /

Adviser's signature	
Date	/ /
Adviser's name	
Telephone number	
TAM date	/ /

(* Please delete as appropriate)

ES 3

Name

The types of job I am looking for

I am willing and able to start work

* immediately   within 48 hours   other

within 24 hours   after giving a weeks notice

I want to limit the days and hours I am available for work

* No

Yes

	Earliest start time	Latest finish time	Most hours I can work
Monday			
Tuesday			
Wednesday			
Thursday			
Friday			
Saturday			
Sunday			
Most hours I can work each week			

I am available for work these days and these hours

Other agreed restrictions on my availability and/or agreed restrictions on types of work

| NI Number | | Claim file/cycle | |

What I will do to identify and apply for jobs

* Write to at least ☐ employers a week

* Phone at least ☐ employers a week

Visit at least ☐ employers a week

Contact the Jobcentre at least ☐ times a week

* Ask family, friends and people I have worked with before

* Look in these newspapers and trade papers	How often I will look

Other activities including any steps to improve my chances of finding a job

Our commitment to you

Jobseeker's Charter
If you are out of work and looking for a job, we want to offer you the best possible service.
Our jobseeker's Charter sets out the standards of service we aim to provide. It also tells you how to complain if you are not satisfied. You can get a copy of the Charter from your Jobcentre.

What you can expect from us
You can expect us to

- wear a name badge and give our name when we answer the phone and write
- be polite, considerate, open and honest
- respect your privacy. In most cases we can provide a private room for sensitive interviews
- apologise if we get things wrong, explain what happened and put things right promptly
- deliver our services fairly and to the same high standards regardless of race, sex, disability or religion.

Your views
We regularly ask people what they think of our service and we publish the results. We welcome your comments at any time. If you want to comment or complain, ask for a copy of our leaflet.

Jobs
The vacancies we display should be up to date and available. We will not display vacancies which discriminate unlawfully because of race, sex, disability or religion. We encourage people of all ages to apply for the vacancies we display.

Information
We will give you advice about employment opportunities, training and setting up your own business.
Health problems and disabilities
If you have a health problem or disability which affects the type of work you can do we will tell you about the special help available.

Interviews
You will be asked to attend the office regularly. Each time we will

- talk about your search for work
- make sure your Agreement is up to date
- see what other help we can give you.

If possible you will be seen by the same person or someone from the same team.

Jobseeker's Allowance
If you are entitled to Jobseeker's Allowance we will aim to get the right money to you in time.

Other benefits
We will give you information about other benefits you may be entitled to.
You may get benefit even when you start work, for example, Family Credit.

More about our services
You will find out more information about our services in the leaflet '*Just the job*'

Appendix 2

Limited Capability for Work (ESA) Assessment

SCHEDULE 2   Regulation 19(2) and (3)

ASSESSMENT OF WHETHER A CLAIMANT HAS LIMITED
CAPABILITY FOR WORK

PART 1
PHYSICAL DISABILITIES

(1) *Activity*	(2) *Descriptors*	(3) *Points*
1. Walking with a walking stick or other aid if such aid is normally used.	1 (a) Cannot walk at all.	15
	(b) Cannot walk more than 50 metres on level ground without repeatedly stopping or severe discomfort.	15
	(c) Cannot walk up or down two steps even with the support of a handrail.	15
	(d) Cannot walk more than 100 metres on level ground without stopping or severe discomfort.	9
	(e) Cannot walk more than 200 metres on level ground without stopping or severe discomfort.	6
	(f) None of the above apply.	0
2. Standing and sitting.	2 (a) Cannot stand for more than 10 minutes, unassisted by another person, even if free to move around, before needing to sit down.	15
	(b) Cannot sit in a chair with a high back and no arms for more than 10 minutes before needing to move from the chair because the degree of discomfort experienced makes it impossible to continue sitting.	15
	(c) Cannot rise to standing from sitting in an upright chair without physical assistance from another person.	15

(1) Activity		(2) Descriptors	(3) Points
		(d) Cannot move between one seated position and another seated position located next to one another without receiving physical assistance from another person.	15
		(e) Cannot stand for more than 30 minutes, even if free to move around, before needing to sit down.	6
		(f) Cannot sit in a chair with a high back and no arms for more than 30 minutes without needing to move from the chair because the degree of discomfort experienced makes it impossible to continue sitting.	6
		(g) None of the above apply.	0
3. Bending or kneeling.	3	(a) Cannot bend to touch knees and straighten up again.	15
		(b) Cannot bend, kneel or squat, as if to pick a light object, such as a piece of paper, situated 15cm from the floor on a low shelf, and to move it and straighten up again without the help of another person.	9
		(c) Cannot bend, kneel or squat, as if to pick a light object off the floor and straighten up again without the help of another person.	6
		(d) None of the above apply.	0
4. Reaching.	4	(a) Cannot raise either arm as if to put something in the top pocket of a coat or jacket.	15
		(b) Cannot put either arm behind back as if to put on a coat or jacket.	15
		(c) Cannot raise either arm to top of head as if to put on a hat.	9
		(d) Cannot raise either arm above head height as if to reach for something.	6
		(e) None of the above apply.	0

(1) Activity		(2) Descriptors	(3) Points
5. Picking up and moving or transferring by the use of the upper body and arms (excluding all other activities specified in Part 1 of this Schedule).	5	(a) Cannot pick up and move a 0.5 litre carton full of liquid with either hand.	15
		(b) Cannot pick up and move a one litre carton full of liquid with either hand.	9
		(c) Cannot pick up and move a light but bulky object such as an empty cardboard box, requiring the use of both hands together.	6
		(d) None of the above apply.	0
6. Manual dexterity.	6	(a) Cannot turn a "star-headed" sink tap with either hand.	15
		(b) Cannot pick up a £1 coin or equivalent with either hand.	15
		(c) Cannot turn the pages of a book with either hand.	15
		(d) Cannot physically use a pen or pencil.	9
		(e) Cannot physically use a conventional keyboard or mouse.	9
		(f) Cannot do up/undo small buttons, such as shirt or blouse buttons.	9
		(g) Cannot turn a "star-headed" sink tap with one hand but can with the other.	6
		(h) Cannot pick up a £1 coin or equivalent with one hand but can with the other.	6
		(i) Cannot pour from an open 0.5 litre carton full of liquid.	6
		(j) None of the above apply.	0
7. Speech.	7	(a) Cannot speak at all.	15
		(b) Speech cannot be understood by strangers.	15
		(c) Strangers have great difficulty understanding speech.	9
		(d) Strangers have some difficulty understanding speech.	6
		(e) None of the above apply.	0

(1) Activity	(2) Descriptors	(3) Points
8. Hearing with a hearing aid or other aid if normally worn.	8 (a) Cannot hear at all.	15
	(b) Cannot hear well enough to be able to hear someone talking in a loud voice in a quiet room, sufficiently clearly to distinguish the words being spoken.	15
	(c) Cannot hear someone talking in a normal voice in a quiet room, sufficiently clearly to distinguish the words being spoken.	9
	(d) Cannot hear someone talking in a loud voice in a busy street, sufficiently clearly to distinguish the words being spoken.	6
	(e) None of the above apply.	0
9. Vision including visual acuity and visual fields, in normal daylight or bright electric light, with glasses or other aid to vision if such aid is normally worn.	9 (a) Cannot see at all.	15
	(b) Cannot see well enough to read 16 point print at a distance of greater than 20cm.	15
	(c) Has 50% or greater reduction of visual fields.	15
	(d) Cannot see well enough to recognise a friend at a distance of a least 5 metres.	9
	(e) Has 25% or more but less than 50% reduction of visual fields.	6
	(f) Cannot see well enough to recognise a friend at a distance of at least 15 metres.	6
	(g) None of the above apply.	0
10 (a) Continence other than enuresis (bed wetting) where the claimant does not have an artificial stoma or urinary collecting device.	10 (a) (i) Has no voluntary control over the evacuation of the bowel.	15

(1) Activity	(2) Descriptors		(3) Points
	10 (a) (ii)	Has no voluntary control over the voiding of the bladder.	15
	10 (a) (iii)	At least once a month loses control of bowels so that the claimant cannot control the full evacuation of the bowel.	15
	10 (a) (iv)	At least once a week, loses control of bladder so that the claimant cannot control the full voiding of the bladder.	15
	10 (a) (v)	Occasionally loses control of bowels so that the claimant cannot control the full evacuation of the bowel.	9
	10 (a) (vi)	At least once a month loses control of bladder so that the claimant cannot control the full voiding of the bladder.	6
	10 (a) (vii)	Risks losing control of bowels or bladder so that the claimant cannot control the full evacuation of the bowel or the full voiding of the bladder if not able to reach a toilet quickly.	6
	10 (a) (viii)	None of the above apply.	0
10 (b) Continence where the claimant uses a urinary collecting device, worn for the majority of the time including an indwelling urethral or suprapubic catheter.	10 (b) (i)	Is unable to affix, remove or empty the catheter bag or other collecting device without receiving physical assistance from another person.	15
	10 (b) (ii)	Is unable to affix, remove or empty the catheter bag or other collecting device without causing leakage of contents.	15
	10 (b) (iii)	Has no voluntary control over the evacuation of the bowel.	15

(1) Activity		(2) Descriptors	(3) Points
	10 (b) (iv)	At least once a month, loses control of bowels so that the claimant cannot control the full evacuation of the bowel.	15
	10 (b) (v)	Occasionally loses control of bowels so that the claimant cannot control the full evacuation of the bowel.	9
	10 (b) (vi)	Risks losing control of bowels so that the claimant cannot control the full evacuation of the bowel if not able to reach a toilet quickly.	6
	10 (b) (vii)	None of the above apply.	0
10 (c) Continence other than enuresis (bed wetting) where the claimant has an artificial stoma.	10 (c) (i)	Is unable to affix, remove or empty stoma appliance without receiving physical assistance from another person.	15
	10 (c) (ii)	Is unable to affix remove or empty stoma appliance without causing leakage of contents.	15
	10 (c) (iii)	Where the claimant's artificial stoma relates solely to the evacuation of the bowel, at least once a week, loses control of bladder so that the claimant cannot control the full voiding of the bladder.	15
	10 (c) (iv)	Where the claimant's artificial stoma relates solely to the evacuation of the bowel, at last once a month, loses control of bladder so that the claimant cannot control the full voiding of the bladder.	9

(1) Activity	(2) Descriptors	(3) Points
	10 (c) (v) Where the claimant's artificial stoma relates solely to the evacuation of the bowel, risks losing control of the bladder so that the claimant cannot control the full voiding of the bladder if not able to reach a toilet quickly.	6
	10 (c) (vi) None of the above apply.	0
11. Remaining conscious during waking moments.	11 (a) At least once a week, has an involuntary episode of lost or altered consciousness, resulting in significantly disrupted awareness or concentration.	15
	(b) At least once a month, has an involuntary episode of lost or altered consciousness, resulting in significantly disrupted awareness or concentration.	9
	(c) At least twice in the six months immediately preceding the assessment, has had an involuntary episode of lost or altered consciousness, resulting in significantly disrupted awareness or concentration.	6
	(d) None of the above apply.	0

PART 2
Mental, cognitive and intellectual function assessment

(1) Activity	(2) Descriptors	(3) Points
12. Learning or comprehension in the completion of tasks.	12 (a) Cannot learn or understand how to successfully complete a simple task, such as setting an alarm clock, at all.	15

(1) Activity	(2) Descriptors	(3) Points
	(b) Needs to witness a demonstration, given more than once on the same occasion, of how to carry out a simple task before the claimant is able to learn or understand how to complete the task successfully, but would be unable to successfully complete the task the following day without receiving a further demonstration of how to complete it.	15
	(c) Needs to witness a demonstration of how to carry out a simple task, before the claimant is able to learn or understand how to complete the task successfully, but would be unable to successfully complete the task the following day without receiving a verbal prompt from another person.	9
	(d) Needs to witness a demonstration of how to carry out a moderately complex task, such as the steps involved in operating a washing machine to correctly clean clothes, before the claimant is able to learn or understand how to complete the task successfully, but would be unable to successfully complete the task the following day without receiving a verbal prompt from another person.	9
	(e) Needs verbal instructions as to how to carry out a simple task before the claimant is able to learn or understand how to complete the task successfully, but would be unable, within a period of less than one week, to successfully complete the task the following day without receiving a verbal prompt from another person.	6
	(f) None of the above apply.	0

(1) Activity	(2) Descriptors	(3) Points
13. Awareness of hazard.	13 (a) Reduced awareness of the risks of everyday hazards (such as boiling water or sharp objects) would lead to daily instances of or to near-avoidance of: (i) injury to self or others; or (ii) significant damage to property or possessions, to such an extent that overall day to day life cannot successfully be managed.	15
	(b) Reduced awareness of the risks of everyday hazards would lead for the majority of the time to instances of or to near-avoidance of (i) injury to self or others; or (ii) significant damage to property or possessions, to such an extent that overall day to day life cannot successfully be managed without supervision from another person.	9
	(c) Reduced awareness of the risks of everyday hazards has led or would lead to frequent instances of or to near-avoidance of: (i) injury to self or others; or (ii) significant damage to property or possessions, but not to such an extent that overall day to day life cannot be managed when such incidents occur.	6
	(d) None of the above apply.	0
14. Memory and concentration.	14 (a) On a daily basis, forgets or loses concentration to such an extent that overall day to day life cannot be successfully managed without receiving verbal prompting, given by someone else in the claimant's presence.	15

(1) Activity	(2) Descriptors	(3) Points
	(b) For the majority of the time, forgets or loses concentration to such an extent that overall day to day life cannot be successfully managed without receiving verbal prompting, given by someone else in the claimant's presence.	9
	(c) Frequently forgets or loses concentration to such an extent that overall day to day life can only be successfully managed with pre-planning, such as making a daily written list of all tasks forming part of daily life that are to be completed.	6
	(d) None of the above apply.	0
15. Execution of tasks.	15 (a) Is unable to successfully complete any everyday task.	15
	(b) Takes more than twice the length of time it would take a person without any form of mental disablement, to successfully complete an everyday task with which the claimant is familiar.	15
	(c) Takes more than one and a half times but no more than twice the length of time it would take a person without any form of mental disablement to successfully complete an everyday task with which the claimant is familiar.	9
	(d) Takes one and a half times the length of time it would take a person without any form of mental disablement to successfully complete an everyday task with which the claimant is familiar.	6
	(e) None of the above apply.	0

(1) Activity	(2) Descriptors	(3) Points
16. Initiating and sustaining personal action.	16 (a) Cannot, due to cognitive impairment or a severe disorder of mood or behaviour, initiate or sustain any personal action (which means planning, organisation, problem solving, prioritising or switching tasks).	15
	(b) Cannot, due to cognitive impairment or a severe disorder of mood or behaviour, initiate or sustain personal action without requiring verbal prompting given by another person in the claimant's presence for the majority of the time.	15
	(c) Cannot, due to cognitive impairment or a severe disorder of mood or behaviour, initiate or sustain personal action without requiring verbal prompting given by another person in the claimant's presence for the majority of the time.	9
	(d) Cannot, due to cognitive impairment or a severe disorder of mood or behaviour, initiate or sustain personal action without requiring frequent verbal prompting given by another person in the claimant's presence.	6
	(e) None of the above apply.	0
17. Coping with change.	17 (a) Cannot cope with very minor, expected changes in routine, to the extent that overall day to day life cannot be managed.	15
	(b) Cannot cope with expected changes in routine (such as a pre-arranged permanent change to the routine time scheduled for a lunch break), to the extent that overall day to day life is made significantly more difficult.	9

(1) Activity	(2) Descriptors	(3) Points
	(c) Cannot cope with minor, unforeseen changes in routine (such as an unexpected change of the timing of an appointment on the day it is due to occur), to the extent that overall, day to day life is made significantly more difficult.	6
	(d) None of the above apply.	0
18. Getting about.	18 (a) Cannot get to any specified place with which the claimant is, or would be, familiar.	15
	(b) Is unable to get to a specified place with which the claimant is familiar, without being accompanied by another person on each occasion.	15
	(c) For the majority of the time is unable to get to a specified place with which the claimant is familiar without being accompanied by another person.	9
	(d) Is frequently unable to get to a specified place with which the claimant is familiar without being accompanied by another person.	6
	(e) None of the above apply.	0
19. Coping with social situations.	19 (a) Normal activities, for example, visiting new places or engaging in social contact, are precluded because of overwhelming fear or anxiety.	15
	(b) Normal activities, for example, visiting new places or engaging in social contact, are precluded for the majority of the time due to overwhelming fear or anxiety.	
	(c) Normal activities, for example, visiting new places or engaging in social contact, are frequently precluded, due to overwhelming fear or anxiety.	6
	(d) None of the above apply.	0

(1) Activity	(2) Descriptors	(3) Points
20. Propriety of behaviour with other people.	20 (a) Has unpredictable outbursts of aggressive, disinhibited, or bizarre behaviour, being either:	15
	(i) sufficient to cause disruption to others on a daily basis; or	
	(ii) of such severity that although occurring less frequently than on a daily basis, no reasonable person would be expected to tolerate them.	
	(b) Has a completely disproportionate reaction to minor events or to criticism to the extent that the claimant has an extreme violent outburst leading to threatening behaviour or actual physical violence.	15
	(c) Has unpredictable outbursts of aggressive, disinhibited or bizarre behaviour, sufficient in severity and frequency to cause disruption for the majority of the time.	9
	(d) Has a strongly disproportionate reaction to minor events or to criticism, to the extent that the claimant cannot manage overall day to day life when such events or criticism occur.	9
	(e) Has unpredictable outbursts of aggressive, disinhibited or bizarre behaviour, sufficient to cause frequent disruption.	6
	(f) Frequently demonstrates a moderately disproportionate reaction to minor events or to criticism but not to such an extent that the claimant cannot manage overall day to day life when such events or criticism occur.	6
	(g) None of the above apply.	0
21. Dealing with other people.	21 (a) Is unaware of impact of own behaviour to the extent that:	15

(1) *Activity*	(2) *Descriptors*	(3) *Points*
	(i) has difficulty relating to others even for brief periods, such as a few hours; or	
	(ii) causes distress to others on a daily basis.	
	(b) The claimant misinterprets verbal or non-verbal communication to the extent of causing himself or herself significant distress on a daily basis.	15
	(c) Is unaware of impact of own behaviour to the extent that:	9
	(i) has difficulty relating to others for longer periods, such as a day or two; or	
	(ii) causes distress to others for the majority of the time.	
	(d) The claimant misinterprets verbal or non-verbal communication to the extent of causing himself or herself significant distress to himself for the majority of the time.	9
	(e) Is unaware of impact of own behaviour to the extent that:	6
	(i) has difficulty relating to others for prolonged periods, such as a week; or	
	(ii) frequently causes distress to others.	
	(f) The claimant misinterprets verbal or non-verbal communication to the extent of causing himself or herself significant distress on a frequent basis.	6
	(g) None of the above apply.	

Appendix 3

Limited Capability for Work-related Activity (ESA) Assessment

SCHEDULE 3 Regulation 34(1)
ASSESSMENT OF WHETHER A CLAIMANT HAS LIMITED
CAPABILITY FOR WORK-RELATED ACTIVITY

Column 1 *Activity*	Column 2 *Descriptors*
1. Walking or moving on level ground	Cannot— (a) walk (with a walking stick or other aid if such aid is normally used); (b) move (with the aid of crutches if crutches are normally used); or (c) manually propel the claimant's wheelchair; more than 30 metres without repeatedly stopping, experiencing breathlessness or severe discomfort.
2. Rising from sitting and transferring from one seated position to another.	Cannot complete both of the following— (a) rise to standing from sitting in an upright chair without receiving physical assistance from someone else; and (b) move between one seated position and another seated position located next to one another without receiving physical assistance from someone else.
3. Picking up and moving or transferring by the use of the upper body and arms (excluding standing, sitting, bending or kneeling and all other activities specified in this Schedule).	Cannot pick up and move 0.5 litre carton full of liquid with either hand.
4. Reaching.	Cannot raise either arm as if to put something in the top pocket of a coat or jacket.
5. Manual dexterity.	Cannot— (a) turn a "star-headed" sink tap with either hand; or

Column 1 Activity	Column 2 Descriptors
	(b) pick up a £1 coin or equivalent with either hand.
6. Continence.	
(a) Continence other than enuresis (bed wetting) where the claimant does not have an artificial stoma or urinary collecting device.	(a) Has no voluntary control over the evacuation of the bowel;
	(b) Has no voluntary control over the voiding of the bladder;
	(c) At least once a week, loses control of bowels so that the claimant cannot control the full evacuation of the bowel;
	(d) At least once a week, loses control of bladder so that the claimant cannot control the full voiding of the bladder;
	(e) At least once a week, fails to control full evacuation of the bowel, owing to a severe disorder of mood or behaviour; or
	(f) At least once a week, fails to control full-voiding of the bladder, owing to a severe disorder of mood or behaviour.
(b) Continence where the claimant uses a urinary collecting device, worn for the majority of the time including an indwelling urethral or suprapubic catheter.	(a) Is unable to affix, remove or empty the catheter bag or other collecting device without receiving physical assistance from another person;
	(b) Is unable to affix, remove or empty the catheter bag or other collecting device without causing leakage of contents;
	(c) Has no voluntary control over the evacuation of the bowel;
	(d) At least once a week loses control of bowels so that the claimant cannot control the full evacuation of the bowel; or
	(e) At least once a week, fails to control full evacuation of the bowel, owing to a severe disorder of mood or behaviour.

Column 1 Activity	Column 2 Descriptors
(c) Continence other than enuresis (bed wetting) where the claimant has an artificial stoma appliance.	(a) Is unable to affix, remove or empty stoma appliance without receiving physical assistance from another person;
	(b) Is unable to affix, remove or empty stoma without causing leakage of contents;
	(c) Where the claimant's artificial stoma relates solely to the evacuation of the bowel, has no voluntary control over voiding of bladder;
	(d) Where the claimant's artificial stoma relates solely to the evacuation of the bowel, at least once a week, loses control of the bladder so that the claimant cannot control the full voiding of the bladder; or
	(e) Where the claimant's artificial stoma relates solely to the evacuation of the bowel, at least once a week, fails to control the full voiding of the bladder, owing to a severe disorder of mood or behaviour.
7. Maintaining personal hygiene.	(a) Cannot clean own torso (excluding own back) without receiving physical assistance from someone else;
	(b) Cannot clean own torso (excluding back) without repeatedly stopping, experiencing breathlessness or severe discomfort;
	(c) Cannot clean own torso (excluding back) without receiving regular prompting given by someone else in the claimant's presence; or
	(d) Owing to a severe disorder of mood or behaviour, fails to clean own torso (excluding own back) without receiving—
	(i) physical assistance from someone else; or

Column 1 Activity	Column 2 Descriptors
	(ii) regular prompting given by someone else in the claimant's presence.
8. Eating and drinking.	
(a) Conveying food or drink to the mouth.	(a) Cannot convey food or drink to the claimant's own mouth without receiving physical assistance from someone else;
	(b) Cannot convey food or drink to the claimant's own mouth without repeatedly stopping, experiencing breathlessness or severe discomfort;
	(c) Cannot convey food or drink to the claimant's own mouth without receiving regular prompting given by someone else in the claimant's physical presence; or
	(d) Owing to a severe disorder of mood or behaviour, fails to convey food or drink to the claimant's own mouth without receiving—
	(i) physical assistance from someone else; or
	(ii) regular prompting given by someone else in the claimant's presence.
(b) Chewing or swallowing food or drink.	(a) Cannot chew or swallow food or drink;
	(b) Cannot chew or swallow food or drink without repeatedly stopping, experiencing breathlessness or severe discomfort;
	(c) Cannot chew or swallow food or drink without repeatedly receiving regular prompting given by someone else in the claimant's presence; or
	(d) Owing to a severe disorder of mood or behaviour, fails to—
	(i) chew or swallow food or drink; or

Column 1 *Activity*	Column 2 *Descriptors*
	(ii) chew or swallow food or drink without regular prompting given by someone else in the claimant's presence.
9. Learning or comprehension in the completion of tasks.	(a) Cannot learn or understand how to successfully complete a simple task, such as the preparation of a hot drink, at all;
	(b) Needs to witness a demonstration, given more than once on the same occasion of how to carry out a simple task before the claimant is able to learn or understand how to complete the task successfully, but would be unable to successfully complete the task the following day without receiving a further demonstration of how to complete it; or
	(c) Fails to do any of the matters referred to in (a) or (b) owing to a severe disorder of mood or behaviour.
10. Personal action.	(a) Cannot initiate or sustain any personal action (which means planning, organisation, problem solving, prioritising or switching tasks);
	(b) Cannot initiate or sustain personal action without requiring daily verbal prompting given by someone else in the claimant's presence; or
	(c) Fails to initiate or sustain basic personal action without requiring daily verbal prompting given by some else in the claimant's presence, owing to a severe disorder of mood or behaviour.
11. Communication.	(a) None of the following forms of communication can be achieved by the claimant—
	(i) speaking (to a standard that may be understood by strangers);

Column 1 *Activity*	Column 2 *Descriptors*
	(ii) writing (to a standard that may be understood by strangers);
	(iii) typing (to a standard that may be understood by strangers);
	(iv) sign language to a standard equivalent to Level 3 British Sign Language;
	(b) None of the forms of communication referred to in (a) are achieved by the claimant, owing to a severe disorder of mood or behaviour;
	(c) Misinterprets verbal or non-verbal communication to the extent of causing distress to himself or herself on a daily basis; or
	(d) Effectively cannot make himself or herself understood to others because of the claimant's disassociation from reality owing to a severe disorder of mood or behaviour.

Appendix 4

Schedule 2 – Prescribed Degrees of Disablement

Description of injury	Regulation 11 Degree of disablement per cent
1 Loss of both hands or amputation at higher sites	100
2 Loss of a hand and a foot	100
3 Double amputation through leg or thigh, or amputation through leg or thigh on one side and loss of other foot	100
4 Loss of sight to such an extent as to render the claimant unable to perform any work for which eyesight is essential	100
5 Very severe facial disfiguration	100
6 Absolute deafness	100
7 Forequarter or hindquarter amputation	100

Amputation cases – upper limbs (either arm)

8	Amputation through shoulder joint	90
9	Amputation below shoulder with stump less than 20.5 centimetres from tip of acromion	80
10	Amputation from 20.5 centimetres from tip of acromion to less than 11.5 centimetres below tip of olecranon	70
11	Loss of a hand or of the thumb and four fingers of one hand or amputation from 11.5 centimetres below tip of olecranon	60
12	Loss of thumb	30
13	Loss of thumb and its metacarpal bone	40
14	Loss of four fingers of one hand	50
15	Loss of three fingers of one hand	30
16	Loss of two fingers of one hand	20
17	Loss of terminal phalanx of thumb	20

Amputation cases – lower limbs

18	Amputation of both feet resulting in end-bearing stumps	90
19	Amputation through both feet proximal to the metatarsophalangeal joint	80
20	Loss of all toes of both feet through the metatarsophalangeal joint	40
21	Loss of all toes of both feet proximal to the proximal inter-phalangeal joint	30
22	Loss of all toes of both feet distal to the proximal inter-phalangeal joint	20
23	Amputation at hip	90
24	Amputation below hip with stump not exceeding 13 centimetres in length measured from tip of great trochanter	80

25	Amputation below hip and above knee with stump exceeding 13 centimetres in length measured from tip of great trochanter, or at knee not resulting in end-bearing stump	70
26	Amputation at knee resulting in end-bearing stump or below knee with stump not exceeding 9 centimetres	60
27	Amputation below knee with stump exceeding 9 centimetres but not exceeding 13 centimetres	50
28	Amputation below knee with stump exceeding 13 centimetres	40
29	Amputation of one foot resulting in end-bearing stump	30
30	Amputation through one foot proximal to the metatarsophalangeal joint	30
31	Loss of all toes of one foot through the metatarsophalangeal joint	20

Other injuries

32	Loss of one eye, without complications, the other being normal	40
33	Loss of vision of one eye, without complications or disfigurement of eyeball, the other being normal	30

Loss of:

A.   Fingers of right or left hand

Index finger –

34	Whole	14
35	Two phalanges	11
36	One phalanx	9
37	Guillotine amputation of tip without loss of bone	5

Middle finger –

38	Whole	12
39	Two phalanges	9
40	One phalanx	7
41	Guillotine amputation of tip without loss of bone	4

Ring or little finger –

42	Whole	7
43	Two phalanges	6
44	One phalanx	5
45	Guillotine of tip without loss of bone	2

B.   Toes of right or left foot

14	Great toe –	
46	Through metatarsophalangeal joint	14
47	Part, with some loss of bone	3

Any other toe –

48	Through metatarsophalangeal joint	3
49	Part, with some loss of bone	1

Two toes of one foot, excluding great toe –

50	Through metatarsophalangeal joint	5
51	Part, with some loss of bone	2

Three toes of one foot, excluding great toe –

52	Through metatarsophalangeal joint	6
53	Part, with some loss of bone	3

Four toes of one foot, excluding great toe –

54	Through metatarsophalangeal joint	9
55	Part, with some loss of bone	3

Note: for any injury not covered by these Regulations, a government-appointed doctor will examine the claimant and make an assessment of the degree of disablement as a percentage.

Appendix 5

Working Tax Credit – Disability Which Puts a Person at a Disadvantage in Getting a Job – Part 1 of Schedule 1

1   When standing he cannot keep his balance unless he continually holds onto something.

2   Using any crutches, walking frame, walking stick, prosthesis or similar walking aid which he habitually uses, he cannot walk a continuous distance of 100 metres along level ground without stopping or without suffering severe pain.

3   He can use neither of his hands behind his back as in the process of putting on a jacket or of tucking a shirt into trousers.

4   He can extend neither of his arms in front of him so as to shake hands with another person without difficulty.

5   He can put neither of his hands up to his head without difficulty so as to put on a hat.

6   Due to lack of manual dexterity he cannot [with one hand, pick up] a coin which is not more than 2½ centimetres in diameter.

7   He is not able to use his hands or arms to pick up a full jug of 1 litre capacity and pour from it into a cup, without difficulty.

8   He can turn neither of his hands sideways through 180 degrees.

9   He is registered as blind or registered as partially sighted in a register compiled by a local authority under section 29(4)(g) of the National Assistance Act 1948 (welfare services) or, in Scotland, has been certified as blind or as partially sighted and in consequence registered as blind or partially sighted in a register maintained by or on behalf of a regional or island council.

10   He cannot see to read 16 point print at a distance greater than 20 centimetres, if appropriate, wearing the glasses he normally uses.

11   He cannot hear a telephone ring when he is in the same room as the telephone, if appropriate, using a hearing aid he normally uses.

12   In a quiet room he has difficulty in hearing what someone talking in a loud voice at a distance of 2 metres says, if appropriate, using a hearing aid he normally uses.

13   People who know him well have difficulty in understanding what he says.

14   When a person he knows well speaks to him, he has difficulty in understanding what that person says.

15   At least once a year during waking hours he is in a coma or has a fit in which he loses consciousness.

16   He has a mental illness for which he receives regular treatment under the supervision of a medically qualified person.

17   Due to mental disability he is often confused or forgetful.

18   He cannot do the simplest addition and subtraction.

19   Due to mental disability he strikes people or damages property or is unable to form normal social relationships.

20   He cannot normally sustain an 8 hour working day or a 5 day working week due to a medical condition or intermittent or continuous severe pain. [Note that HMRC state that a person should not fail the test simply because the job exceeds 8 hours per day or 5 days per week. The test is whether a person is disadvantaged in getting a job in the open market. A person may work more than 8 hours per day or 5 days per week if the job has been adapted to suit his needs.]

21   For initial claims only, as a result of an illness or accident, he is undergoing a period of habilation or rehabilitation. [The habilation and rehabilitation criteria apply only

to initial claims, ie a claim for the disability element by someone who has not qualified for it in the two years immediately preceding the claim. Guidance from HMRC states that rehabilitation is helping somebody to do something again which they could do before the illness or accident. Habilitation means enabling them to do something they have not done before. Rehabilitation following illness or injury may involve making a person fully effective throughout the working day. The person may be too weak, or recovering from a psychiatric illness, to work a full day. Time off for physiotherapy or some other form of treatment may be needed. The person may take longer, or need extra, rest periods, or have to avoid stress. Part-time working may be appropriate. Habilitation could be training a person who cannot do his previous job because of an accident or illness, to be able to do a different job. A person who has never worked before can receive habilitation following illness or injury.]

Appendix 6

Welfare Benefits: Reciprocal Agreements

	AA	BB	CA	CB	DLA	IDB	JSA	MB	SP
Barbados		X		X		X		X	X
Bermuda		X				X			X
Bosnia-Herzegovina		X		X		X	X	X	X
Canada				X			X		X
Croatia		X		X		X	X	X	X
Guernsey	X	X		X	X	X	X	X	X
Isle of Man	X	X	X	X	X	X	X	X	X
Israel		X		X		X		X	X
Jamaica		X				X			X
Jersey	X	X		X	X	X		X	X
Macedonia		X		X		X	X	X	X
Mauritius		X		X		X			X
New Zealand		X		X			X		X
Philippines		X				X			X
Serbia and Montenegro		X		X		X	X	X	X
Turkey		X				X		X	X
USA		X							X

Index